WITH EVERY
MOUSE
& MAN

A Novel About One of the Most Heroic and Tragic U-boat Mysteries of the Second World War

DAVE GARWICK

Cover illustration and layout by Heidi Sutherlin

This novel is dedicated to the one who inspired it, Margarita Maria Francesca Lucia, the finest storyteller who left every listener unable to untangle fact from fantasy.

 This was the emblem of the 2nd Flotilla of which U 156 was a member. Only three boats carried this emblem.

 This was the emblem which only U 156 carried.

ACKNOWLEDGMENTS

This is the most dangerous part of any book because of the very real risk of inadvertently omitting the names of people who have been so helpful. Beyond any doubt, the single greatest source of help was the work of Gudmundur Helgason and his associates at Uboat.net. Beta readers whose perspectives were invaluable included, Rebecca Damron, Michael Damron, Mary Anne Damron, Chris Foley, Greg Donnelly, Rebecca KenKnight, Joan Murphy, Steven Nesser, Meg Newswanger, Nina Olsen, Chris Steele, Leon Stier, Gunnar Svavarsson, Bob Tesarek, and Ron Wipf. My literary editor, Norah Sarsour, was my trusted writing coach who provided such insightful perspective all along the way. Heidi Sutherlin was not only my cover artist and final copy editor, but my professional morale officer. Over the long years of dreaming and writing, I was especially sustained by the patient encouragement of my daughters and their husbands, Karen and Karl Oberjohn and Kirsten and Michael Childe, and most especially my wife, Ann.

Thank you, Thank you, Thank you!!!

CONTENTS

KEY CHAPTER LOCATIONS

TIMELINE

July 1914 – November 1918   WORLD WAR I

28 Jan 1917	*Amiral Magon* sunk	ch 2
25 Feb 1917	*Laconia* sunk	ch 3
19 Jul 1918	*USS San Diego* sunk	ch 4
25 Sept 1918	*U-156* sunk	ch 4

September 1931 – September 2, 1945   WORLD WAR II

1 Jul 1937	Niemöller arrested	ch 7
20 Nov 1938	Hartenstein takes *Seeadler*	ch 9
Oct 1939	Hartenstein takes *Jaguar*	ch 11
10 Jul - 31 Oct 1940	Battle of Britain	ch 12
4 Sept 1941	Hartenstein takes *U-156*	ch 13
7 Dec 1941	Pearl Harbor	ch 13
26 Jan 1942	U.S. troops to England	ch 14
24 Jun 1942	*Willimantic* sunk	ch 13
1 – 27 Jul 1942	1st Battle of El Alamein	ch 16
May 1942	Japanese in Madagascar	ch 19
27 Aug 1942	*Clan Macwhirter* sunk	ch 20
12 Sept 1942	*Laconia* sunk	ch 26
8 Mar 1943	*U-156* sunk	ch 45
6 Jun 1944	D Day on Normandy	
8 May 1945	Germany surrenders	
6 Aug 1945	Atomic bombing of Hiroshima	
15 Aug 1945	Japan surrenders	

FOREWORD

"I think it is better to do right, even if we suffer in so doing, than to incur the reproach of our consciences and posterity."

General Robert E. Lee
Commanding General, Confederate Army
U.S. Civil War

PROLOGUE

Near the south-central border of Germany, a small city named Plauen lies on the White Elster River in the state of Saxony. It has survived over a thousand years of plagues, wars and fires. In the center of that city lies an old church. In the center of its cemetery is the memorial of a war hero to both the Nazis and the Allies.

PART I
IN THE BEGINNING
1917 – 1926

CHAPTER 1

HIS FIRST U-BOAT

Opening weeks of 1917
The Hartenstein home
Plauen, Germany

S ometimes a crystal ball is made of paper.

Wernie had been inseparable from the huge book that he had received just yesterday on his ninth birthday.

German wartime economy was in a death spiral, but Werner's father had managed to pick up a copy of *Twenty Thousand Leagues Under the Sea*. Export merchant Herr William Hartenstein was the local expert in connecting products with buyers. The city of Plauen was world renowned for its lace industry, and local artisans were having an almost impossible time getting their products out of the country which put Werner's father in high demand. Local lace craftsmen who needed his export services unfortunately did not have an abundance of cash with which to pay him. It just happened, however, that one of them had a fine keepsake edition of the beautifully illustrated tale. In the barter exchange system, William normally would not have traded for something like this, but a birthday was right around the corner for a boy who always seemed to have his nose in a book.

"But Mutti, I'm right in the middle of my stitching," said twelve-year old Thea. "Why can't Wernie go? He's not doing anything."

"I am too!" came an indignantly defiant protest from the living room couch.

His mother, Selma, called out from the kitchen where she had been negotiating legal terms with Thea for a grocery errand. "What are you doing in there, Wernie? You're so quiet all of a sudden."

There was no answer from the reader dreamer. "Werner, are you still there?" said his mother who stood impatiently in her pale blue apron that was dusted with flour and stained with grease.

"I'm reading my favorite book!" was the impatient reply.

"Well, I'm making your favorite cookies," said Mutti. "Could you run over to Mrs. Gunther's for some salt for my baking?"

"But I'm reading!"

"It would be good for you to get outside for some exercise. How about two more pages and then take a break for my errand?"

"But I don't get some of the words."

"Thea can help. Then you can return the favor and help me."

This idea was twice as bad as far as Thea was concerned. Not only did this still interrupt her sewing project, but it meant that now she also had to actually do something with her irritating little brother.

"But Mutti, that's not fair!" cried Thea. She stood a head taller than her little brother and was already beginning to look like an emerging young woman. Werner still looked like a freckled little boy. Even though she jealously defended her superior position of birth order, she still acted like Werner was a real threat. She had her mother's wavy brunette hair and petite frame, but her father's temper-stoked, flushed face.

"It's either that or getting the salt for me *yourself*," advised mother.

With eye rolling exasperation, Big Sister huffed off to serve her sentence with Little Brother. She stood in front of him and folded her arms. "OK, what words are too hard for you?"

Werner ran his finger along the page. "It says, '*For some time past, vessels had been met by an enormous thing, a long object, spindle shaped, occasionally phosphorescent, and infinitely . . .*' What does 'fosferscent' mean?"

When Thea read on her own, she was always asking her mother what this word or that word meant. But when she read to her nine-year-old brother, she answered his questions with authoritative imagination. "Scent means how you smell. Fospher means a big nose."

His eyes grew big. "Oh Thea! Look at that boat!"

"It called *The Nautilus*."

"I know that. I can read, you know. But look how it's going under the water!"

"Don't you know anything? It's a U-boat. They call it a U-boat because it goes *under* water."

"Why do they do that?"

"I don't know." Thea turned the page to reveal a sea monster that was larger than the U-boat. Its greenish, suckered hide was more hideous than Werner's most terrifying nightmare. The leviathan's flaming red eyes and rows upon rows of saber teeth guaranteed an exciting, sleepless bedtime tonight. "Maybe so they can go after things like that."

Werner had seen drawings of fire-breathing dragons that could fly. Brave knights with huge swords would ride gallant steeds to do battle with those kinds of creatures. But he had never heard of dragons that could swim in the oceans. No wonder you needed boats like *The Nautilus*.

"What do you mean 'go after'?" said the little brother.

The senior sibling flexed her authority. "What do you think? They have to kill things like that."

"How do they do that?"

"In school, they told us that U-boats shoot things called torpedoes that blow things up," said Thea.

"That's what I'm going to do," said the boy with a mission. "I'm going to be a U-boat captain and shoot torpedoes to blow up monsters."

Only a big sister could pour water on an underwater dream. "You can't. We don't live by the sea."

"We do too."

"Do not."

"Do too." Wernie was thinking about the little creek a couple blocks away. In fact, that stream had long been where he had sailed the oceans in other dreams. Why couldn't it take him to seas of conquest now? "That's where the Muhlgraben goes. Doesn't it, Mutti?"

"Does what do what?" asked Selma, who was somewhere in her own thoughts in the kitchen.

"Thea said I can't be a U-boat captain 'cause we don't live by the sea. But the Muhlgraben goes into the sea, doesn't it?"

Again, Thea expressed her considered opinion as she rolled her eyes in exasperation. What in the world would the Muhlgraben have to do with oceans and monsters and U-boats? To the twelve-year-old girl, the riverside park was about

6

dreamy summers beside a lazy stream that smelled of cotton candy where the happy sounds of children filled the warm air.

Mother looked thoughtful. "Well, I think it actually does. It flows into the big White Elster River at the edge of town. Then I think it empties into bigger and bigger rivers all the way to the North Sea near where Auntie Katie and Uncle Otto live in Hamburg."

"See?" said victorious Werner to vanquished Thea who exhausted another sigh, closed the book, plopped it into her pest's lap, and moved off to something else.

Werner also moved somewhere else. He was already sailing the high seas all the way to the kitchen, where Selma was busy baking. In the pantry, the young explorer was making a furious racket of pots and pans as he searched for something seemingly urgent. "I found it!" he said as he dragged out the extra-large roaster pan. "Mutti, can I use that jar on the top shelf?"

"That depends. What do you want to do with it?"

For the next hour, he showed her. It took eleven jars of water to fill up the big roaster. Then the jar became a boat that the young Captain Nemo could submerge again and again and again. Finally, Selma thought of a way to break the nerve-scraping monotony.

"Hey sailor, I still need that salt from the high seas. Be sure to say thank you."

With no further excuses, the boy ran out the door. Selma went upstairs to see how Thelma was coming on her sewing project. She didn't notice her son dash back into the house for a moment.

She was back in the kitchen when William returned home from his day at work. He gave her a little kiss on the cheek. "Something smells good. Is that supper?"

His wife didn't look up from mashing ingredients beside the sink. "It is, if you managed to pick up that tallow that I asked you to bring home."

For the last three years, meat had been in very short supply. By mashing together rice and grains glued together by an egg, the mixture could be fashioned together around a wooden stick which gave the appearance of a bone-in lamb chop. When fried in mutton tallow and garnished with a little imagination, it almost smelled and tasted like the real thing.

It had been a long time since this breadwinner had brought home the bacon, but William proudly presented Selma with a small, paper-wrapped package. "For the best cook this side of Plauen, mein liebschen."

That piece of chivalry was rewarded. After the extended embrace, William suddenly realized that they had not been interrupted. "What are the children up to?"

"Oh, Thea's up in her room working on a little sewing project. I sent Captain Nemo off to Mrs. Gunther for a little salt." She looked at her watch. "Strange, he should have been back a while ago. I would have expected him to rush right back so he could sail his *Nautilus* in that tub of water over there."

William gave a confused look.

"He has such an imagination. He kept pestering me with one question after another about the Muhlgraben."

"The Muhlgraben?"

"That's how our little Captain Nemo plans to sail away to do battle under the sea," said Selma. "The tub of water is just for practice and pretend. The Mulgraben, you know, is for real."

William casually asked, "How long has he been gone?"

"Perhaps an hour or so."

He turned his face to the stairs and yelled for Thea to come down.

From her room, Thea said, "What? What did I do?"

Selma tried to allay the girl's fears. "You did nothing wrong, young lady. Your father is simply trying to find your brother."

Father was direct. "Do you know where your brother has gone?"

"No. Is something wrong?"

Father said, "We can't find your little brother. Nobody knows where he is."

Thea had long ago learned that the best defense was a strong offense, whether one was needed or not. "I was supposed to watch him?"

"Nobody's blaming you for anything," said Papa. "He's old enough that he doesn't need to be watched."

Just then, Selma came in from the kitchen. "Funny, the jar he was playing with is gone."

"What does that jar have to do with anything?" William asked.

"Werner was pretending that it was a U-boat in that roaster full of water," said Selma. "He must have submerged it a hundred times. I was hoping that he would get bored before I went crazy."

William looked up in surprise when he remembered how a boy thinks. "That's it. He knew where he could find a lot more water, where it would be a lot more fun."

"What are you …?" Then it dawned on the little boy's mother. "No, he wouldn't dare go down to the creek by himself. He knows better."

"Yes, but yesterday was his birthday, and he asked if he was now old enough to play down by the creek," said William. "We told him that we'd think about it."

Thea, hearing her parents think aloud, began to realize the seriousness of the situation. "I could go down to the creek to see if he's there."

If Werner were in trouble, his mother did not want to be waiting for news when she should be there doing what was necessary. Also, she did not want young Thea to be alone if there was trouble. To put the best face on things, Selma stretched her lips into her best imitation of a smile and said, "Why don't we all take a stroll?"

Thea began to sense something when Papa suggested that he would scoot ahead and let them catch up. "Could Wernie be in trouble, Mutti?"

"I'm sure he's fine," said Selma, although she picked up her pace. "It's just that the weather has been so warm, that the creek is really high and fast with the winter melt."

Thea took that in and thought out loud, "And Wernie's not all that good a swimmer."

By the time that Selma and Thea caught up to William, he had just come back from having checked out the right creek bank. "There's more foliage down by the creek shore on the left. Let's head down there."

He hurriedly shuffled in his boots, as the crisp grass bent with the weight of his worry. They hadn't gone two minutes before Thea pointed.

"Look! There's something by the water."

"Oh no! Don't let it be! Please don't let it be!" cried Selma.

All three broke into a run with William in the lead. A dozen meters ahead of them, he suddenly stopped and ran back to the other two. He gathered them in an embrace and turned them away from the creek.

"Don't look. Don't look."

Selma broke loose to spin around and look herself. All that the father could see were two little legs on the shore pointing away from the creek. A motionless head was face down in the water. William doubled over in grief as Selma and Thea scrambled past him toward the still form of what looked like a small child. William was unnerved by a deep mechanical voice he had never heard from his wife as she chanted on the run, "no-no-no, no-no, no-no-no, no-no."

Alerted by the strange sounds, the boy rolled over to prop himself up on one elbow and gaze in terror at his whole family rushing towards him.

Mother and sister stopped in mid stride. "You're alive!" cried Thea. Selma rushed forward to scoop up Werner.

"Mutti be careful! It might break!" he said. "Hi, Papa! Thea, look at this! Just like a U-boat."

He waved her over to the bank and carefully inserted the jar vertically into the water. He then bent over to place one eye over the mouth of the jar and look through the bottom into the water. "Try it, Thea! You can see everything under the water even!"

William quietly came up beside Selma. The dazed parents simply stood side by side, gazing at their playful river otters.

Almost as if he was talking to himself, William said, "Like in church yesterday."

"Huh?" said the shock-exhausted mother. "What about church yesterday?"

"About when Jesus was twelve years old."

Werner's voice penetrated the fog of their minds, "Come on, Thea! It's my turn! You've got to share!"

"I have no idea what you're talking about," said Selma.

Again, Werner yelled at his sister. "If you don't share, I'm going to tell Mutti and Papa!"

"For three days, remember?" said William. "When he was twelve, wandered away from his folks."

"Alright, alright!" said Thea as she thrust the jar back at Werner.

Selma's terror was beginning to twist into something else. "But they didn't kill him."

"Probably wanted to," said William. "I think Mary yelled at him or something."

"Thea, come down over here by the branch and see what's swimming under the water!" said Werner.

Selma slowly shook her head in exhausted confusion. William said, "Something about how his parents didn't understand."

Selma let out a long breath. "That part I understand."

CHAPTER 2

JUST WAR

Opening weeks of 1917
Deck of the French troopship SS Amiral Magon
Central Mediterranean midway between Crete and Malta
1100 hours

While a little boy was playing at sailing under the water, sailors not that much older than he were doing it for real. Germany had been at war now for three years and its U-boats had already hit over twenty-five hundred ships. So stealthy were these new weapons that some of the men they killed never even knew they had died.

To the French troops sunning themselves topside on the *Amiral Magon*, the war seemed very far away. These men had just risen from the human slime-mud of over three hundred thousand decomposing corpses at Verdun. Having survived one killing field, these men did not know that they had used up all their good luck and were now about to roll their one last last die.

But now, in the sweet Mediterranean breezes, there were no hills, no gnarled fingers of hands and twisted trees and no structure behind which lurked some steady rifle barrel aiming to take off someone's head. There were no trenches and gashes on the visible surface of an unusually placid sea. None of the gentle swells was wrapped up in the endless curls and coils of barbed wire.

It seemed that every soldier was straining to catch fresh air, topside on the deck. The ship's master felt a little uneasy about these bathing beauties advertising the extremely valuable troop load he was carrying. The truth is that it would not have mattered if the troops had been kept below decks. The cargo value of the *Amiral Magon* was clearly signaled by the fact that it was being escorted by three of France's newest destroyers.

Soldat First Class Henri Noblet was just one of a couple dozen French troops basking in the late morning Mediterranean sun. "Ha, I finally get to sunbathe on the Mediterranean!"

"If you call standing in a sweater sunbathing," said another.

Noblet said, "Compared to where we've been, it is."

"After all that freezing mud, I'd wear a sweater in hell," said his buddy.

"Not too bad for a bunch of Frogs, eh?" said Belland, his squad leader, who aped what the British Tommies liked to call them.

"Wonder how cold this water is?" said Prevost. Before he took his next breath, he found out, but never knew.

All three soldiers were instantly brewed into the Mediterranean by a heat eruption that carbonized their remains in a flash. They and two hundred other souls were casualties of the 112th sinking of the Kaiser's second-deadliest U-boat.

Ten minutes later, the only trace of the massive liner was the flotsam of eight hundred survivors splashing for their lives.

U-39
Two Kilometers South
Submerged at periscope depth

Kapitänleutnant Walter Forstmann was victorious. "Well, boys, it looks like two did it. She's on her way. Take a look, Martin."

Oberleutnant Martin Niemöller looked through the scope. "I only see a few lifeboats in the water, Sir. Looks like a destroyer changing course to close for a rescue."

"Well, let's tuck in a little closer to make sure that they don't," said the captain.

Niemöller wasn't sure he heard correctly. "Sir?"

"What we are going to do, Oberleutnant, is to keep those rifles from coming back another day," said Forstmann.

Indeed, it was that simple.

Three hundred meters above the sinking SS Amiral Magon

Guardiamarina Francoise Archambault was one of many who was on his own in the water. Somehow, he had to keep himself afloat with only one functioning arm until something came his way. Something did. The flames of burning oil slicks illuminated the wake of something slicing its way toward him. Did sharks patrol even in flames? One did. But this one did not project a fin. The ensign found himself staring into the advancing single glass eye of some kind of cyclops.

His scream distracted four others who were busy with a bloody oar, braining a desperate man who had made the mistake of trying to cling to their overloaded lifeboat. They saw the wake bear down on Archambault.

"My God! Look! Sharks!"

When everyone leaned forward to see, the shifting weight capsized their lifeboat, offering up every soul to the hungry prowler. The merciless oarsman clung to his wooden hope which now could not save him, even as his agitated thrashing washed the brainy gore off the bludgeon oar. He grabbed on to a floating object, but the sinking corpse of the man he had just murdered returned the favor as both sank beneath the chaos.

Through all the screaming, a foghorn could be heard from their escort less than a mile away. The destroyer would be their savior. But every time it seemed to get closer, the U-boat would raise its periscope in the midst of survivors who were swimming for their lives. Time and again, the destroyer deflected its rescue to chase off the bait. Each time the destroyer got too close, *U-39* quietly slipped away out of sight as did most of the exhausted swimmers.

U-39
Submerged 100 meters
Officer's Wardroom

Two hours later, the exhausted U-boat skipper was asleep in his private berth. His officers, however, could not sleep. In the day room, they struggled in hushed voices.

The Navigator, Niemöller, cut to the chase, "I don't know about what we did back there."

The Third Watch Officer summed it all up. "Fifty-five hundred tons, Marty, plus God only knows how many riflemen sent to the bottom. On just two fish yet!"

"Always tonnage, isn't it?" Niemöller half-said to himself.

"What else matters?" asked the Chief Engineer.

Even though Karl Dönitz was the junior officer, he weighed in. "She was a troopship, Otto. You've got a brother in the Army, just like them, don't you?"

"Yeah, bright boy, but now none of those guys will be shooting at him."

Niemöller capped the thought. "Or seeing their wives, or kids, or parents or brothers."

"So what's gotten into you all of a sudden?" said the machinist. "We've done this, what, a hundred and eleven times before? Can't take it anymore?"

Niemöller stared down into the table. "We have never done *this* before."

"What, kill the enemy?"

"No, murder the enemy." Niemöller kept his eyes on his folded hands as if in some sort of confession. "We've never murdered the enemy the way we did tonight." Slowly, Niemöller raised his eyes to lock the warrant officer in the crosshairs of his stare. "We simply stood between them and their rescue until they drowned."

The Quartermaster was in charge of the boat's inventory of emotionless objectivity. "But war is war. You die in war, you kill in war. You're just as dead, no matter how it happens."

Young Dönitz would not let it go. "Isn't it enemy equipment and supplies that we go after? We talk tonnage. If people die in the process, then that is an unfortunate price. But do we go out of our way to kill people who can no longer harm us?"

"They are as dangerous as the equipment they will use on our families," said the Petty Watch Officer. "They are pigs who would not show us any mercy!"

"Keep it down!" whispered Niemöller who did not want the dozing captain to hear. "They are no different from us."

Otto said, "Listen to that crap! Maybe you ought to be standing in a pulpit, not a conning tower, Father Martin."

Niemöller looked up and let out a sigh of resignation. "It's just that I was thinking of our own brothers. If any of them wind up floating in the water like that, I hope somebody will give them more of a chance than we did tonight."

CHAPTER 3

THE FIRST LACONIA

Weeks later, early 1917
RMS Laconia
North Atlantic, due east of County Cork, Ireland
2300 hours

Ironically, in this third year of the war, it was the effectiveness of Germany's U-boats that was about to trigger the beginning of the end for the Kaiser. On April 2nd, American President Woodrow Wilson called Congress into Special Session and announced:

"[Last month] I officially laid before you the extraordinary announcement of the Imperial German Government that . . . it was its purpose to put aside all restraints of law or of humanity and use its submarines to sink every vessel ... of every kind, whatever their flag, their character, their cargo, their destination, their errand ... to the bottom without warning and without thought of help or mercy for those on board. The world must be made safe for democracy."

And with that, the hammer of the United States fell on Germany. American passengers like George Fairfax now understood that they themselves were fair game, especially on the high seas. He leaned over the deck railing. Not to jump. Not to throw up. Just to see what wasn't there. The pitch-blackness hid everything from sight on this moonless night.

A stranger took up station beside him. With no need to fill the space with chatter, the two kept silent vigil for several minutes. Orley Bainbridge broke the inky silence with a sigh. "Ah yes," said the Brit. *'The light shineth in the darkness.'*"

"Beg your pardon?" said Fairfax.

"I say, the Gospel of John," said Bainbridge, "about how the light is supposed to shine in the darkness and not be overcome by it."

"Not on this ship, pal," said Fairfax.

"Quite. You can't see one blessed thing out there. Not one single deck light, every bleedin' porthole blacked out and red lights in all the doorways. Can't even see the waves."

"Smoke?" Fairfax took out a pack of Lucky Strikes, wrist-slapped it to pop out a cigarette, flicked out his lighter, flared the flame, and sealed the fate of the *RMS Laconia*. Indeed, the darkness did not overcome *this* particular light.

U-50, surfaced
Three kilometers northwest of the Laconia

It was from the surface that *U-50* stalked its prey, for at least two reasons. First of all, the hunted was faster than the hunter and the U-boat moved fastest on the surface. Also, torpedo shot mathematics were much simpler to plan in the two dimensions of a surface trajectory than for a three-dimensional underwater solution.

Kapitänleutnant Gerhard Berger was still further out than he preferred for the attack. "Steady as she goes, Ernst," he whispered to the navigation officer, Oberleutnant Klaunig. Referring to the tiny orange flash from the target, he said, "Let's not spook our little glow fish, eh?"

The moonless night provided perfect cover in the pitch-black late hours. Even the breezes cooperated, placing the U-boat and its noises downwind from its prey.

Hunger pains focused the crew in the belly of the iron shark. She had not had a meal in days. The Cunard liner was about to be her twenty-third. Four dozen men were the internal organs of the killer: its stomach, its eyes and ears, its heart and lungs, and most importantly, its brain. It had no soul. For hours, it had stalked a prey three times longer, eighteen times heavier and still twice as fast. But only the shark knew that a chase was on, ever closing the distance by intersecting each zig and every zag of the wary prey.

"Tubes one and four ready, Kapitän," called out the junior Watch Officer, Helmuth Knoke.

Deck of the Laconia

Orley sucked in his first draft, and the orange tip of the cigarette glowed four times brighter. "No need to see the waves anyway. It's what moves under the waves, like the ocean currents. That's what really makes the difference."

That's why Captain Irvine had scheduled a routine evacuation drill that afternoon. Most of the passengers had been irritated at the unnecessary interruption.

"What *is* the point?" said a chronically inconvenienced passenger. "After all," said Mrs. Wilson, "did we not just tolerate this foolishness when we left harbor? Is he afraid we're just going to tip over or something?"

Her husband didn't worry so much about the boat tipping over, as much as he was concerned about his wife losing her balance. "My dear, I'm sure there's nothing to worry about at all. Like the Captain said, just routine. The insurance companies are probably just being a little cautious since that *Titanic* affair and all the problems with lifeboats."

The evacuation drill had not been lost on everyone. "Don't you think the *Lusitania* is more to the point?" said a portly gentleman who was caught in the crush beside them.

"Now, sir, that kind of talk is only going to frighten the women. There is no point in borrowing trouble."

The historian offered a faint smile of amusement. "I'm just saying that icebergs don't go after you. U-boats do."

Another man tried to shut down the fear monger. "Pardon me, sir, but what would you know about it?"

"Only what I read in the papers," said the messenger they were trying to shoot. "Something like two thousand people torpedoed right off County Cork, Ireland." He let out a breath. "Which is where I figure we ought to be right about now."

Throughout the day and into the evening, the whispered fears echoed off one anxious heart to another. The Captain assured his passengers that everything was nothing more than routine procedure.

In the dining room, some quieted their nerves with spirits of one sort or another. Five men at the bar drank theirs. At a nearby table, Reverend Gomseth called on a different spirit. The little circle of souls sent up prayers for safety on the rolling seas.

Not far down the corridor, Mary Perth was preparing three-year-old Lyn for bed. Already, people had been commenting how much the little girl resembled her mother. Mary herself had the look of a young girl, petite with long, dark hair and large, dark brown eyes. Her slightly olive skin was always accented by bright red lipstick, the only feature not shared by her little copy.

Mary could just barely make out the chorus from Reverend Gomseth's little band of prayer warriors:

"... is well, with my soul,
It is well, it is well, with my soul."

She, of course, had no way of knowing the depth of those words. She might have found less solace to know how the lyrics had come to be written, not too far from where the singers were this very night.

Lyn's tiny voice barely broke through Mary's concentration. "Mummy, I'm scared."

"Why is that?"

"Some boys say that boats under the water are going to get us."

"Oh, hush now! Those boys are just being silly. Do you hear those people singing? They don't sound scared. They sound happy, don't they?"

"I suppose."

"OK now. Do you want me to say your bedtime prayers or do you want to?"

"You."

"OK then. Fold your hands and close your eyes: *Now I lay me down to sleep, I pray the Lord my soul to keep. If I should die before I wake, I pray the Lord my soul to take.*"

Before the night was over, her prayers would be answered.

U-50
Surfaced
1 kilometer northwest of the Laconia

The predator knew nothing of a little girl's dreams. The man at the periscope was lost in his own darkness as he waited to carefully close the distance for the kill. When there was nothing to do but wait in silence, he often drifted to another place. He glanced at his watch: 2230 hours. For his family, that would be half past eleven back home in Bremerhoff. His heart watched over Katie and their four-year old, little Maria, snuggled together under the heavy quilts, safe in the journeys of their own dreams.

"Kapitän?"

His wife Katie had written in her last letter that, since his departure, Maria had insisted on sleeping with her again. She told how his "ladies" closed each day, kneeling beside the bed to say a prayer that she had written for her hero beneath the waves:

"Now I lay me down to sleep
I pray the Lord my soul to keep

Keep our papa through the night
Safe and sound till morning light ".

"Kapitän? Sir!"

The commander was snapped back to his grizzly task. "Yes, Ernst."

"We have closed to within one kilometer, Sir."

The firing solution was double-checked and Berger pronounced sentence on the unsuspecting victim. The "whoosh!" of compressed air that launched the torpedo began the countdown to eternity for a dozen souls.

RMS Laconia

Below the waterline inside the target, three men shoveled coal into the furnaces of the ocean liner for hours upon endless hours. Each stoker worked in a monotonous trance to shut out the sweltering heat and deafening noise of the massive turbines. Suddenly, silence. Forever.

But topside, above the point of impact, a machine gun rip of popping rivets riddled a steward who neither heard nor saw a thing. A volcanic ejection of molten metal rocketed far above the bridge before cascading down upon the crewman it vaporized.

Shattered glass sliced human meat that had not been thrown off its feet fast enough. The bellows of hell throttled every molecule of air.

Almost a football field away from where the iron shark took its first bite out of the eighteen-thousand-ton behemoth, mother and child had just tucked into their berths. A vague clang and gentle bump did not penetrate their slumber. But the commotion in the hallway did.

"Mummy? Mummy!" Mary awoke to her little helper whispering in her ear.

"What is it, love?"

"I can't sleep," said little Lyn. "Lots of people are talking too loud outside."

She was right. There seemed to be all kinds of activity outside their stateroom. People were running back and forth through the corridor. Mary could make out frantic knocking on door after door. "Everybody wake up! Please don your life jackets and report to your boat station."

What? A drill again? At this time of the night? This really was too much. Suddenly it was their door that was being hammered with demanding fists. "Everybody wake up! Please don your life jackets and report to your boat station."

"Mummy? Mummy!"

Mother did not answer.

The child's questions became a command that slapped Mary out of her daze. "Mummy!" She screamed this time, "Mummy! I'm scared!"

The mother now tried to calm two terrified little girls, one beside her and the one inside her. "I know, love. Everybody is making so much noise." She tried to shield her little one by turning fear into an exciting game. "I know," she said, "let's get dressed and put on those funny jackets and go see what all the noise is about, shall we?"

What most frightened the young mother was that the corridor was now completely silent. Had they been left behind? Her trembling fingers tangled the strings as she tried again and again to tie Lyn's lifejacket. Before opening the door, she stopped to collect her thoughts as well as a tube of lipstick. She fumbled the lipstick and dropped it on the floor. Strangely, it rolled away with increasing speed toward the porthole wall. Her world was turning upside down.

The little helper got down on the floor to chase the lipstick, but Mary screamed at her, "For the love of Pete, let it go! Stop it! Right now! Get over here! Now!" Her own outburst shocked mother as much as the child who broke into a wail of confused sobs.

Mary rushed to Lyn and gathered her in her arms. "Oh, baby, I'm so sorry. I didn't mean to yell at you. You were being so helpful. I guess that sometimes I go too fast and I say things I don't mean. I love you so, so much."

Through sniffled sobs, the child comforted the grownup. "That's OK, Mummy." Her little hand opened and revealed the retrieved treasure. "We'll be OK. Right?"

One more big hug and then to the door. It would not open. Mary worked the handle again and again. The handle operated well but the door seemed jammed. In a frantic shove, Mary forced the door open. The corridor floor was inches deep in water.

U-50

One hundred meters away, the U-boat floated motionless as its commander watched the stricken liner through binoculars. "She's dead in the water and listing to starboard. I think it's about time to put her out of her misery, yes?"

27

Leutnant Knoke said, "Sir, we have only two fish remaining."

"Thank you, Helmuth. But no matter. The potatoes in the hold are rotten anyway."

"Sir?"

"All our fresh provisions are exhausted. We've been gone long enough. I'm not even sure that we are adequately hosting the mice that have stowed aboard. No need to be frugal. It's about time to wrap up this little adventure anyway."

Not only were the potatoes rotten, but the unwashed men smelled that way too, bathed in cologne to kill the putrid odor of a patrol that was well beyond its shelf life.

"Aye, Sir. Tube four ready," called out the watch officer.

"Send her on her way, Mr. Knoke."

The U-boat hissed and lurched as it fired its last nail into the coffin.

RMS Laconia

By the time Mary and Lyn got outside, the deck was already beginning to tip seaward. The reason was not evident. Men and women were rushing in all directions, calling out for one another. The ship's foghorns called out to the darkness again and again in long, plaintive bass tones.

Mary asked a woman next to her, "What happened? Did we hit something?"

"We're sinking! That's all I know."

Somehow, a crewman managed to stand above the crowd to direct the herd of aimless passengers. "Please proceed in an orderly manner to your assigned boat stations. There is nothing to worry about. This is just a precaution."

Behind him, two crewmen perched atop the siderail to guide a large open rowboat over the edge. As it dangled from a hoist, the sailors tried to stabilize the craft in midair to prepare for the loading of its pre-assigned passengers.

The child clung like a tiny vise clamp to her mother's hand and tugged at her skirt. "Mummy?"

Mary did not answer because she was preoccupied in her frantic searching for where they were to go. Lyn screamed, "Mummy!"

Mary knelt down to eye level with her little one. "What is it, love?"

Just then, several flare rockets arched into the sky and exploded in star clusters.

"Where is everybody going, Mummy?"

"People are trying to find the boat they are supposed to go to."

"Do we have a boat too?"

"We do, honey. But we came out a different door and I'm trying to find our boat." She directed the child's attention to one lifeboat that was already being filled with passengers. "You see those people? We get to go on a ride just like they do. Doesn't that look fun?"

The young mother's brave façade instantly melted as that very lifeboat was engulfed in a storm of fire. A thundering earthquake slammed everybody to the deck, into the bulkheads and into one another. Unconsciousness spared both mother and child the horror of a screaming human torch next to them which flung itself into the sea. When the child awoke minutes later, she was still under the protection of a comforting arm. But as she sat up, the limb fell away.

It was the toddler's blood-curdling scream that blasted Mary awake. She embraced Lyn in a clutch of terror. "Oh baby, you're all right! Mummy's here. Mummy's here."

"Lady, we've got to get the child off this ship! We're going down and there's room for one child in the only lifeboat that we can get to!"

Mary scooped up the dazed child and followed the officer, over tangled bodies to a full lifeboat. "Here, hand her to me!" called out the crewman who was manning the boat.

"I love you, baby!" sobbed the young mother who kissed her child through streaming tears.

Mary's whole world clung to her neck and wailed more horror with each cry, "Mummy! Mummy! Mummy! Mummy!"

Three passengers gently pried loose the tiny fingers and carried the hysterical child to a new life. As the lifeboat descended out of sight, the frantic cries of her child faded away. Mary collapsed on the blood-slick deck to await her own destiny.

That destiny was now to lose what she had tried so hard to save. She had been so close to reassembling their little family which the Great War had torn asunder. So close. The shrieks and screams of the departing faded from her awareness as she relived how this all came to be.

The baby had been just a year old when Jack had been swept up in England's enlistment fervor of Kitchner's Army. The Secretary of State for War, Lord Kitchner, had promised that pals could enlist and serve together. The smoky streets of Accrington instantly emptied every able-bodied, young man into the Accrington Pals. At the ripe old age of twenty-four, Jack became "Pop" to many of the others. The problem was that he already was Pop to someone else. He said he was going, in order to keep England safe. But to keep his young family safe, he was the one who had insisted that Mary take their newborn and stay with relatives across The Pond.

When his part of the York & Lancaster Regiment left for Egypt early last year, Mary and the baby left for her aunt's home in New York. It was December before she heard news of Capt. Perth. So many fragments of rumors just added to the confusion. Apparently, he and his unit had somehow found themselves back in Europe. Perth had been seriously wounded somewhere in northern France and had been transported to hospital in London. Newspapers reported that over eighty per cent of his outfit had been killed or wounded in the first twenty minutes of fighting over some French town that she had never heard of. She had been unable to learn of his condition, only that he was still alive. With help from her aunt and uncle, mother and child booked passage on the first available ship back home to be with Jack.

Waiting on the deck, she now took solace in the thought that at least two in their little family would soon be together. She was only mistaken about which two. As if knowing that all had now been said, the deck tipped seaward and tucked her into the deep as the ship turtled over.

All who lived to tell about the sinking of the *Laconia* came home from the seas on February 28, 1917.

H.M.S. Laburnum docked in Liverpool with the survivors. A strange mercy had been granted the *Laconia*. Instead of the three thousand people she could have been carrying, this trip had carried only two hundred and seventeen crew and seventy-five passengers. Miraculously, the double torpedoes and the dangers of the open sea had claimed only twelve lives. Dozens of anxious, welcoming dockside relatives listened to the excited accounts of the surviving men and women and especially the children. But not from one motherless little girl. Tiny lips would not utter another sound for the next four years. Memory would mercifully not grant her access to the horrors of that night.

August 1917
The home of Robert and Ann Campbell
Birmingham, England

"Annie, do we quite fully understand what we're proposing here?"

"No, I'm not at all certain that we do, Robert. But when do we ever fully understand anything we do? If either of us had truly understood the risks of my return voyage, I would still be back in the States, and God only knows when we would next have seen one another."

"But that's different, isn't it? I mean, we already were a family when this whole mess started up."

"Yes, but didn't our families caution us about getting married when the whole world was in such a turmoil? Didn't they tell us to wait until things settled down before getting married? My own mum was insistent when she said, 'Who knows what could happen to him if he finds himself overseas in hostilities?' And look which one of us did get stuck overseas."

"That was a fluke, and you know it."

"Exactly, Robert! Best laid plans and all. But things happened. And we survived. And along the way, something else happened. A little girl has come into our lives, Robert."

"Yes, dear. A little girl. What do we know about this little girl? Where she came from? What her background was?"

Annie put hands to hips, "As though we ourselves are royalty."

"Annie, you know that is not what I was saying."

"Then what are you saying?"

"I was only saying that we have no idea what she was used to. Would we even be able to provide what she is used to, on the salary of a shipping clerk with Midland Red?"

The most promising path to privileged wealth was probably not his. He worked as one of thousands for the gigantic automotive manufacturer, Birmingham & Midland Motor Omnibus Company. The locals called it Midland Red.

"Robert! For heaven's sake! She is only three years old! What she was used to was having a mum and a dad. She watched one die and then came home to a father who had died of battle wounds before she and her mum had even boarded the ship to rush home to him. They were simply three desperate souls trying to be together as a family. And now only two of them are together. For some reason, it was my arms that she found herself in. Does that tell us anything, my love?"

In fact, it had not been Annie Campbell's arms into which little Lyn Perth had been placed that horrible night six months ago. When *RMS Laconia* had been sent to the bottom by the Kaiser's U-boat, those two had not even been in the same lifeboat. Both of their shells had capsized. Having lost her floatation vest, Annie had just about given up her struggles to stay above water when she grabbed for the only thing floating by. It was the body of a motionless child in a life vest. Scruples drown faster than a body. Without a second thought, Annie set about freeing the vest from the child who no longer needed it. Until the little girl sputtered to life.

"Dear, I know that you saved this little girl," offered Robert.

"Robert, she saved me. She saved us."

"Annie, I understand all that. But is this the time that we can afford another mouth to feed?"

There was a pause. Annie looked into her lap. Without lifting her gaze, her subdued reply was, "Husband, we had already decided to do exactly that."

"Yes, we had, but that was when you were . . ." Now he wished that he had not started that sentence.

"Go ahead. Say it. When I was whole, right?"

"I didn't mean it that way, Annie, and you know it," he said.

"Before the injuries in the sinking made it impossible for me to conceive."

Robert countered, "Well, maybe that's a sign that we're not supposed to have a child."

He regretted those words, too, the instant they came out of his mouth. Instead of the emotional return fire that he expected, his wife brought him to his knees with gentle understanding. "I know that you almost lost me. I know that we did lose the dream of having our own child. Now you have me back. Our own child can never be. I know it can be hard to love again, to love another whom you could lose again, Robert. But what if the sea, which took the child we never had, is now giving us another child? For Christmas?"

As if struck in the gut, Robert doubled over in spasms of quiet sobs. She moved over to him, took his face to her bosom and comforted the childless father.a

CHAPTER 4

THE FIRST U-156

19 July 1918
10 miles off Manhattan
1000 hours

Three months after *U-50* had sent the *Laconia* to the bottom, the next of Germany's three hundred and seventy-five U-boats was born. This one was *U-156*. In its short life, this boat would sink forty-five ships, but even this would not compare with sister boats that sank as many as two hundred and fifty vessels. She would destroy over sixty-four thousand tons of enemy material, but a far cry from boats that sank a million tons. Nevertheless, *U-156* would score a victory that none other ever did.

The *USS San Diego* was a proud old gal. The fourteen-thousand-ton armored cruiser was almost the length of two football fields and her crew of eight hundred and forty-five men could push a speed of twenty-two knots. She had recently served as the flagship of the United States Pacific fleet. Her only casualties had been three years ago when boilers exploded, killing six crewmen. But even that had added to her charmed reputation since that incident resulted in two Congressional Medals of Honor.

Captain Christy pulled aside his Executive Officer. "Gerry, I've got a feeling about this one. I think we might just lose the Gibbons Curse."

Back in 1911, the ship's pay clerk, Charles Gibbons, had been arrested and later convicted of having embezzled $3,000. In naval tradition, his shame reflected on the honor of the entire ship and crew. When he was arrested, Gibbons cursed the ship. The legend grew that, because of Gibbons's Curse, the honor of the ship could never be redeemed. That is why, throughout two wars in two oceans, the cruiser had never yet fired any of its fifty guns in combat.

A faint smile betrayed a respectful playfulness from Lt. Cmdr. Gerald Bradford. "Wishful thinking, Sir?"

"Could be. What day of the week is this?"

"I believe it's Friday, Sir."

"Very well," said the Captain. "That will have a nice ring to it."

"Beg your pardon, Sir?" said the second-in-command.

"All the papers are still talking about Black Sunday, aren't they?" said Christy.

"Yes, Sir. That U-boat that took down six ships on one Sunday last month," said Bradford.

"That happened right around here. I think we're the biggest bait that shark has had since then. I wouldn't mind if we got the honor of returning the favor by making this their Black *Friday*. Let's go to battle stations and evasive zigzag maneuvers."

"Aye, aye, Sir!"

Thirty-four minutes later, the Gibbons Curse came to a flashing end as several portside, three-inch, fifty-caliber rapid fire guns opened up on something moving on the surface. The suspected U-boat periscope quickly disappeared beneath the waves.

U-156

Kapitänleutnat Richard Felt snapped the periscope handles shut to quickly drop the glass eye out of sight below the waves. "Dive! Dive! Depth four zero meters. Course two niner zero."

To his second-in-command, the captain said, "They took the bait!"

Yesterday, the U-boat had completed a mine laying operation parallel to and five kilometers off the coast. The Captain's plan now was to make sure that the target see and hopefully pursue them right into the minefield.

After thirty minutes, the commander gave the order to come to periscope depth. He rotated his field of vision all around until he spotted the target advancing coastward toward him and the waiting minefield.

"Prepare to descend back to four zero meters on my command. Helm, stand by to correct course to zero five degrees on my command. Engines full ahead." He wanted to stir up enough froth around the periscope to make sure the target saw them again. But he did not want to venture further into his own minefield. He hoped that a brief run coastward before submerging would give the unwary pursuer the incentive to follow their extrapolated course right into the minefield. Meanwhile, the submerged and unseen *U-156* would veer north, away from the killing field.

He kept careful watch on the cat. "Aha! She is blowing heavy smoke now! She sees us again. Drop depth now!"

The Weapons Officer said, "Depth now at four zero meters, Sir."

"Very well," said Felt. "Navigation, make course correction now."

USS San Diego

At precisely 1105 hours in the boiler room, Enginemen Second Class Clyde Blain and Jim Rochet ceased to exist. Machinist Mate Second Class Andy Munson was last seen oiling the port side gears, and he also disappeared. Inside of three minutes, the ship listed ten degrees and the smoke stack toppled over and crushed to death Seaman Second Class Paul Harris.

At 1121 hours, the Captain gave orders to abandon ship. This became the actual moment that the Gibbons Curse was cancelled. This time, the pay clerk was one J.D. Gagan whose first action was not to save himself. He immediately went to the payroll safe and transferred all the paper cash to a canvas bag. Even before donning his life preserver, he went over the side with the bag in one hand and his flotation in the other. He saved the United States Navy the funds that the first pay clerk had pilfered, plus the same amount for every year since.

The youngest officer was the newly commissioned Ensign J.P. Hildman. He had just finished double-securing the depth charge racks to prevent accidental catastrophic explosions among the eleven hundred floating survivors.

"Henderson!" he yelled to the Boatswain. "Are the men of your department accounted for?"

"Aye, Sir!"

"Then get overboard!"

"Aye, Sir!" said the senior enlisted man who then ignored the order and immediately headed toward the stairs. The nineteen-year-old junior officer had no idea how to control a man who was older than his own father.

The older man made his way to a mountain of lumber on the next level, cutting it loose so that it tumbled into the ocean. He followed it all overboard and then led the nearby floating seamen to lash timbers together into floating rafts.

First Division Officer Lt. F.G. Kutz called out to the leader of a nearby firefighting crew, "Davis, there's no point anymore. Get your men into that lifeboat and get it away as fast as you can!"

As soon as that boat hit the water, the next descending lifeboat went swinging into it, crushing the skull of Fireman First Class Tom Davis.

At 1130 hours, when he determined that all hands had evacuated, Captain Harley H. Christy walked across the partially submerged deck, turned to salute the ship, and jumped into the water to swim for outstretched arms in a raft. He did not know that Second Class Machinist Mate Tom Fraziee had been trapped in the crow's nest when the ship rolled over, making him the sixth and last fatality of the *San Diego*'s only battle.

Thirty-two more vessels would experience the *San Diego*'s fate before *U-156* was out of torpedoes. But if the crew was out of ammo, it was over-stocked with pride. It had now earned the right to affix another thirty-six victory banners to the previous nine, which fluttered from the top-side suspension cables.

It wasn't just the number of kills that was spectacular. These men had sunk the only American capital warship of the entire war. They had every reason to celebrate. And celebrate they did on this last day from home port. The captain had ordered the cook to outdo himself in creating the most elaborate cake possible. The decoration depicted the sinking of the *San Diego* buried bow-first up to her command bridge in waves of dark blue frosting. Beer rations were liberally distributed and Fatherland was serenaded from one end of the boat to the other. The only casualty was vigilance.

Clearing the Northern Passage around the UK, all the men were in perfect unison as they sang,

Es war einmal ein treuer Seemann, (A faithful sailor without fear)

Der liebt' sein Mädchen ein ganzes Jahr, (He loved his girl for one whole year)

Ein ganzes Jahr und noch viel mehr, (For one whole year and longer yet)

Die Liebe nahm kein Ende mehr." *(His love for her, he'd ne'er forget).*

Der Knab' der fuhr ins fremde See, *(This youth to foreign seas did roam)*

Derweil ward ihm sein Mädchen krank, *(While his true love fell ill at home)*

Sie ward so krank bis auf den Tod" *(Sick unto death, she no one heard)*

One last time in unison, all seventy-seven men halted the ballad as they were all blown a hundred and fifty meters into the air. Just like she had done to the *San Diego*, the U-boat herself had stumbled into a surprise of four submerged mines.

Every U-boat sailor knew the poor odds of returning home. In the U-boat service, it was a foregone conclusion that when a boat went down, so did every single living thing aboard it, including the mice that always stowed away with the fresh provisions at the start of a cruise.

So without warning and in mid-verse of a homesick song, the *U-156* ended its first life, as U-boat sailors say, "with every mouse and man."

CHAPTER 5

WERNER: IF AT FIRST

April 1926
Hartenstein home
Plauen, Germany

All afternoon, the Hartenstein house had been saturated with the increasing fragrance of Selma's dinner-time preparations. Even though the temperature outside was still a little cool, windows were open just a bit to let in the cleansing air of early spring. From a block away, everybody in the neighborhood knew what everyone else was having for supper. Frau Hartenstein was preparing a schnitzel dish that the family had eaten a hundred times. But two parts appetite added to one part anticipation was a recipe that could turn a routine dish into a culinary masterpiece. The cooking smells made waiting more difficult by the minute.

Once everyone was seated at the table, the prayers were said. Then the serving dishes were passed around and everyone began sharing their stories of the day. Thea, the eldest, had graduated the year before and was now working for the family of one of the town doctors. "So Thea," said Papa, "are those six little wild ones minding you any better?"

She let out a little sigh. "Let's just say that they are little angels when their parents are in the room. I am so glad to have the evening off and to be able to come home for supper!"

Charlotte was the youngest, at fifteen years old. "I can hardly wait until I'm done with school and can get a job."

Mutti said, "So what kind of a job do you have in mind?"

"I don't know," she said. "Maybe work in the office for a doctor or a lawyer."

Thea said, "You know, that probably would mean a little more school for things like typing and bookkeeping."

Charlotte pushed the food around on her plate. "Well, it would sure be better than the classes I have to take now."

"Werner, you have been awfully quiet tonight," said his mother. He didn't even seem to be following the conversations. "Is everything alright?"

"I guess I'm just tired of waiting. That's all." Nobody responded but gave him room to say more. "I applied the day after I turned eighteen. We're graduating in a few weeks, and I can't make any plans."

His father weighed in. "I know you've worked really hard for this, son."

"It's all I've ever wanted to do. To be a naval officer. Ever since I was a kid, I've read everything I could put my hands on about the Navy. I even spent all last summer with a tutor to bring up my math scores."

Because Werner was looking down, he didn't notice Selma and William cast a look at each other. Selma nodded at her husband for him to go ahead and do it.

Papa said, "You know, Werner, ever since Versailles, the Navy has not had a whole lot of openings for new naval personnel."

"But if they didn't need new officers, why are they taking applications at all?" said Werner.

"I'm sure there is always a need for new officers," said William. "All I'm saying is that there may not be as many openings as we might like. One of my business contacts told me yesterday that his own son got a rejection notice. The young man, like you, had good qualifications."

Charlotte was getting bored with a conversation that had nothing to do with her. "Can I be excused? I've got homework to do."

Selma looked at William while she addressed the girls. "That would be fine, Charlotte. Thea, could you help me clear the table?"

When only father and son were at the table, William cleared his throat. "Werner, this came this afternoon for you." He handed across the table an official looking envelope.

Werner slowly received the envelope and looked at it for several seconds. Then he opened it. He read it to himself. He closed his eyes. "May I be excused, Papa? I've got homework, too."

CHAPTER 6

LYN: TRANSFORMATION

May 1926
Birmingham Children's Hospital

"**M**rs. Campbell, little Lyn is progressing remarkably well. As we had hoped, the incomplete fractures to her vertebrate do not appear to have bruised the spinal column. Before much longer, I expect that we shall allow some careful steps."

The consulting orthopaedist allowed a subdued smile as Annie's formal composure began to erode with a stream of tears. "Please forgive me. I was so terrified that there would be something else."

"I beg your pardon?" said the doctor.

"Oh, I mean, she has already been through so much in her young life, that I just can't bear the thought of her having to weather other storms as well."

"What, specifically, were you afraid of discovering here, if I may ask, Mrs. Campbell?"

"Oh, that maybe there might have been further injuries, like internal injuries."

The physician looked down as he searched for a gentle way to broach the next subject. "Um, Mrs. Campbell, at Children's here, we discover that mothers sometimes actually sense things before we know them, ourselves."

"I'm sorry, doctor, but I'm not at all sure that I follow."

"Not all internal injuries are physical, you know."

Annie stared at the doctor for several seconds. Then she stared through the doctor, through the walls, beyond the hospital, all the way to a point in the North Sea seven years in the past.

"I wonder if perhaps you suspect particular internal injuries that may not be physical ones," confirmed the doctor.

Annie said, "That is the real reason why she broke her back."

"Now I'm afraid that I am the one who does not follow," said the specialist. "Wasn't this caused by an accidental fall?"

"She fell because she was running from other children who were teasing her about not talking, about not playing like the rest of them. Then they tried to take her lipstick away."

The doctor was confused. "Her lipstick?"

"The only thing she seems to play with. That is when she ran, when they chased her, when she fell down all those stone steps."

"And what is her anxiety all about?" asked the physician.

"I'm sure I don't know. She has always been like this since we adopted her. I assume it is trauma from the sinking. She and her mum had stayed with relatives in the States for half a year before the disaster. She was only two. In letters, the family does not recall any unusual behavior."

"Mrs. Campbell, I feel that I can be more certain of Lyn's spinal recovery than I can be of her psychological issues. We know so little about such things in children. Sometimes these things change and sometimes they don't."

"Then what?"

Without skipping a beat, the healer filled in the correct answer. "Why, then it would become necessary to begin thinking about an asylum where she could receive more appropriate care."

"Does it never end for this child? Annie said angrily. "She is plucked from drowning only to become an orphan, then rescued from that fate only to face the possibility of a paralysis. And now she heals from that only to face another kind of prison."

"There does indeed seem to be a pattern there," said the physician.

Mary looked down and sniffled, "A pattern of hopelessness."

"Oh, yes, I see," said the slightly embarrassed doctor. "Well, I was noticing perhaps a second pattern as well."

Annie didn't know whether to brace herself for hope or disappointment. "Second pattern?"

"Well, yes," he said. "It does seem that each time little Lyn approaches a cliff, somehow or other the road seems to change in her favor, don't you see? I might suggest a pattern of hope there, wouldn't you?"

Indeed, that did become the pattern which clearly emerged over the next four months. Lyn's spinal injury healed so well that she emerged as an ideal candidate for the new outpatient clinic at Birmingham Children's Hospital. Ironically, it was her psychological progress that was too good for discharge from the hospital. Hence the meeting.

The physician opened the consultation. "Mr. and Mrs. Campbell, it is so good of both of you to be here today. There are some developments that I think we should address." Both parents, in their Sunday finest, looked at each other with shared and concerned confusion.

The doctor then introduced the fourth person in the meeting who was a young, slender, slightly olive complexioned brunette in a nurse's uniform. "I have also asked Nurse Cummings to join us because, as you know, she is probably the most important person of our staff from little Lyn's perspective."

The young nurse offered a warm smile and nodded her head. "Mr. Campbell, Annie, it's good to see you."

Annie needed to get right to the point. "Is there something wrong?"

"Oh no, quite the contrary," assured the doctor. "We have an opportunity before us. As you know, our hospital has just opened one of England's first outpatient clinics. This new clinic could make it possible for Lyn to remain home and come in for appointments instead. That's why they call it 'outpatient', for patients who are treated out of hospital."

Robert excitedly asked, "Are you saying that Lyn could receive her care through that out-clinic?"

"Outpatient clinic," corrected the doctor. "Yes, as a matter of fact, that is true. If that is what you want."

Annie was confused. "Why would we not want to bring Lyn home?"

"Well, that is why we wanted to talk with both of you. You certainly can bring her home. You also have a different opportunity, as well. Nurse Cummings, this was your idea. Perhaps you might explain it to Mr. and Mrs. Campbell?"

"Yes, doctor," said the nurse. "We wonder if perhaps we should want to keep Lyn *in* hospital for a bit longer. Since she is doing so well."

Robert Campbell was beginning to strain. "Forgive me for not quite following. You say that Lyn is doing so well that she should stay *in* hospital?"

The nurse said, "Not for her spine. That could very well be handled outside the hospital. But it's her speech, her social skills that have shown the most amazing growth."

"Remember a few months ago, Mrs. Campbell?" said the physician. "Back then, I said that I couldn't be as sure about Lyn's psychological improvement as I was about the prognosis for her spine? Well, presently, I confess that I don't quite know what to say."

When the doctor saw that he was creating even more confused looks, he said, "I personally have never witnessed such a wonderful awakening as we are seeing in Lyn, though this sort of thing has occasionally been reported among young children. Their systems can have an uncanny resilience to all sorts of insults."

Annie was equal parts wearied and wary. "Well, then, why do you want her to remain in hospital if she has made such a good recovery?"

"To be perfectly forthcoming," said the physician, "I do have to admit that not all my colleagues here are of the same mind on this. In fact, mine may well be the minority position, especially with the opening of the new outpatient facility here. I am in agreement that as far as her spine is concerned, things could do quite nicely with monitoring through that clinic."

The father was almost at his wits' end. "Then why not allow her to come home?"

"Certainly that, of course, is what we'll do if that is your wish. But let me ask what you have noticed about how Lyn's talking has emerged," said the doctor.

"Well, it was like her language suddenly appeared fully developed," reflected Annie.

"Precisely. And what were the circumstances when this happened?"

Annie had to catch her breath and she blinked back tears when she recalled the exact moment. "I will never forget how she looked up at me with such bright, excited eyes for the very first time I can ever remember. And out came this whole sentence, right then and there!"

The doctor gently prodded. "Do you recall what that sentence was?"

Annie pursed her lips to hold back a sob as she remembered the day when Nurse Cummings had very objectively reported all the ways Lyn had helped that day. "What Lyn said was, 'Mummy, look! I'm a nurse!'"

Her father reflected, "It was almost like she waited to talk until she thought she had a good reason to."

"The thing is," said the nurse, "at first, all her talking was just with me. But after a couple weeks, she also started talking with one of my assistants as well. Slowly, she seems to be allowing others into her circle."

"Yes, I have noticed as much," said Ann. "But what does all of this have to do with keeping her in hospital?"

"Well," said the doctor, "it has to do with what she is choosing to do and with whom. Nurse Cummings, please explain further, if you would be so kind."

"Certainly, doctor. You see, Mr. and Mrs. Campbell, so far, Lyn does not seem to be interested all that much in other children. Her play is not like that of most little girls her age. Her interests seem rather specific to her nurses and to what these nurses do. To encourage her new-found development, we have been playing to her interests. So, we have allowed her to shadow me at times, as my little helper."

Lyn's father was even more confused. "That's good, isn't it? It sounds like you're saying that it's *not* good."

The doctor and the nurse looked at each other as though silently determining which of them should explain things. Nurse Cummings took the cue. "Oh, you are certainly correct. Lyn is doing marvelously, indeed. The thing is, little Lyn thinks she's a nurse like me. She needs to think that she is a little girl like the other little girls."

"That is where University comes in," said the doctor. "As you know, our hospital is associated with University of Birmingham next door here. We provide training opportunities for their students and in turn we have the benefit of some of their research expertise. Lyn's sudden blossoming is really such a remarkable thing, that your little girl caught the attention of one of their consultants here. So, he's been looking in from time to time, and he had an interesting thought. This is really why we wanted to talk with you this morning."

Both parents appeared to be leaning in with interest, so the physician continued. "Well, the consultant was wondering if we could channel Lyn's natural interests. Mrs. Campbell, you just said that the reason Lyn landed here in the first place was that the other kids were teasing her because she wasn't talking and playing with them. Well, this is precisely where we are at the moment. Though she has shown remarkable progress with adults and adult-like tasks, what she still needs to do is to learn to play with other children. Our thought would be to have her assist Nurse Cummings here in bringing toys, for instance, to much younger patients."

The nurse said, "I might show Lyn how to teach a small child how to play with a particular toy or game. Eventually, Lyn might work with older kids until she finds a peer with whom she becomes a friend. Then, just as she included other nurses besides me, she might naturally widen the number of children with whom she plays."

The father connected the dots. "And that is why she would remain in the world of hospitals."

"Perhaps for a few more weeks until she begins expanding her circle," said the physician. "Then she could go home to see if she continues expanding that circle in her own neighborhood and school."

Their daughter would indeed remain in hospital. But, before long, not as a patient.

PART II
EMERGENCE 1937-1945

DAVE GARWICK

CHAPTER 7

WERNER: CONSCIENCE

12 June 1937
Saturday evening
German Naval Officer's Club
Berlin

E leven years earlier, Werner Hartenstein h
rejected for the officer naval cadet program.
the first time he had applied. Shortly
rearmament efforts accelerated and so did the demar
naval officers. Hartenstein's second application was
In seven short years, he rapidly rose through five r
now earned him a place at the table.

The person next to him at the table was less thar
with their position. "What a waste of a Saturday nig
sights on a real establishment of fine dining." (
Rasner had the look of someone who already ha
experience with establishments of fine dining. C
waves of prematurely receding dark brown ha
paunchy pale face. Through small wire rimmed

d eyes stared balefully at his watch. "And by this
oped to be on another mission. How long is this
ir supposed to go on?"

senior officer is good and ready to leave for *his*
of the evening." The newly promoted
Werner Hartenstein chided his friend. "This is
r dues, aspiring young officer."

or officer was a contrast to Wilhelm Rasner in
om a distance, Hartenstein looked like his
t 'hard rock'. At six feet one, his slim build
an face with an angular jaw and a gaze that
. When he was not in a command situation
'd also have a twinkle of playfulness.

junkets to Berlin would be a little more
lid get any free time," Willie said.

er, "don't see anything on the schedule

elmed. "Great. A Sunday."

king of taking in a sermon," said

ad been
That was
hereafter,
d for new
accepted.
nks which

lot of fun on a long cruise," his friend
you, make you trade in your guts for
utnant? As for me, I would have
."

see that whiff of black smoke on
sed those well placed shots about
val heroes?"

impressed
ht. I had my
Oberleutnant
d too much
lose-cropped
ir framed a
glasses, even

re talking about. Went right over

. "If you want to rise in the
well to read the waves. They
guy again."

Willie spread his hands in open emptiness. "I'm at a loss."

"Niemöller was one of the U-boat hot shots back in the last one. He's now one of the most controversial pastors in Germany. Right here in Berlin. My home is half a day from here. When our family would holiday in Berlin, we often visited that very church. They say that half of the Führer's men go there now. You want excitement, Willie, that's where you might find it tomorrow."

Rasner was a little less than inspired. "Yeah. Right."

"I don't know," said Werner. "Never heard a U-boat preacher before, much less one playing against the big boys. I'd like to hear for myself, since we're stuck here anyway."

Willie held up his hands in mock surrender. "I don't want to get anywhere near that. If they're warning old war heroes about loyalty, I don't want my face anywhere near those bright, shiney Gestapo cars or whoever they're watching. I figure that to have a future in the Kriegsmarine, you first have to have a future. If you know what I mean."

As though the front tables had been eavesdropping, the senior officers and their escorts rose as one and began filing out of the hall. The obligatory entertainment was accomplished. Rasner wiped his mouth, folded the linen napkin, placed it on the table and rose to pronounce, "Let the evening begin! Say a confession for me in the morning, choirboy."

13 June 1937
Sunday morning
Jesus Christus Kirche
Dahlem, outside Berlin

"Martin! For the love of God, don't do this!" Franz Gottlieb was the senior lay leader of the congregation. He actually looked more like the head butler of the venerable institution. Pastors would come and go, but old families like his had anchored this part of the Body of Christ for generations. If the pastor was the shepherd of the congregation, then Gottlieb saw himself as shepherd to the shepherd. And he had shepherded many, including more than one who had shot himself in the foot with holy righteousness.

"That is precisely why I do this, Franz," answered Niemöller. He went back to looking over his text of the sermon, making a change here and there as the head deacon went on.

"Martin, don't let your namesake go to your head. You will have no Frederick to spirit you away." Herr Gottlieb was not only the keeper of the congregation's stories, but the histories of the Church, as well. He was referring to how Frederick the Wise of Saxony had kidnapped and hidden Martin Luther in protective custody. Luther had thereby escaped execution for heresy against the Holy Roman Emperor, Charles V, in 1521.

Niemöller did not take his eyes off the script. "Ah, but my good friend, if it comes to that, you as head deacon will have to be the one to remind the flock that the name 'Martin' does indeed mean martyr."

The portly Gottlieb saw himself as the protector of whatever pastor was under his tutelage. Lately, he found himself needing to protect Niemöller from himself. "If you really knew what that could mean," and here he paused for effect, "Martin, even you would not wax so philosophical."

The pastor kept making little changes to the text as he commented, "Have they touched Bonhoeffer? He was teaching against the Reich, in London of all places. He returned two years ago and not a thing has happened to him. You're overreacting, Franz."

Herr Gottlieb grasped his hands behind his back, slightly bent over the seated pastor and lowered his voice into a confidential tone. "Martin, you yourself are still pinched by what happened last night. Don't pretend otherwise."

Niemöller did not look up and feigned indifference. "What happened?"

"Not a thing happened to you. That's the point, Martin. Has the Naval Officer's Club ever failed to invite the heroic Kapitänleutnant Niemöller, holder of Iron Cross First Class, to a command staff affair?"

The old hero waved away the suggestion, "Ach, a simple oversight, I'm sure. Besides, it was my Saturday night sermon preparation. I couldn't have wasted the evening."

Franz baited the hook. "Then you haven't heard."

Niemöller stopped his editing, but still focused on the paper. "Haven't heard what?"

"Well, apparently you were not overlooked after all."

Suddenly, the pastor looked up for the first time. "Stop playing games with me, Franz. Spit it out."

"Oh, well now we seem to have gotten your attention!" Gottlieb said.

Martin remained silent, looking straight into the deacon's eyes, waiting for the commanded explanation.

Herr Gottlieb seemed to be enjoying his success when all of a sudden he was jolted to the task at hand. "It seems, Martin, that in his dinner speech, Konteradmiral Raeder made a glancing reference to the loyalty that is expected of all German naval officers. Active duty and retired."

Gottlieb paused after each remark. "'No matter where or to whom they find themselves preaching', he said. 'Whether they had commanded a desk or a U-boat and even held the Iron Cross First Class', he said."

That stopped Niemöller for a moment's reflection of the old days when Raeder had been a peer. "Well, Finke always did have a certain flair for the dramatic when he got into his cups a bit. So, how did you come by this juicy bit of gossip, Franz?"

The pastor's protector rejected the premise of the question. "It's not gossip, Martin. That is the reason I came to see you before church. Two of our members, who wish to remain nameless, happened to be at the dinner for some reason or other. They were so concerned that they came straight to my home at ten o'clock last night. They wanted me to warn you. They insisted that I rouse you out of bed immediately so that you could change your remarks for today. But I wanted to think about all this so as to not 'overreact' as you say. But I could not sleep at all, the more I thought about it. I've been waiting all night so I could talk to you."

"And so you have, good friend. Just don't try catching up on that sleep during my sermon," teased the pastor. "And in all seriousness Franz, I do thank you from the bottom of my heart for taking my welfare so seriously. And I promise you that I will ponder your advice."

"Martin, please don't underestimate what I am saying. It's not just you that I worry about. If you bring down the wrath of the Reich, it may not just fall on you, but on this entire congregation and all who are associated with you."

"Yes, Franz, but if I as a preacher and this congregation fail to stand up for what's right, then what is the point of either?"

"But if both are silenced, then who can speak anything for God?" countered Gottlieb.

"The Lord somehow managed to get by without me before," said Niemöller who looked at his watch. "Now I need a few moments to organize things. Service is about to start."

"All I can say is, God be with you, Martin."

"He always is, Franz."

The door announced a fervent double tap. The parish secretary, Frau Eberlein, spoke through the door in a strained whisper. "Pastor, there is something you should see."

Franz opened the door and the assistant rushed into the study. "Pastor Niemöller, please come quickly! Herr Gottlieb, you too!"

Without a word, both men followed behind her out of the study, down to the end of the narrow hallway where large windows overlooked the church entrance two stories below. Three black sedans were parked directly in front of the steps. Six men all in identical black fedoras and long black leather overcoats loitered on the sidewalk. They were not entering the church. Three were smoking cigarettes and two appeared to be taking notes as they made a point of observing every arriving worshiper. One agent nodded a sinister acknowledgment to each worshiper.

Children who stared back in curiosity were jerked straight ahead by parents who were nervous about standing out. One family half a block away saw the vultures and turned back.

"Now will you finally listen to me, Martin?" demanded the deacon.

"Franz, they've been here before. Though maybe not so obviously."

"Of course! That's when they started keeping an eye on you. What do you think it means that they are now bold enough to show themselves like this?"

A scene materialized in the cinema of Martin's mind. For some pastors, one of the most painful things in Scripture had been a famous clash between Jesus and the one he had just chosen as his chief apostle. Jesus has just explained that he himself is going to be martyred. Peter stands up to defend Jesus by saying that nothing like this could ever be allowed to happen. Instead of appreciating Peter's loyalty, Jesus turns on his friend and rebukes him by saying, "Get behind me, Satan, for your thoughts are on the side of man, not of God." People who thought of themselves as apostles often identified with Peter and felt like he got a raw deal for simply trying to stand up for Jesus.

For the first time, the pastor saw his own chief defender as a Peter. Pastor Niemöller took on the command presence of Kapitänleutnant Niemöller. "All it means, Herr Deacon, is that they are trying to intimidate us into silence. Your job and my job is to speak the truth, not to silence it. Do you understand me?"

Gottlieb registered the rebuke and it stung.

The old captain had more to say. His outward stature had diminished since his days on the bridge. But his inner strength had redoubled in those same years of standing watch in the pulpit.

"By showing up like this, they are doing us a favor, Franz. Now people can see for themselves what I have been saying. The Reich wants to stand at the door of the church itself so they can be what the people see! The church will worship Jesus Christ alone or it will cease to be the church, and I will cease to be its servant. But for now, I have a job to do." He forcefully planted his fountain pen on the blotter, as he quickly pushed away from the desk, rose to attention, smoothed down his shirt and shouldered his way past Gottlieb. "Excuse me as I get ready." He may as well have said, "Dismissed!"

Frau Gottlieb was old enough to be Niemöller's mother and may have been the only one who would have dared chide him. "Shall I fetch your robe, Pastor, or your shining suit of armor?" The battle was met.

One of the many who filed into the church was Kapitänleutnant Werner Hartenstein. His self-appointed mission was to observe what the provocative remarks had been about at last evening's officers' dinner. But to enter the church, Werner found himself having to pass in front of the most feared observers in all Germany, the Gestapo greeters of Heinrich Himmler. He didn't know it, but Himmler's hawks had been sent there personally by their master as a personal favor to his own lord and master, Adolf Hitler.

As he entered the spacious sanctuary, Werner was immediately aware of a tension in the air. There was no customary silence of worshipers in meditation. Instead, there was the pervasive thrum of a hundred hushed conversations that not even the pipe organ prelude could mask. As if in competition with the distracting noise, the organ rose in a building crescendo.

As the music soared, the majestic flight was shot down by the stoic, staccato footfalls of five black, leather-clad Gestapo agents advancing down the center aisle in uniform cadence.

They took their places in the front row by kindly inviting the already seated worshipers there to find some other pew. In a space of less than sixty seconds, the father's confusion was replaced by indignation which instantly turned to fear and then to flight. The displaced family stood, side-stepped out of the pew, and quickly filed down the side aisle, and right out of the church.

Pastor Niemöller appeared up front from a side door to take his place at the altar. He then pronounced the customary invocation in a very uncustomary way. He focused directly and solely at the Gestapo pew, and paused for several seconds of deafening silence.

"In the name of the Father." Still looking at them, he paused and spoke the next line, "And the Son." He paused again with his eyes locked on the visitors, "And the Holy Ghost." One last pause noticeably longer than the others. "And *no other*. Amen."

Then the pastor announced: "My dear friends, with your kind indulgence, I am going to alter our course of worship a little this morning. Normally, we begin with a hymn, with the sermon following later in the service. With the indulgence of our gracious organist, I would like to begin, instead, with the words of Jesus. We are here because of God. We are here to worship God. We are here to do what His only Son did and to say what His only Son said.

"When the authorities tried to silence Him, when they tried to replace Jesus, when they tried to intimidate Christ, when they insulted the Prince of Peace," and now the pastor looked straight at the front row interlopers, "when they told the Son of Man to move over, this is what the King of Kings said, when God himself walked this earth among us:

Blessed are the meek, for THEY shall inherit the earth. Blessed are the merciful for THEY shall obtain mercy. Blessed are the pure in heart, for THEY shall see God. Blessed are the peacemakers, for THEY shall be called the sons of God. Blessed are those who are persecuted for righteousness' sake, for THEIRS is the kingdom of heaven."

Then Niemöller paused and searched the congregation for the face of his head deacon. He slowly panned the sanctuary with searching eyes while everyone else awaited the next expected line of the Beatitudes. There was Franz, far in the back. The preacher raised his gaze, locked eyes with his old friend, and continued,

"Blessed are YOU when men revile YOU and persecute YOU and say all kinds of evil against YOU falsely on My account. Rejoice and be glad, for your reward is great in heaven, for so men persecuted the prophets who were before them."

Niemöller was able to see Head Deacon Franz Gottlieb shake his head in resignation and walk right out the door. It was held open for him by the sixth Gestapo agent.

Two of the Gestapo observers in the front row were stenographers, furiously recording everything Niemöller said. When he noticed this, the pastor looked at them and said, "I hope you got that. I hope you got every word of that. For these are not my words but the words of the only God we worship."

Then he raised his eyes to the congregation. "Dear friends, allow me to beg your patience once more as I apologize for not preaching the sermon I had prepared. I had planned to share with you the one experience of the War which had the biggest impact on my decision to leave the Kriegsmarine and seek a place in the pulpit. I must leave that story to another time. Because of recent developments, the Spirit seems to be moving me to share another message with you.

"I would hazard a guess that not everyone will be saddened that my message will be unusually brief. I want to be sure that you are awake and attentive throughout, to hear the entire message. The text for this next message is from the twenty-second chapter of Saint Matthew, the twenty-first verse, where Jesus said, '*Render unto Caesar the things that are Caesar's and unto God the things that are God's.*'

"I served the state with zealous honor, placing my life on the line as a U-boat commander in the War. I have always been a faithful son of the Fatherland. And I firmly believe that from citizens, much is due Caesar. Indeed, our Lord says that we are to render unto Caesar all that belongs to Caesar.

"But the place of God does not belong to Caesar. The First Commandment itself is that we are to worship God and no other. We are to love the Lord our God with all our heart and all our soul and all our mind. In the biggest questions of life, our first loyalty is to the commands of God. What we render unto Caesar is everything else that does not conflict with the will of God.

"It is because we worship Jesus that we love our enemies. Why? Simply because He commanded us to. It was the God we worship who said, '*You have heard that it was said, 'You shall love your neighbor and hate your enemy,' but I say unto you, 'love your enemies and pray for those who persecute you.*'

"Does your enemy insult you even with a slap to the face? It was Jesus who said, '*Do not resist one who is evil. But if any one strikes you on the right cheek, turn to him the other also.*'

"Does someone presume to take your pew in worship? Again it was Jesus who said, '*If anyone would sue you and take your coat, let him have your cloak as well.*'

"So, we of all people, can certainly spare a pew, no? After all, did not Jesus himself share His Last Supper?" The pastor slowly and deliberately shot a sustained stare at the front row, "Even with Judas." He took a long pause as he acknowledged the gravity of his guests. "I welcome the messengers of Caesar."

68

The worship service probably continued for a little while after that. Hartenstein would not have known. Niemöller had just poked a stick right in the eye of the Gestapo.

Somehow, the young officer found himself standing in line to be greeted at the door by Niemöller himself. The pastor's attention was caught by the trim six-foot-tall uniformed naval officer.

Hartenstein addressed him by his old military title. "Kapitänleutnant Niemöller, Sir, would there be any possibility that you could sacrifice even the briefest time to share with me the thoughts you had prepared about the War?"

"Well, young man, I would be honored, though being seen with me might not be the smartest career move for you. Maybe you would be wiser to hear the story along with the rest of the congregation next week, so as to not stand out?"

It had been some while since the twenty-nine-year-old commander had been called a young man. His torpedo boat crews usually referred to him as The Old Man, though certainly not to his face.

"I do appreciate your concern for me, Pastor, but I will be returning to base in two more nights. It will probably be some time before I return to Berlin, and by that time. . ."

"I myself might not be here, you mean," quipped the preacher.

Years of trained military stoicism had never been able to erase Hartenstein's honestly expressive face. Truly horrified at having offended a senior person, the visitor quickly said, "Oh no, Sir! Please forgive me! I meant to say that, by that time, you probably would have already preached that sermon."

"Of course, of course. I was simply teasing you. This day has been far too serious. Tell you what, son. I know that if you are worth your salt as a naval officer, you will pursue your goal until you have closed with it anyway. So why not stop by my quarters after dark, say at 2200 hours, and perhaps we can get better acquainted. You might do well to make sure that you are not being watched. If you do not show, I will certainly understand. Please take no risks, my young friend."

Werner Hartenstein had been on vulnerable torpedo boats long enough to learn a thing or two about stealth and evasion. He employed those skills in planning his reconnoiter with the old veteran. When time and circumstances allowed, one of the most effective ways to avoid ambush and maybe set one yourself was to arrive on station long before those hunting you.

"Is this a little overdramatic?" thought Werner to himself. He was simply going to a pastor's residence for a casual late night conversation. Yet, he himself had seen the provocations of six Gestapo agents and the way that Niemöller had kept waving a red flag before them. Last night, he had heard the not too subtle disparaging allusions to Niemöller from the high command. No, Hartenstein decided, he was not at all being overdramatic. There was real drama going on here. And he knew that it was far bigger than anything he could appreciate. Years on a torpedo boat had taught him to regard every unidentified ship as hostile until proven otherwise.

So, Hartenstein left the church to take a casual stroll around the neighborhood with the Niemöller residence nearby. Within sight of both was a small guesthouse called the Schwarzhaus.

Though he had no luggage, his uniform convinced the proprietor that the naval officer would go back to base to retrieve his overnight bag. "And how many nights, sir?" asked the man.

"Just tonight. There are a few other spots in town that I need to visit."

"Forgive me, Kapitänleutnant, but under such circumstances, we do have to ask for payment in advance. We have an inexpensive room in the back area."

The tall, handsome officer tilted his head in a shy smile and lowered his voice. "I was kind of hoping for a room looking out the front. In fact, the reason that I chose your fine establishment is that it looks out on the church I attended this morning. I guess I'm a bit of a romantic, but it is that view which brings me the peace I need before putting out to sea again."

The manager hesitated, "I . . . don't know. We try to keep those available for our regular returning guests."

"I certainly understand," replied the cooperative officer. "For that reason, I would happy to pay a little extra to . . . secure the privilege?" Hartenstein's eyes smiled as he laid out a large bill which the manager made invisible with his beefy sleight of hand.

With the other hand the clerk materialized a room key. "I think we may have one of those rooms that you may find quite adequate."

"I had hoped you might," winked the officer. "I shall now fetch my overnight bag and return within a couple hours."

As Hartenstein exited the lobby door, he noticed the three black Gestapo sedans still parked in front of the church, even though all worshipers had long since gone home for their Sunday dinners. "I hope the good pastor is still here for our evening conversation," he said to himself.

A blast of snowy wind seemed to answer his question and propel him back, away from the sinister sedans. He re-entered the lobby, telling the manager that he first needed to take a brief nap before heading back to the base. From his second floor window, he kept an eye on the outside of the church, trying to imagine what was going on inside the church.

Niemöller was hanging up his vestments when one of the Gestapo agents quietly walked into his office. The other five waited out in the hallway.

"Herr Pastor, we certainly would not presume to intrude upon your well-earned rest, after conducting such a . . . what shall we say . . . courageous service out there. But you were so insistent on extending a welcome to the, how did you call us, the 'messengers of Caesar?' It would have been rude of me to ignore such a gracious invitation, no?"

"Indeed, please do make yourself comfortable Herr . . .?"

"Major Ernst Dietrich, Secret State Police, at your service, kind Pastor."

"And how can I be of service to you, Herr Major?"

"You were prophetic in your remarks this morning, Herr Pastor. You referred to us as messengers of Caesar. As it happens, that is exactly why we are here this morning: as messengers of Caesar. Hah! Is that not inspired?"

"I am at a loss, Herr Major. I am quite sure that I do not know what you might be referring to."

Like a snake with no eyelids, the serpentine agent did not blink as he eye-locked his prey. "Yours is a prestigiously visible congregation where many of the state's officials worship. Their involvement here is a public testimony to the good will of the Reich."

"That may be the conclusion of some, but I hope it is not the reason these people participate. Some of those officials are among the most faithful worshipers I have," said the pastor.

"Be that as it may," said the stalker, "your position as pastor here, salaried by the state, and your prominence as a national war hero, also bestowed by the state, carry with it certain obligations to be rendered unto Caesar, as you so eloquently put it."

"I quite agree, Herr Major."

Dietrich clapped his hands together in a prayer stance. "Excellent! Then I am sure you would want to be the first to know that membership in your congregation for the Himmler family would be seen by the Führer himself as a personal favor to him and a service to the Reich."

Niemöller was a little less jubilent. "As I said earlier this morning, Herr Major, in case you might have missed it, the place of God does not belong to any mortal, even Caesar. This is a place of God, not a social registry. Membership is for those who swear allegiance to Jesus Christ. Herr Himmler has refused such allegiance on grounds that his allegiance is only to the Führer. He is the one who has excluded himself from membership in the church of Christ. Membership is not granted as a favor to the Führer but only for the sake of God."

The Gestapo agent concluded the audience, "As I said, Herr Niemöller, you certainly do have a way of being prophetic. But you would do well to not forget what you yourself, or should I say your God, said about prophets: *For so they persecuted the prophets.* You see, we *did* indeed get it all down. Every single," and here he paused for mocking effect, "last word of it. Good day to you, Herr Niemöller."

From his window perch, Hartenstein saw the Gestapo sedans pull away from the church. He watched ten more minutes to be sure that no other official observers returned. Then he left for the hotel where he and his friend Willie Rasner were sharing quarters. It was now 1400 so he hoped that Willie had returned and sobered up from whatever "mission" he had been on the night before.

As Werner approached the hotel, he fabricated an untraceable alibi that would explain his anticipated absence this evening. It was important that he plant the fish tale with Willie who then could honestly provide him false cover. The nature of their relationship was perfect for this particular fiction. Nobody knew them to be particularly close friends. They had only made each other's acquaintance the previous week when Willie had been assigned to Werner's unit. It would make perfect sense for them to have been doing different things on their free time and for Rasner to only know what Hartenstein happened to share with him.

The lobby of the Kaiser Wilhelm dwarfed the entire guesthouse where Werner planned to stay in the hours leading to his meeting with Niemöller. The ceilings alone rose almost two stories, with a dozen chandeliers that each might have suspended at least half a ton of reflective crystal. Scarlet, upholstered, overstuffed mahogany thrones were arranged throughout the lobby in half a dozen clusters for private conversations.

The doormen would not allow an officer to strain himself opening any lobby door. These guards of hospitality wore uniforms that seemed to outrank the dozens of bemedaled officers of every service who were temporarily billeted there.

Hartenstein opened the door to his shared room and called out, "Willie, you here?"

The only reply was a moan from under a mountain of blankets. Rasner was still hung over from the night before.

Hartenstein chuckled derisively, "Willie, would you please get your sorry corpse upright? I need to talk to you." It was imperative that Willie get the message right so that he could convey the story-line if necessary. If some Gestapo goon asked Willie where his roommate had been, Willie needed to be able to truthfully tell the lie. If Willie had no idea where Hartenstein had been, then there would be no alibi.

Rasner was hopeless. There was no chance that he would even remember that he had seen his roommate, much less recall what had been said. Werner decided to write a huge note to his roommate explaining that he had "met a special friend with whom he planned to spend the night" and would catch up with Willie the next morning at the opening conference. It occurred to him that the written message might even be better by way of providing a story that was documented. "Be sure to use your cursive hand to verify that this was really written by you," Hartenstein reminded himself.

He didn't like portraying himself as some kind of womanizer, but such a farewell dalliance could seem totally believable, especially to Willie. Besides, he was not lying. He was indeed spending the night with a new special friend. But if it came to having to say that it was with a prostitute, then so much the better, because Werner could say that he had no idea who she was. The story would be irrefutable.

There was another advantage to Willie's hangover: Werner would not have to waste precious time talking with him. The March sun still set rather early and Hartenstein wanted to get

75

back to the Schwarzhaus with plenty of light remaining to observe the Niemöller residence.

When he entered the lobby of his temporary new residence, the officer made a point of greeting the proprietor by showing off his overnight bag. "Good to see you back, Kapitän," was the homecoming. "Dinner will be served at six o'clock. Will you be joining us?"

"Unfortunately, no, Herr Sievers. I thank you for the kind invitation, but I have been invited to a friend's for refreshments later this evening."

"As you wish, my friend. Have a good evening," acknowledged the owner.

Hartenstein would have to earn this good evening with a few hours of preparatory observation. Endless hours of monotony were nothing new to a shipboard officer. A specialty was that of remaining vigilant to the slightest clue on changeless seas after hours of seeing absolutely nothing. This would be child's play by comparison.

On the other hand, he couldn't shake the feeling that all of this cloak and dagger business was a little silly. He would be embarrassed if anyone were to see him sitting in front of sheer curtains watching the street. There was, in fact, little else a person could do in this room. There was no music, nothing to read. Just a bed, a chair, a desk, a drawer and one window. And time. There was not even a pattern to count on the wall covering.

Then he noticed it. A man standing in front of the church, looking up at its massive, double-wrought iron doors. He did not seem to belong to a car. He was simply enjoying a smoke. In twenty-degree cold. The man seemed to be pacing back and forth in front of the church, occasionally looking at his watch as though he were expecting something.

If that man were Gestapo, standing out in the open would be a strange way to surveil somebody. Just then, a small black car driven by a woman with long golden hair stopped at the man. He looked up and down the street as though to make sure that no one saw him getting into the car. A sexual rendezvous in front of a church? He could imagine the guy defending himself to his wife: "Do you think I would be crazy enough to have an affair in front of a church?!" This was the avenue of alibis for everybody, it seemed.

Then it dawned on the novice spy that, for all his machinations, he was observing the wrong side of the street! If that last guy would have been stupid to stand right in front of the church to spy on it, then Werner was just as stupid expecting to see a spy on that same spot. If someone were keeping the church under surveillance, he would have to be doing it from the same side of the street as Werner, maybe even under his window! Now he was doubly glad that no one knew what he was up to.

In order to scan the correct side of the street, Werner himself was going to have to be the idiot standing in front of the church so he could monitor the guesthouse side of things. For the next three hours, he made up one excuse after another to leave the lobby and walk around the neighborhood, "enjoying the fresh air as any sailor likes to do."

By 2200 hours, he had strolled through every inch of the immediate block, precisely six times in the dark. There had been no sign of anyone showing any attention to the church. So, he knocked at the door of the Niemöller residence. It was immediately answered before the third rap.

The light inside was dim so as to not illuminate the night. "Please come in immediately Kapitänleutnant," said the pastor who pulled him in. "Please forgive my neurotic behavior, young man. I must be a little paranoid after my visitors this morning."

So, this is what a pastor's home is like, thought the grown-up Sunday school student. He had never been in a pastor's home. He felt like he had stepped behind the altar into the sacred space of the holy of holies where few mortals would ever dare tread: the serene quiet, the low light, the smell of leather, the walls lined with books and the overstuffed chair of contemplation. Everything seemed to set the backdrop for the small end table nearby piled with opened books stacked six deep.

Niemöller recognized the familiar disorientation of unfamiliar visitors who seemed mesmerized by the thought that they were standing on holy ground. "Please feel comfortable, my young friend."

Werner said, "I did as you advised and took precautions to ensure that I was not being followed."

"Are you sure?" said the pastor.

Werner thought for a moment. "As sure as any target can be."

The former U-boat officer slowly nodded in deep thought. "No offense intended, but I'm not sure that such an assurance gives me total confidence. Once upon a time, I sank upwards of seventy-five ships whose captains thought the same thing."

The young naval officer reverted to his normal stance of humble deference. "Pastor Niemöller, I do not want to add to your troubles. You don't even know if I might be an informant. I would be more than willing to leave," assured Hartenstein.

Niemöller could not suppress a chuckle. "My rudeness again. I'm not laughing at you, but I am afraid I have misled you. I am not concerned about myself being observed. I am already a matter of public record, as you saw this morning. It is *you* whom I don't want being observed in my presence. I am obviously already under suspicion. Hopefully you are not."

"Speaking of such things, Kapitän, I am extremely interested in hearing that story you alluded to this morning," said Werner. "That is, if I am not intruding."

"Don't worry, young man. One of the reasons I invited you over at such a late hour is that, by this time, Frau Niemöller will have retired for the evening." He chuckled again, "I use the late hour to save her from hearing the same old story, in the same way that I hope the late hour will save you from unwanted attention."

Hartenstein was eager to get to the point. "Sir, I was surprised to hear you refer to an incident in the War that eventually turned you in another direction. It has always been my understanding that your service was quite . . . productive?"

"'Destructive' would be a little more accurate. I think you might be referring to *U-39*. Its record was not my doing. Legends grow as heroes are needed. I was only part of its story, not the commander at all, but the navigator for a time on that particular boat. I later assumed another command, but *"the 39"* is the one which eventually gained some notoriety. Became our second-deadliest U-boat in the War. One hundred and fifty-seven confirmed kills in nineteen missions."

Hartenstein said, "On torpedo boats, I myself have just begun to get a little combat experience. Was it the combat that drove you out of the Service?"

"No, I don't think so, Werner. When the survival of hearth and home is at stake, killing is sometimes one of the unpleasant necessities. I have learned to live with that."

Werner was growing more intrigued by his own confusion. "But if it was not the combat, then what was it?"

"What eventually got to me," said the former captain, "was one particular action that happened – no, something we deliberately did - on the very boat you asked about. What we did in that one incident became a wound that remained and festered. When I was no longer needed to command, I was able to attend to the wound. That is when things came to a head."

"Pastor Niemöller . . . "

"Please call me Martin."

"I am honored, Sir . . . I mean, Martin." The younger officer was clearly uncomfortable with the more casual way of addressing any senior person, even the occasionally older seaman under his command. "What was it then that wounded you, Sir?"

"The truth is that it may have wounded at least two of us," confessed the pastor.

"Did he survive the War?"

"Oh, not only did he survive the War, but you've probably heard of him."

The officer was getting more confused by the moment. "Excuse me?"

"Well, let's just say that if I were still in the U-boats, he would be my supreme commander."

"You don't mean Karl Dönitz?"

"One and the same. Karl was junior to me on that boat. I have never actually heard him speak of this incident. But he and I were the two officers who wrestled most with what our boat did."

"Wrestled with what?"

Niemöller paused and bowed his head in deep reflection while covering his mouth as if to keep the story from tumbling out. "January 28, 1917."

"You remember the exact date?" asked Hartenstein.

"Not of most things, Werner, just of particular days that never seem to go away," said the old sailor. His eyes stared down and away for some point of infinity that would never focus. Several seconds of silence passed. The visitor respected his host by giving him the time he needed to return.

Slowly Martin's eyes came up and he recognized the visitor before him. "Frau Niemöller will be very unhappy with my lack of manners if she awakens in the morning to find no cups and saucers in need of washing. Please relax, my young friend, while I return with the incriminating refreshments."

Hartenstein was not the least bit hungry for food. But it was clear that his host did need the intermission. So, as Martin returned with the cookies and tea, Werner waited in silence until the elder decided to continue.

"As I was saying, before I so rudely interrupted myself, we spotted an entire convoy that was escorting two large liners. We decided that the liners were somehow especially significant because they were so heavily protected. No less than three of the most modern French destroyers."

Hartenstein was not about to interrupt the momentum that was building.

"So naturally," Niemöller said, "we took our shot at the closest of what we figured must be troopships. Twenty seconds later, 'Boom!' Our target is sinking by the stern. Two of the destroyers are making off at top speed with the remaining troop ship. The remaining destroyer is closing in, trying to fish out what few survivors it can."

"All seems quite routine to me," said the younger man.

"And it was. Until what happened next." Martin let out an exasperated breath, "You see, Werner? I'm still doing it. I still cannot bring myself to say that this is something that we did. It did not just 'happen.' We did it."

"I'm sorry, Sir, I still don't follow. What is it that you did that is supposed to have been so bad?"

"Supposed? Supposed to have been so bad?" Niemöller slowly shook his head again and again, as he closed his eyes and bowed his head into his hand that cupped the tears. "No, no, no, my dear new friend. You are kindly trying your best to excuse me from something that was so awful that only the death of God himself could pay. Don't you see? That is what I came here for in the first place."

The young naval officer was way, way out of his depth. He had no idea what Niemöller was talking about. "I . . . I truly beg your pardon, Sir. Please accept my apologies. I clearly do not know what I am talking about." The younger officer began to rise. "Perhaps I have stayed my welcome too long."

Now it was Niemöller's turn to sputter. "Please, Werner, sit down." He needed to catch his breath. "Please. I . . . I am the one who needs to do the apologizing to you."

The preacher chuckled once again. "My goodness, you almost got smacked in the face by a sermon on the propitiatory sacrifice of Jesus Christ! Not too many people come around here late at night to hear another one of my sermons. Unless they're trying to fall asleep." Hartenstein was too gun-shy to do any more than smile respectfully.

A silence followed until Niemöller said, "Do you know what a confessor, is, Werner?"

"I don't believe so, Sir."

"A confessor is someone who hears a confession." Niemöller smiled apologetically. "Tonight, I'm afraid, that's you. God's forgiveness is the only medicine for this kind of pain, Werner. I tell people that Jesus died to forgive those who do not deserve it. But I have a hard time practicing what I preach. Sometimes, medicine is hard to swallow. In my case, I sometimes think that it's hard to swallow because I don't deserve to be forgiven at all." Niemöller paused to search for a thought. "Someone once said that church is a hospital for the soul. Well, that may be part of why I checked myself in."

The novice confessor just smiled respectfully.

"What we did, Werner, was that we tried to keep that destroyer from rescuing our helpless victims. Kept drawing off that destroyer every chance we got. We succeeded, as we plowed through the swimmers and ran them down, one by one."

The confessor made the rookie mistake of trying to help the penitent feel better by minimizing the sin. "But these were enemy combatants who would live to fight another day, to kill your brothers on the front and your own women and children at home."

Niemöller waved off the help, "Yes, yes, yes. That is exactly how our Kapitän reasoned. It does make some sense. But over all these years, it has never convinced my conscience. Some say that this is what drove the almighty Kapitän Niemöller from periscope to pulpit." Then he paused in reflection. "Hmm. Has a nice ring, does it not? *Periscope to Pulpit.* I should have used that for the title."

"Sir?"

"The story I'm telling you is one that I've just submitted for publication. But I called it *From U-boat to Pulpit.* Should have been *From Periscope to Pulpit,* don't you think?"

Hartenstein's signature dimples simply acknowledged the comment. "So that is what made you a pastor?"

"Well, that may been what finally drove me here. But hopefully, it is not what has kept me here. I hope that what keeps me here is something larger than myself."

"You said that what your commander did may have made some measure of sense."

"Of course it did. I believe that most people like to think that they are doing good. Our Kapitän was not a vengeful man. He was making an objective tactical decision in a life and death situation."

Now the confessor bore in. "Would you have made that same decision?"

"I hope not. I pray to God about that all the time. It tore my conscience as we did it."

The confessor spoke. "But you did it."

"Now you understand."

Hartenstein was still feeling the novice confessor temptation to protect Niemöller from his self-judgment. "But you yourself were simply following orders."

"Precisely. Which is why I do not automatically do that anymore with the orders of men, especially men who do not follow the orders of God."

"Which is why you get the visits you do from the police."

This was Niemöller's turn to faintly smile.

CHAPTER 8

WIN: BY ANY OTHER NAME

14 June 1937
Birmingham, England

Whamen she was a twelve-year-old patient at Birmingham Children's Hospital, the little girl who called herself Win had decided to become a nurse. Less than twelve years later, she realized that dream and took her first position at the very same hospital.

Now it was her place to bless another's dream come true. Win looked straight through the middle button on the shirt of her fiancé. "Why, that's, that's wonderful."

Pilot Officer Roger Ensfield was revved up like a hot engine. "I can't believe it. Right out of flight school and I get picked to fly the newest fighter!"

Win displayed a forced smile.

Roger was flying high. All by himself. "She's more than I ever dreamed of!"

Win raised her eyebrows with another stretched smile.

"You ought to see this Hurricane, Hon. She's absolutely the most beautiful thing I've ever seen!"

She hesitated to respond and looked down.

Roger finally picked up. "Are you all right? I thought you'd be more excited."

She put the best face on it that she could. "Just a little confused is all."

"About what?"

"About us, I guess," she said.

"Now I'm confused," Roger said. "I was talking about . . ."

Win cut him off. "About another woman."

"Huh?"

"It sounds like you're talking about another woman: how *she* is so beautiful, how *she* is all you've ever dreamed of."

The new flight officer tried to fly above her clouds. "Aww, she's jealous, she is!"

"Well, I suppose I might be a little," Win said. "You're the most important thing in *my* life. I'm just afraid that something else is taking first place in yours."

"Hon, is this the same thing we talked about when I enlisted?"

"You never even told me that you were going into the military! Just one day you told me that you had already done it!"

"But Win, you never asked me about your decision to go to nursing training."

"I was not saying that you had to ask me. You never even talked to me about wanting to fly. I talked to you all the time about wanting to be a nurse. When I applied to nursing school, that was no surprise to you at all."

Roger took a deep breath. She had a point there. "You're right. I wasn't thinking on that one."

Win said, "When we started talking about a future together, I chose schooling at home in Birmingham so we could be together. But then you decided on your own to do what you wanted, and it took you away."

"But I'm not gone."

"So much of the time you are gone," Win said.

He raised a pointer finger in mock instruction. "Away but not gone."

Quietly, her hot tears began to flow. "When you left for the RAF, I was so afraid I was going to lose you, the dashing young flight officer and all."

"But you didn't. You could never lose me. I love you Win. I always have. Besides, I can't get lost. They don't let you become a pilot unless you have a good sense of direction. I know where I'm going. And it's with you."

Win sniffled back the tears and blinked through wet eyes. "But now you're going to be a fighter pilot. That's dangerous. I really could lose you."

"Listen, if it were all that dangerous, we wouldn't have an air force. In hospital, how many crashed pilots have you ever seen? And how many car accidents are there? I was in more danger just driving here to see you."

Her tears were subsiding. "Oh, I'm so daft. I know I can't always be afraid of losing you to every single thing that could happen in life."

"You just need to remember than I'm really a very safe chap. After all, I am marrying my own nurse."

She looked up and to the right as though she were searching for something. "I don't know why I'm always so terrified about losing people."

"Well, I guess you see a lot of hard stuff in your line of work, don't you?" he said.

She gave this some thought. "I suppose so. But come to think of it, we really do save a lot more than we lose. If anything, I should think that my work would make me less afraid."

"And being a nurse, you could do all of that in London as well as here, couldn't you?"

"Why London?" she asked.

"That's closer to where I'm being sent for the Hurricanes. Number 111 Squadron is based at Northholt, less than an hour out of London. We could take out a flat. I could be home with you whenever I'm off duty."

And that is how a new Hurricane pilot survived his first skirmish. Pilot Officer and Mrs. Roger Ensfield were married on October 24, 1937.

CHAPTER 9

WERNER: SEEADLER

November 1938

Hartenstein had been looking over his shoulder for a year and a half, ever since Niemöller had been swallowed whole by the Gestapo. That had been just eighteen days after he had met with the daredevil pastor late one night. Two nights after that, a message had arrived from a desperate wife:

Kapitänleutnant Hartenstein,

The SS have arrested my husband. You know he is a patriot. Please help if you can.

An electric current of energy shot through his terrified imagination. "My God," thought the naval officer to himself. "Niemöller arrested! I may be next!"

A blizzard of questions almost choked off his very breath. Could she possibly think that he had anything to do with that? How could she have dared send an actual note, knowing that the Gestapo could be monitoring everything she did? This message could lead them right to his door! Or perhaps she sent this in the open to establish his own innocence to prying eyes. Suddenly he was overcome with a chill. Maybe this was not even from her. Maybe it was Gestapo bait.

As soon as he could get out of sight, Hartenstein immediately burned the note. Then he ground the ashes into the dirt again and again as if each carbon flake were a wasp that just would not die and could rise up to bite him. For thirty seconds he ground the ashes to a fine powder that not even Hitler's hornets could reassemble. Then, to be doubly sure, Werner carefully spread out the darkened soil, mixing it with lighter-colored dirt. What else could he do to erase any trace of the ashes which could lead to a conviction, which could lead to a firing squad, which could lead to his own ashes?

For fourteen months now he had been waiting for that knock on the door. He obsessed to the point of paranoia, even while trying hard to not look over his shoulder with every breath he took. His clandestine meeting with an enemy of the Gestapo may well have lit a silent fuse that was sparking its way to the detonation of his career and maybe even his very life. The fact that he could perceive no movement was more terrifying than if he could see the glowing eyes of a predator. Like a cat with a cornered mouse, the Gestapo liked the game of prey-play, to warm up the blood of its victim with the terror of patient stalking. Were they simply waiting to give him enough rope to hang himself?

His worst fears came true. A black-goggled military courier throttled his motorcycle to a dusty stop menacingly close to Hartenstein who was preparing to board the torpedo boat.

"Kapitänleutnant Werner Hartenstein!" demanded the soldier.

Hartenstein was shaken to the core by the arrival of this fearless grim reaper. He bolstered his command presence with an air of arrogance. "Of course. Is it customary for couriers to refuse to salute a superior officer?"

"Sir!" came the immediate salute from the courier who jolted to attention in the sitting position. "An urgent telegram for you to report immediately to headquarters in Berlin." The courier first snapped the envelope and then a second salute to the officer, and then immediately roared away.

Hartenstein felt the pale coolness of all the blood sinking to his feet. He stood motionless, without needing to open the communiqué. Little solace came from reflecting that he would not be the first commander to torpedo himself from a poorly aimed shot that came back around.

No one was more surprised than he when, five days later, he was still among the living, and boarding a different torpedo patrol boat. This time, Kapitänleutnant Werner Hartenstein was the new commander of the *Seeadler*.

CHAPTER 10

WIN: TAKING FLIGHT

December 1938
The dinner table of Robert and Ann Campbell
Birmingham, England

When she worked the third shift like tonight, it was always nice to start her day with a home cooked supper with Mum and Dad. She hoped that tonight would not be an exception. It was probably not going to be easy.

"It's always nice to have you home for supper," said her father.

Win continued arranging the silverware around the dinner table. "Well, Daddy, I only live and work a couple kilometers from here."

"I've said it so many times before, but I still never get over how things worked out," her mum said. "How you became a nurse at the very place where you first got the idea as a little patient. Then you marry your school sweetheart, a handsome young fighter pilot, and set up your first home close by. My goodness! Nurse Win Ensfield!"

By the time she was able to say her proper name, the family had already surrendered to Lyn's habit of calling herself Win.

"We're so glad that you've chosen to settle down so close to home," said her father.

"Well, at least for now, Dad. Who knows what will come?"

Few things got by dad. "Did you hear that, Annie? I wonder if our little girl is trying to tell us something here."

Her mother seemed to pick up the pace of placing cups and saucers around the table. "So," said her mother, "what is this 'for now' all about? Are you trying to tell us something?"

Win cocked her head playfully. "Well, yes and no."

Robert gave up trying to read the newspaper which headlined something about the commissioning of Britain's newest aircraft carrier, *HMS Ark Royal.* News about warships could wait. News about daughters could not.

He surrendered. "All right, you've got my attention. What is it?"

The teakettle sounded the alarm in the kitchen. Ann said, "Let me bring in the tea and we can sit down to dinner to hear what this is all about."

The interlude provided everyone an opportunity to prepare for something, but not too much time to let imaginations run away.

The table was ready, all were seated and father assumed his customary role to offer the prayer of thanks. "For what we are about to receive, may the Lord make us truly thankful. And may we always be mindful of the needs of others, for Jesus' sake. Amen."

The courses were passed around with no sound except the clinking of serving ware. The silence was a pressure cooker.

"Well," said Win's father.

This is it, the young nurse thought, as she silently took a deep breath to open the subject.

"Well, my dear," said Robert, "you have outdone yourself as usual. This is delicious." Win tried to not sound like a deflating balloon.

His wife said, "This is Win's favorite recipe from Granny." With her mouth full, Win smiled and nodded.

"And how was work today?" said Ann. Win was relieved that finally there was the opening to what needed to be discussed. But when she looked up, she noticed that Ann was directing the question to Robert, not to her.

He nodded his head. "Nothing particularly special. About the same."

"And you, love?" Ann said to Win.

Win almost missed the pitch. She was beginning to wonder if she would ever get to bat.

"Well," Win said, "that's kind of what I wanted to talk with you about."

"Could you pass the milk, please?" said Robert.

That is not the next line that Win had anticipated. But she should have.

"Of course," said Ann.

Robert poured the milk into the tea very, very, very slowly as he stirred the mixture. And stirred and stirred. And added a little more milk. And stirred some more.

Ann said, "Sugar, also?"

"Yes," he said, "that would be good."

The same protracted exercise ensured an evenly dispersed sweetening of what he was about to swallow. "Ahh," he said, "that should do it."

"You mean, without lemon?" said Ann. "You never go without lemon."

Robert said, "Well, it was my father who taught me how a working man should drink his tea. Lemon, he always said, was a good finisher. But a working man should periodically learn to enjoy the unadulterated thing."

Ann looked puzzled. "That's strange, Robert. I've never heard you tell that story."

He gave up. "OK then, pass me the lemon, after all."

"Well not if you really don't want it," his wife said.

Silence. The endless, mindless twaddle had numbed Win into forgetting that she had ever wanted to say anything at all. She stopped eating and stared vacantly through her parents. They both looked up and smiled at her. They kept eating.

The silence snapped Win awake and she tried to open the conversation one more time. "You were wondering about my work."

Both parents looked at each other.

Win took the plunge. "I have a chance to take a job in London."

"Of course," said her mother. "Near Roger."

"Well, we knew that this is what you two were hoping to do. And as it should be, after all," said her father.

Ann was not quite so willing to concede. "But what if the RAF should relocate him?"

"Well, he's a Hurricane pilot at a Hurricane base," said Win. "They don't seem to be moving these blokes around too much. Besides, if I don't move near him because he could be transferred, we would never live together."

Her dad raised both eyebrows and nodded. "Umm ... quite so. You do have a point there." Her mother swiveled her sights right between his eyes.

"The timing just seems right," said Win. "Did you hear about the Kindertransport?"

"That sounds German," said her mum.

"It is. Well, sort of, Mum. It's all those little Jewish children who are being evacuated from Germany. Things are getting scary for Jews, with Hitler and all."

Father nodded toward the paper he had folded up on the chair. "I was just reading about that. We're going to be taking in thousands of these kids. They say the first group just came in at Harwich."

Ann said, "I'm sure I don't know what that has to do with you, Win."

"Well," said the young nurse, "they're recruiting paediatric nurses for St. Bartholomew's Hospital in London where these kids are first going. They're not coming with any adults, so they need to be checked out and treated before they get placed in foster homes."

"But why does that have to be you?" said her mother. "The way things are going these days with Germany and all. I just don't want you so far from home. So close to where everything could happen."

"Mum, you of all people! You risked your life to save me when I was a little orphan in the last war. In fact, if memory serves, I think that was a war with Germany?"

"I think that is what your mum is thinking about," said Robert. "After everything we have been through and all the blessings we have received. To just . . . I don't know."

"Daddy, could you please repeat the table prayer that you just said?"

He said, "Let's see … *For what we are about to receive, may the Lord make us truly thankful. And may we always be mindful of the needs of others, for Jesus' sake. Amen.*"

"It's that last part, Daddy."

He said, "I see your point. But why do you have to leave home to be mindful of others? Aren't there other ways to help?"

"Daddy, you and Mum took me in. That is a big part of who I am. Who else better to do this?"

Her mother said, "But what if there's another war? London would be the most dangerous place to be."

"Mum, the Queen herself was just standing with Chamberlin at Buckingham talking about that new peace treaty with Germany."

"What do we know about a treaty?" Ann said. "What is that supposed to do?"

Robert said, "I don't know. There's quite a bit about it in the papers. I think they call it something like The Munich Treaty? Chamberlain says that it will give us, how did he put it, 'Peace in our time.' It says that, in the future, all disputes with Germany will be resolved through diplomacy. Not arms."

Ann put down her fork and stared at Robert. "So that's why the government was just passing out gas masks to everyone in London? I read the paper too, Robert."

"Mum, it's not like the Germans are going to fly over and bomb London!"

Ann quickly pushed her chair back from the table. "Who promised you that?" She placed both hands on her hips and shifted weight. "The Lord High Chamberlain?" She collected her dishes. Just *her* dishes. Supper was over.

CHAPTER 11

WERNER: JAGUAR

8 October 1940
2210 hours
Wardroom of torpedo boat Jaguar
Waters off the eastern tip of the Isle of Wight

At thirty-two years of age, Werner Hartenstein was now in command of his second torpedo boat, the thirteen-hundred-ton, predator class *Jaguar* with a crew of one hundred and twenty-five men. Together with the four other boats of the Fifth Torpedo Flotilla, he prowled the waters off the eastern tip of Britain's south coast island, the Isle of Wight.

As Hartenstein entered the room, the casual conversations among the ship's officers came to an abrupt halt. Everyone snapped to attention.

"Be seated gentlemen," said the commander. "Welcome to Operation Mousetrap.

"Our flotilla is presently off the eastern tip of the Isle of Wight, on Britain's southcentral coast. On the north coast of this island is a shipyard that manufactures destroyers and light cruisers. Intelligence tells us that one of these ships has completed outfitting and is preparing to get underway. Our five ships are about to conduct an operation to lure that mouse into our trap.

"The operation will be conducted in a sequence of three movements. The first step will be for each of us to lay mines in our respective sectors. This phase will commence precisely at 2300 hours under strict noise discipline, since coast watchers are looking skyward for our bombers on the way to London tonight. These mines will be the mousetrap itself, laid right across the door where that new destroyer will exit to pursue us.

"That mouse will pursue us, gentlemen, because our flotilla itself will be the cheese. When moonrise provides coastal vision, all five boats will bombard the antiaircraft command bunker near the egress channel. Hopefully, this bombardment will draw out the enemy through the channel exit where they will run afoul of our waiting mine field. Those who evade the mines will be greeted by our torpedoes.

"To be blunt, gentlemen, we will be picking a fight with someone who is not our size: to their advantage. We are going to be engaging a hardened, dug in battery of two 9.2-inch guns. These guns have twice our range, they send a shell nine times larger than ours and they may have coastal defense radar that can zero in on us with precision."

Hartenstein did not miss the quiet throat clearing among the officers.

"To balance the scales, our flotilla will be five rapidly mobile firing stations with eighteen guns of our own. Frankly, we are not expecting to do them much serious harm. All we are trying to do is rattle their cages a bit, in order to pick a fight with a destroyer that hopefully will take the bait.

"Our strategy will have to capitalize on our mobility and speed. Unlike land-based artillery, we will not have the luxury of sitting in one place and using several rounds to adjust fire. At 0445 we will advance to within visual range of the target. At precisely 0500 our five boats will lay down a full fire-for-effect barrage from all eighteen of our 105's, and continue firing."

He turned to his gunnery officers. "Guns, draw as many non-operational personnel as needed to aid ammo handlers in order to maintain the heaviest sustained fire possible."

To his Chief Engineer, "Max, as soon as we begin firing, I want maximum speed and I want that speed maintained until I order otherwise."

"Bridge, be prepared for a zigzag evasive course immediately on our first volley. I want each zig and every zag to be at varying, non-parallel angles to the shore so that their gunners have to adjust each shot for both range and bearing. Take special care to stay within our assigned sector so as to not risk collision with our other boats."

The commander took questions and suggestions. He looked at his watch. "Mine laying begins in seventeen minutes. Gentlemen, let's get to it."

Flying bridge outside command deck
0450 hours

The seas were unusually calm with a light, southerly-running breeze that made the night air particularly pleasant. Hartenstein hoisted the heavy naval binoculars to scan the eastern coast of the island. Not everything was dark. In the village of

Bembridge, a tiny twinkle or two could be detected. "Hmm, apparently not everyone is asleep," the captain said to the man next to him.

Executive Officer Hans Schiller said, "Probably the baker, Sir."

Hartenstein picked up his command mic. "All ahead two thirds."

Hartenstein was taken off guard by an actual answer. "Hmm? What did you say?"

"The baker, Sir."

Still focusing forward through his binoculars, the captain was having a harder time focusing on the conversation. "A baker? What baker?"

Schiller said, "I was just saying that the only one up at this hour is probably the baker."

Hartenstein kept the binos in position as he turned slightly to look quizzically at the junior officer.

"My dad was a baker. By ten years of age, I was, too," said Schiller. "We always rose at midnight and baked all through the night so the rest of you had fresh bakery every morning."

"Strange," said the captain. "I always grew up sleeping through these hours. How many people even have a clue what goes on in the middle of the night in their own little towns?"

"Only the baker's family, Sir."

Hartenstein said, "So how do you know that we're not looking at the constable doing his rounds?"

"I can smell the bakery on the breeze, Sir."

With an almost imperceptible smile, Hartenstein just stared incredulously at the junior man. "You do have a nose for this, don't you?"

"Well, Sir, it's just that Dad and I never had any company at all in these hours. In my experience, the village cop never wanted to be up at this hour. Unless there was some kind of emergency."

The commander looked at his watch. "Well, he'll have one tonight. I think he's slept long enough. The guns are yours, Hans. Wake 'em up."

At Culver Downs station most of the 118th Battery of the 527th Coast Regiment was asleep. Only the cooks and the two lookouts were up at 0459 hours. But only the cooks were really awake. The lookouts were at the far sleepy end of their watch and they were both looking down when the light flashed by them, unnoticed, at 186,000 miles per second.

At two and a half miles out, each torpedo boat in its assigned sector began firing at precisely 0500 hours.

The flash warnings were long gone, and the sound of the firing explosions had not yet arrived, when eighteen artillery rounds burst like dirty geysers in front of, behind, to the left and to the right of two dazzled soldiers. One round of that first volley found the lookout platform with what cannoneers refer to as "that last loud rushing sound in your ears".

The entire battery automatically sprang to action like the spring-loaded machine it was. But like any machine, it had no idea what was attacking it. Explosions continued and continued as though from Luftwaffe bombers. It was only a year ago that Ventnor Station down the coast had been destroyed by a double attack of Junker 87 and 88 bombers. Particularly as an antiaircraft command center, it was aerial attack that was constantly on the mind of these men. But their antiaircraft radars showed nothing in the air.

The explosions continued and continued and continued. It took fully ten minutes for the battery to realize the seaborne nature of its troubles. The explosions went on and on and on. They were surprised to discover that they had as many attacking targets as they might have had with an aerial squadron. Each of its two guns chose its own target and answered with a volcanic eruption.

Jaguar

Kondor and *Jaguar* were the first two torpedo boats of the flotilla to draw the short straws, to receive Culver Battery's delivery: packages that each weighed close to two hundred kilos.

The air split overhead but held intact well enough to carry the warning command at deck level. "Heads down. Incoming mail!" bellowed Schiller. Twenty meters seaward of them, a ten-meter geyser of water rocketed skyward.

Hartenstein called in on the mic. "Bridge, immediately take your next diagonal zig after each incoming round. Watch your sectors and the minefield."

The ship responded instantly and was far beyond where it had been in the forty-five seconds that it took the next projectile to arrive. There was no air ripping sound this time as the warhead shot up a geyser landward of their location.

"Sir, they've got us bracketed," said Schiller.

"Only if we were in the same position. They don't have the same spot to bracket. Stay on those guns, Hans. I don't want our rate of fire to drag."

The whole point of this ruckus was to draw out some newly minted destroyer to play with. But just like many eager mousers learn, now that they were in position, no feckless mouse emerged to take the bait.

"What does it take to draw these guys out?" said Schiller.

Hartenstein said, "Well, you know, mice do learn from each other. Maybe they just don't want to be the first mouse."

The Executive Officer was reticent to appear either slow or insolent. "Begging Captain's pardon, Sir?"

"They say that it's the second mouse that gets the cheese," said the mentor.

Schiller dutifully smiled and nodded his head, in acknowledgment if not comprehension. He was a good junior officer, not an imaginative one.

Throughout the gunfight, Culver Battery took thirty-two rounds for every two they fired. After *Jaguar's* first lucky shot, no one on either side hit anything, but a good time was had by all.

Nevertheless, it was this extended sea bombardment that would bring Werner Hartenstein to the attention of U-boat Command. Strategic planners were already beginning to envision ways of using U-boats to attack shore oil installations in the far reaches of the North American theatre.

CHAPTER 12

WIN: BATTLE OF BRITAIN

October 1940
St. Bartholomew's Hospital
London, England

It had taken less than a year before Ann Campbell's worst fears came true. Nine months after their short-lived supper, Germany dropped its peaceful façade, and Britain declared war. Nine months after that, the *Luftwaffe* began carpet-bombing London.

Less than three hours away from Werner Hartenstein's bombardment, Nurse Win Ensfield was herself at war.

"But Mum, I am just fine! Please don't cry," pleaded Win.

Win noticed two nurses showing grave concern as they monitored her end of the phone conversation. She instinctively turned away and bowed her head into the phone for some semblance of privacy.

Both nurses were three or four years younger than the twenty-five-year-old Win, who was therefore regarded as a very much older sister. Rebecca was actually Sister Rebecca who, like many Catholic girls, had been dedicated from early years by her parents to a future of religious service. Therefore, the necessary preparation at Catholic girls' schools meant that she had lived many of her formative years away from family. This is why she cherished the family roots which Win seemed to ignore.

"The very picture of discipline and decorum even when she has to piece together her terrified mum. Where do her parents live?" asked Nurse Florence Hathwick.

"Outside of Birmingham, not that she ever speaks anything of her personal life," said Brown. "You would think she was an orphan with the little she has to say about her roots."

"You went through Nursing with her," said Flo. "Did you know anything about her family?"

"Not much, really," Rebecca said. "She's always pretty much kept to herself. Nice enough and all. But no one knows much about her personal life. Has always kept her nose to the grindstone. And her hands on the lipstick."

"She's always done that?" said Flo. Upon further thought and much, much deeper reflection, she pondered one of life's ultimate questions. "Since we can't wear lipstick around here, and no one has ever seen her out socially, I wonder what color that lipstick might be?"

"Well," said Rebecca, "if it's any clue, her nickname back in school was Red, although some say it was because she grew up in Birmingham where her dad worked for Midland Red."

Even in hushed tones, Win's remarks could be clearly heard. "I understand, Mum. But all phone lines have been down since the raid. Even our emergency operations have been seriously hampered." There was a silence for only three seconds. "No, Mum, nobody here has been able to communicate with their families." Five more seconds. "Mum, none of us has even slept in the last forty-eight hours since our nurses' quarters were hit." Three seconds. "You had not heard about that? Oh, now I've made things so much worse." Another five second pause. "Mum, there is nothing to worry about. Bart's has already been taking precautions since the outbreak of things. Sure Mum, put him on.

"Hi, Daddy. Yes, I'm doing fine. No, nobody was hurt. Yes, Daddy. Just one bomb. Well, it hit on the east side. Went through a basement wall in the nurses' quarters. Nobody was there. Well, yes, they say a fair amount of damage to the building, to the water and gas mains and such."

A short silence while her dad talked. Win said, "Well, that's because they already moved all the nursing students out to another location in Northwood, Dad. And about half a year ago, sometime before Christmas, they moved most of the staff nurses to a couple other locations away from the main hospital."

Win neglected to mention one little detail. Since she had been one of the nurses who did not have a family of her own, she volunteered to be one of only a hundred and thirty-three who remained behind at the previously bombed Smithfield location of the hospital. These nurses formed an emergency evacuation center for the growing stream of victims from the daytime bombing raids.

"Daddy, I do have to go. We are terribly busy here. Give Mum my love. I will try to be good and do a better job of staying in touch. They are taking good care of us. Don't worry. I love you too, Daddy."

Tuesday
17 September 1940
Saint Bartholomew's Hospital

London's world changed overnight. Two days ago, British Spitfire and Hurricane fighters had resolutely put a flaming end to Hitler's daylight bombing raids over the city. The Führer replied with the start of nighttime bombings upon the sleeping city. Civilians in their nightgowns and nightcaps, unaccustomed to middle of the night bombing, were being roasted by the thousands.

Coping routines had not yet evolved for an entire city engulfed by a nighttime hell. Street lamps were out. Phone lines were out. Off-duty doctors, nurses, constables, fire brigades and ambulance crews were in their well-rehearsed pattern of sleeping during the night hours to prepare for expected daytime raids.

St. Bart's became one massive triage station. The screaming, the moaning, the crying, the silent, the quick, the dead, the vertical and the horizontal all were piling up a block in all directions. Up-reaching arms of staggering figures were backlit by a hurricane inferno.

"Hey, you! Lipstick Lady!" some physician yelled out to Win.

"Are you talking to me?" said the smudge-faced nurse.

"I need something to mark with," said the doctor. "Can you give me a hand with that bloody lipstick you're always carrying around?"

He was trying to sort out victims according to which ones were most seriously injured, who might have the best chance of surviving with medical help. "I need you to mark their foreheads with the number I call out to you."

For the first time in her career, Nurse Win Ensfield used that ever-clutched tube of lipstick in an actual nursing function.

They came to a man whose broken arm was protruding away from his body at a ninety-degree angle. Bedside manner was now beside the point and the doctor spoke to his new assistant without acknowledging the patient. "This one will keep. Write a 'two' on his forehead."

Through a face caked with dust and cinders, the man cocked his head and peered plaintively at Win. "Here, sir," she said as she used her hand to wipe away some of the grime from his forehead. She tried to engage him with a little kindness. "I'll bet we've never worn lipstick before, have we?"

She carefully labeled him. He tilted his head quizzically again. "This is good news," she said in a cheerful voice. "What I wrote on your forehead means that the doctor says you are going to be just fine."

The doctor blasted open the tender contact Win had just established. "We don't have time for you to hold hands, Florence Nightingale! Over here!"

Win gently touched the man's good hand. "Someone will help you soon, love."

She scooted to the doctor. 'Over here' was an unconscious little boy whose blond hair was blood soaked. He was cradled by his young mother, whose cinder-covered face was streaked with tears. "This one gets a 'three.' Nothing we can do."

The mother's eyes snapped open in shock.

As the doctor moved on to the next victim of his brutal care, the enraged nurse dashed over to confront him. She took him by the elbow and pulled him to the side. With flaming eyes and a strained whisper, she attacked him. "Look here you! You can try to humiliate me with all the names you like. And I don't care if this costs me my job. But you will not treat people like this! Not if you want me to help you. You just tore the heart out of that desperate, young mother!"

He calmly looked at her but did not answer. There was no change of expression to indicate if any of this had registered. A massive explosion brought down the better part of a whole city block a kilometer away. The doctor just moved on to the next. And the next. And the next. Win moved alongside him. He gave her the number. She gave each patient two things: a number on the forehead and some promise she couldn't keep.

Five hours later, the earliest rays of dawn saw the medical duo still at it. "Win, would you change the designator on this chap?"

Had he actually asked her? And even used her name? Maybe he was just slowing down from exhaustion. He looked all rung out, like the tattered, makeshift bandages on so many who were brought to him. What really was wearing him down was that he didn't feel like a doctor at all. He wasn't curing anybody tonight. All he could do was maybe offer some tincture of comfort. The doctor was learning to be a nurse. He was even taking a little more time with some of the patients.

"What should it be, doctor?" she asked her new colleague.

"I want him upgraded from a two to a one. Talked with him for a moment and his vitals picked up."

Win expressed mock surprise. "You did what? You actually talked with him?"

He rolled his eyes. "Alright, don't let it get out, but even old docs can learn new tricks."

A bedraggled nurse simply answered with a pursed smile and an incredulous shake of her head.

PART III
THE SECOND LACONIA

CHAPTER 13

RESURRECTION OF U-156

June 1942

O ver in the Pacific, it was now only six months after Pearl Harbor. This was the month that America faced down the Japanese in the pivotal naval engagement which came to be called the Battle of Midway.

In the Atlantic, however, United States naval forces suffered the worst defeat in American military history. In June, Germany's U-boats sank the six-hundred-and-ninth merchant ship since January along America's east coast. Berlin referred to the whole thing as *Der Paukenschlag*. The Drumbeat.

Not far off, the undead trolled the depths. German U-boat *156* had been mined to death twenty-four years earlier in the closing days of what was now remembered as The Great War. Now another *U-156* had been reincarnated as one of the world's deadliest weapons of the Second World War. This Class IXC long distance killer had sunk five ships and damaged two others on its first operational war patrol since its birth only seven months earlier.

At the helm was another who had been brought back from the grave. After his clandestine association with Hitler's "personal enemy," Werner Hartenstein somehow found himself not in front of a firing squad, but in command of a U-boat. That may have been a distinction without a difference, since eighty-five per cent of all German submariners would be killed anyway in the boats that came to be known as iron coffins.

24 June 1942, Wednesday
South Atlantic, 700 miles east of Bermuda
SS Willimantic Radio Room
0734 hours

Third Radio Operator, George Ellis, opened a new line of chatter. "How much longer is the old man going to keep us on double watch? I'm about ready to drop."

"Captain's been up all night himself, George," the senior man said. The very much older twenty-one year old Senior Radio Officer, Francis E. Youds, was from the tiny hamlet of Babbington near Nottingham, about as far from the sea as you get in England. About this same time each day, his widowed mother would have her morning tea and gaze at a global map and try to guess where in the world her only son might be.

The understudy gave it some thought. "Yeah, the First Mate's been up on bridge all night as well. We're all going to be a sorry lot if we have to snap to and actually do something. Been like this since 1600 yesterday, ever since Captain Everett thought he saw something. I swear, he's been acting like he saw a ghost."

"It's *all* about ghosts," said the older one. "Three merchants go down in this neighborhood, one right after the other – boom, boom, boom. Then not a thing for what, two weeks now?"

"I'll bet the old man is seeing ghosts all right," said the junior man, Ellis.

"Ever hear about the *Bonheur* a couple years back?" asked the one who knew all the stories.

Ellis looked upward as he searched his memory. "Doesn't ring a bell with me."

"I think it's ringing his all the time," said the old-timer. "A captain never fully comes to terms with losing a ship."

"What are you talking about?" asked the junior man.

"Everett got his *Bonheur* torpedoed and sunk off Northern Ireland back in '40 sometime," the storyteller said. "Then a year later, he got hit again, this time by a torpedo plane. I think his ship was the *Swinburne* or something like that."

The youngster had already picked up a mariners' penchant for superstition, such as the fear that saying frightening things out loud could make them come true. He was almost afraid to ask. "Lose anyone?"

"Not sure," the boss said. "But they say he's been a whole lot edgier ever since."

The assistant let out a breath and said, "Being out here all on our own without escorts, I guess I'd be seeing ghosts too."

The more experienced sailor had long ago learned to search clouds for silver linings. "Yeah, but with all the heavy traffic further north, just maybe we'll get by unnoticed, being off all by ourselves this far south."

This ship was a maritime needle in a haystack, with two special advantages. First off, the massiveness of the ocean made them more like a pine needle on Mt. Everest. Perhaps even more important was the simple fact that, unlike the proverbial needle in the haystack, no one was actively looking for the *Willimantic*. They would only be found by accidentally happening to occupy the same point in time and space as some U-boat. And what were the odds of that happening?

"Didn't do the *Lillian* much good a couple weeks ago," said the youngster. "Or the *Alegrete* two days before that. Or the *Norman Prince* two days before that." In the communications room, they heard it all and they heard it as it happened.

One rap on the door by a heavily tattooed arm, and a sailor with peach fuzz facial aspirations handed in a piece of paper to the radio men. Just seven years earlier, this same kid had played with a pirate's voice that he now tried to summon up with a gravelly pretension. "Latest position, you blokes. New course."

Youds asked the messenger, "We ziggin' or zaggin' this time Smitty?"

Up on the bridge, the captain was playing a cat and mouse game. He and his ship were the mouse: nothing to fight with but wits and luck. Every tasty critter instinctively knows, and, in this case, every man instinctively knew, that predators are never far away. But not every mouse and man sees it coming. Captain Everett was one of those rare mice that had survived the cat often enough to learn that the one to fear was the one you couldn't see. That's why he navigated his ship as unpredictably as he could and always notified the radio room of course corrections. That way, they could be ready at any moment to broadcast a distress call with their precise location in the event of an attack.

The young messenger answered the radioman's navigational question. "I wouldn't know a zig from a zag. All feels the same to me. But I guess it breaks the boredom."

Trapped under his ever-present headphones, Francis was a little envious. "Well, we're glad you boys up there get to play with your toys. Radio silence down here is deafening, mate. All we get to do is listen. To absolutely bloody nothing."

The less experienced George Ellis filled the monotony with a rookie's nose for excitement. "You know, kind of a rum do, it is," he said. "Haven't heard a thing for, what, five, six hours? Too quiet. Maybe the Krauts think they've fished out these waters and have gone off looking somewhere else. Maybe there's nothing out there."

The more experienced Youds just stared in wide-eyed amazement at Ellis. "Ever done much fishing, Georgie Boy?"

Ellis said, "What's that got to do with it?"

"Fishermen catch fish by being real quiet and real patient, making the fish think they're not there. Captain doesn't get tricked by things being quiet."

The radiomen had no way of knowing that a fifteen hundred kilo steel cylinder of high explosive had just flashed past them. It had just granted Francis Youds and George Ellis twelve minutes and fourteen seconds more of earthly existence.

24 June 1942, Wednesday
Control Room
U-156
Thirty meters below the surface
1024 hours

Korvettenkapitän Werner Hartenstein draped both forearms over the periscope control handles as he kept his eyes locked on his prey.

The Watch Officer said, "Kapitän, two minutes and forty seconds, Sir. We should have heard something ten seconds ago, Sir."

"Thank you, Hans," replied the commander with the courtesy that was reported even among his surviving victims. "She probably ran deep."

No one was greatly surprised. Their last fish had been an impact torpedo, notoriously flawed for running deeper than it had been set. But after sixty-two days on their third and longest patrol, the U-boat had been down to its last fish and had nothing to lose by giving it a try.

He snap shut the periscope handles and turned to his Third Watch Officer, "Mister Fischer, prepare for surface gunfire attack."

For the last sixteen hours, the crew had been at battle stations stalking the prey that no one but the captain could see. In addition to torpedoes, they were low on everything else, including fresh air. To conserve fresh water, everyone had long since forgone shaving. The ersatz deodorant of Eau de Cologne was almost strong enough to mask the noxious diesel fumes. Even with the success of eleven kills on this patrol alone, the men were tired. The order to surface for fresh air and the hope of an exciting gunfight breathed new life, at least for the U-boat crew. This would be an uneven fight against a virtually defenseless merchant ship. In truth, it would be no more of a fight than a typical deer hunt.

The instant the U-boat breached the surface, the top-side crew scrambled to its battle stations.

They could see the crew of the *Willimantic* do the same thing.

"Herr Stegemann, please place one round just forward of her bow. Be sure to give her lead," commanded Hartenstein.

The 105-mm cannon split the air with a thunderous roar which was answered by a geyser thirty meters in front of the doomed merchant. Since flight was out of the question, the caged prey fought. Instead of heaving to, she spit back with fifty-caliber tracers. Immediately, *U-156* answered with even more powerful shells from her 37mm antiaircraft gun. Merchant gunners Donald MacNiel, Harry Kenneth Hartley and Hassan Ali were shredded. So were the port lifeboats as well as Ordinary Seaman Charles James Mummery.

Hartenstein was disappointed that his gentler offers had been rebuffed. "Time to cut off the head. Herr Stegemann. One to the bridge."

24 June 1942, Wednesday
SS Willimantic Radio Room
1111hours

On the command deck, the master of the *Willimantic* saw it all coming around again. He was about to lose his third ship in just two years.

"For crying out loud, what is Wingnut shooting at?! Get word down to him to aim at the sub's gun, not the conning tower! Billy, call down our current position for Radio to transmit!"

"Aye, Sir! Radio, you there?"

According to well-rehearsed drill, Radio was waiting for the ship's location coordinates to broadcast for rescue. "Let's have it, Billy."

"Reading coordinates as 25.55N, 51.58W - Grid DQ 1188."

Now more than ever, pinpoint accuracy was a life and death matter. So was speed. Heaven and earth would be separated by eleven seconds which were measured by each keystroke of the senior operator who tapped out the SSS alert signaling a U-boat attack.

"SSS . . . SSS . . . (first second gone) SSS . . . SSS . . . (two more seconds gone) GVXT 25.55N, (fourth second gone) 51.58W - Grid DQ 1188, (six seconds gone) SSS . . . SSS . . . (seven more seconds gone) SSS . . . SSS (eight seconds gone) . . . GVXT 25.55N, (nine seconds gone) 51.58W – (Ten seconds out) Grid DQ 1188." Time was up.

The high explosive artillery round terminated the call. And the lives of both radio men.

Captain Everett's bitter experience had taught him that most of his men could survive if only he would allow the ship to die without struggle. "Engines, all stop," he commanded.

Peering through large binoculars, Leutnant zür See Fischer observed the *Willimantic's* cessation of bow froth. "Target vessel appears to be stopping, Kapitän."

Hartenstein said, "Very well, Max. Prepare a boarding party."

"Aye, Sir. Shall I await your orders or proceed immediately?"

The commander was about to ruin someone else's day. "Ah, Maxie, this will indeed be your time to shine. I do believe your resume' could use a little more time at the helm."

Fischer didn't know what to think. "Sir?"

"When you have the boarding party ready, I'll take them over," said the skipper.

The junior officer wanted to protect both his future and that of his captain. "But Sir, with all due respect, do you think it is wise to expose the commander like that?"

Hartenstein respected Fischer's dignity. "I appreciate your concern, Max. Tactically correct, as always. But there is no honor in hunting where the hunter bears no risk."

Ten minutes later, Hartenstein was in the bow of the boarding craft with ten armed crewmen. He handed the bullhorn to his interpreter, Boatswain's Mate 2nd class Theo Gruber and had him hail the stricken *Willimantic*: "All hands are to be top-side and all weapons cast overboard to avoid being fired upon by superior heavy weapons."

Upon boarding, Hartenstein was received with a smart salute by his vanquished opponent, Captain Leon Otto Everett, who offered his personal sidearm in surrender.

Hartenstein returned the salute and received the revolver. Keeping his eyes locked on Everett, the U-boat commander said, "Herr Gruber, please inform the Captain that he may retain his personal weapon as a sign of my respect." As Gruber conveyed the message, Hartenstein emptied the pistol of its ammunition, clicked his heels together, bowed and, on two opened hands, offered back the symbol of command to its owner.

Everett removed his cap and nodded a humble thanks.

Hartenstein kept facing his counterpart while he spoke to the interpreter. "Furthermore, ask the Captain to inform his assembled crew that everyone will be allowed to safely leave with necessary provisions and charts while the Captain will remain as our guest. And Mr. Gruber, make sure that the Captain gives his crew the accurate message."

Gruber translated to the Captain who then looked to Hartenstein for permission to address the crew.

Hartenstein informed the Captain that the crew would be permitted to board their lifeboats after Everett provided a manifest of crew names and after each man had been accounted for.

When the U-boat commander received the manifest, Everett explained that both of his radio operators and four able seamen had been killed by the gunfire.

Hartenstein said to his interpreter, "Mr. Gruber, inform the Captain that I will address the crew."

The Master of the SS *Willimantic* ordered his surviving crew to attention, and then the U-boat victor spoke through Gruber. "I am Korvettenkapitän Werner Hartenstein, commander of *U-156*. From one seaman to another, I wish to sincerely apologize for the tragic loss of your comrades. Please know that it was not our wish to cause any loss of life. You are now dismissed to board your remaining lifeboats. If you would row to my boat, my crew will provide you with charts and provisions for safe return to your families. God speed, gentlemen."

After conducting a brief inventory tour of the *Willimantic,* guided by its Master, the U-boat commander and his crew took Everett to the U-boat. Everett was given hot coffee and invited to either go below deck or remain topside to witness the coup de grace of his last command. Like a brave prisoner refusing a blindfold, Everett chose to witness the execution of the old merchant. He took quiet pride to see that it took one hundred and seventy-five rounds to finish her off. At 1145 hours, the *Willimantic* became the second of three merchant ships put down that day by U-boats, which would do the same thing more than sixteen hundred times that year alone.

CHAPTER 14

IN LOVE AND WAR

27 June 1942
St. Bartholomew's Hospital
London

T he antiseptic atmosphere of the nurses' prep room was cut by the injection of a little girlish teasing.

"That Yank leftenant is out there again asking for you, Win."

Head nurse Sally Baker nodded toward the subdued chaos of the patient waiting area. Every chair was occupied by questions, interrupted schedules, anxieties, pains, irritations, and the uncertainties of two dozen oxymorons called patients. In contrast to the sterile whiteness of the treatment area, the waiting room tried to settle nerves with subdued green and brown walls that never saw the light of day.

The young nurse feigned disinterest before her supervisor. "I'm sure I have no idea to whom you're referring."

Baker furrowed her eyebrows. "He says he's got the itch real bad, and that you promised to take care of it," she teased in mock seriousness.

Win began to protest. "And you are off your blinkin' rocker, is what you are, if you think . . ."

She was cut off in mid-sentence by a melodramatic plea. "Oh please, I can't take this any longer! My whole back is itching like a million fleas are driving me mad! Oh please help, Nurse Win! Only you can save me!" wailed the American officer.

Win threw down a bandage she was rolling and marched into the waiting room. "If it isn't the heroic gladiator come from across The Pond to suffer the battle wounds of, let's see, self-inflicted discomfort, is it?"

"Ouch!" said the American. "You rub salt into the wound of a gallant warrior who serves a noble cause greater than I myself."

The nurse couldn't resist. "Which would be?"

"You, of course!"

"Well," said the clinician, "your misery all of a sudden seems to have miraculously abated, Lt. Corbetta."

He took advantage of the opportunity. "You see? I knew what I needed!"

"What you need is a cold shower, is what you need," said Nurse Ensfield.

His bluff was called, but the soldier appealed his case of the worst sunburn he had experienced in his entire life. "Seriously, ma'am, I do think something's wrong with my back. At first, I couldn't feel a thing at all . . ."

". . . because you fried all the nerves, you silly fool. Your back was laid out like raw meat. What did you expect?" said the nurse. Sally tried not to show her amusement as she listened to the officer meeting his match.

Pain overruled the officer's comedy. "But now it's like a million ticklers through every pore of my skin! It's driving me nuts!"

"That's simply the nerves waking up, love. There's not much to do. Maybe find some way to distract yourself," suggested Win.

The young artillery officer had experience as a forward observer. In both love and war. He didn't miss the opportunity. "But that's why I'm here, me lady!"

"So then, consider yourself distracted. Seriously distracted, if you ask me," said Nurse Win. "Now off with you. I've got real patients to attend, Yank." Then she handed him a packet of aspirin. "Here, these might help a bit from time to time. Cheerie-bye, then." Win hustled back into the ward to continue her patient cares. She didn't even take notice of the soldier's reaction.

She returned to what she was doing, but now flew into the task with enough intensity to force away all other thoughts, feelings, and people. Since Roger, she worked hard to not let most people get too close.

For some reason, she had allowed Sally to come alongside her. "It's too bad you have to keep putting up with that kind of silliness, it is."

Without looking up, Win said, "It never ends. I probably should put my wedding ring back on as a sign for everyone else to back off."

"Maybe you took off your ring for a reason," said Sally. "It is coming up on two years, after all."

Win just wound the bandages even faster.

"Listen, Win, our shift is over in a couple hours. Why not go home early? I owe you one anyway."

Win's private thoughts found voice. "Why doesn't it ever go away?"

Sally did not answer what she knew was not a question. She also knew that Win wasn't referring to this incident, but to another one altogether.

"I am so bloody angry at him!" the younger erupted as the bandage roll popped out of her hand and rolled across the floor. "What right did he have to do this to me!"

"Sometimes, it's easier to be angry at someone than to be heartbroken," offered one who had had too much practice. "Listen, you can't even roll bandages right now. Get out of here for the day."

In search of something to dull her own pain, Win Ensfield did something that no self-respecting woman would usually do. But respecting herself was not at the top of her list at the moment. She wandered her way to the pub only a block from the hospital. She took a booth all by herself and ordered a pint of bitters. Then another. Then a third.

"It's no good for a woman to drink alone."

She did not have to look up to recognize the voice of the plucky Yank leftenant. She did not want to look up. Especially at a man. Instead, she took another pull of ale.

"I do not want to intrude," said Lt. Corbetta. "I came here to find something to dull my pain, too." Win continued to ignore him.

The officer persisted one more time. "If you prefer, I'll be glad to lick my wounds at another table. But I will be keeping an eye on you. For your own good." When she refused to respond, he kept his promise.

From a nearby table, he nursed his third highball because this did seem to be putting the awakening nerves back to sleep. The intoxicologist offered the recovering soldier more medicine. "Hey Yank, can I set you up with another?"

"Thanks, but not tonight, Mac. I want to leave here toes forward, if you know what I mean," said Corbetta. The officer peered over the rim of his glass and the gentleman in him realized that he might need to be sober for two.

By now, she was swimming in her fourth pint and she looked like she was starting to go under. She must have realized this because she tried to gather herself together as she fumbled into her coat and then mismatched the buttons. She stumbled once as she walked in the wrong direction before regaining her bearings toward the door.

The bartender noticed that she was walking away without having paid. He started to call her attention when the Lieutenant held up a quid note folded lengthwise. He motioned toward the departing woman, then to himself. "For the lady and me . . . and you too, Mac. Will that about cover it?"

"More than cover it, Yank," said the bar man. "Someone ought to keep an eye on that lassie, they should."

Corbetta fitted his saucer cap. "Yeah, you got that right. I'll make sure she gets home in one piece. Wherever that is."

"An officer and gentleman you are, me friend." The barkeep leaned forward and looked the younger man dead straight in the eye. "Remember that, son."

Normally, the young officer would have taken offense at that as some kind of patronizing remark. But he felt like he was standing before his own dad the night of his very first date:

"Remember son, your first responsibility tonight is to take care of that young lady. If you don't, I will. Then, I'll take care of you. Understand?"

Corbetta never thought that he would be nostalgic about that particular conversation. It was the first bit of home he had felt since putting on this uniform.

He took in the advice, rolled it around in his mind, nodded that he understood and then strolled out. After having spent the last hour in the dimly lit pub, he had to shield his eyes from the glare of the late afternoon sun. It was hanging low in the sky and right at eye level. By the time his eyes were adjusted, he could see no trace of the nurse. The pub was in the middle of the block, so he was as close to one intersection as the other. He sprinted north and then looked up and down the cross street, but found no sign of his charge.

So now he was a full block away from the opposite intersection. He jogged in a casual way, trying not to attract attention. At the intersection, he looked south and spotted the woman a full block and a half distant. Even at this range, he could see her wavering a bit along the sidewalk and maybe stumbling every now and then.

Already, a pack of wolves had spotted the vulnerable prey. Three American sailors were crossing the street to intercept Win. Corbetta picked up his step.

Trailing behind her, one of the swabbies called out to her, "Hey missy! You live around here?" She ignored them and kept stumbling her way along.

One of the other sailors chided the first, "Hey, Sulley, looks like she's giving you the shoulder. She must have class." The others laughed.

The sailors hustled around in front of her and walked backwards as she forged ahead with a more resolute cadence.

"Hey, little girl, I was talking to you," said Sulley. "It's not polite to ignore someone who's speaking to you."

"Hey, c'mon," said Buck, "let's leave her alone. She probably doesn't talk to strangers."

"And ain't no-one stranger than you, Sulley," said Smitty.

Sulley stopped and blocked the woman's advance. "Look, sweetheart, we paddled our dinghies all the way over here just to save your sweet little . . ."

"You want to finish that with me?" called out a command voice. First Lieutenant Corbetta had closed with the wolf pack. They had been so focused on their catch that they had not noticed the officer circle out and come in behind them.

"Get lost, sonny," said Sulley.

"Get lost sonny, *Sir*" said the officer.

"Beggin' lieutenant's pardon," said the gang leader, "but this ain't no business of yours. Sir."

"C'mon, guys, move along and have yourselves a good evening and we'll forget this ever happened," said Corbetta.

"And if we don't?" said Sulley.

"Then you're going to face military justice the hard way, mister. Your choice."

"You talk pretty big for a grunt, all by his lonesome," said the bully.

He was right. Corbetta knew it, they knew it, and they knew that he knew it. A straight beats a full house and three big sailors could beat the crap out of this commissioned punk. Math was never his strong suit, but even Corbetta knew that in this case, three minus one would probably equal zero. Then again, sometimes brain beats brawn.

Inspecting the sailor's uniform, Corbetta said, "Well, Mr. . . . Sullivan, is it?" Then he made an exaggerated effort to read the man's shoulder strip. "From the *USS Bagley*, I believe?

Unless you plan to murder an American officer right here and now, I promise I will find you."

"C'mon Sulley, this half-track ain't worth it," said Buck. A captain wore the double silver railroad track and a 1st Lieutenant wore one silver bar, half a track.

Sulley thought it over as he kept his eyes locked on the Army officer. His gaze beamed the unmistakable message that he could have his way if he wanted to. Then a smile slowly spread across his face. "You and the lady here have yourselves a right pretty evening now. Sir." The pack moved on as Buck secretly pressed a five quid note into Corbetta's hand, whispering, "On us, Sir."

All the while, Win had been standing silent and motionless. Once it was safe, her knees buckled as Corbetta reached out to steady her. "Ma'am, today you took care of me. Let me help you out now. Allow me to escort you to your flat."

Win awkwardly looked down and spoke to the sidewalk. "I'm really quite embarrassed. I have never been like this before. I'm sorry to have placed you in such danger. I'm sure I'll be fine making my way home now. Only a block from here."

"Ma'am, at least allow me the chance to protect what I nearly gave my life to defend," said the soldier in mock melodrama. "Please take my arm before you stumble again and break your ankle."

Win acquiesced for the knight in shining armor to walk her home. The air was beginning to cool as the day set into early evening. Occasional windows were beginning to dimly light the way since street lamps these days were unlit as precaution against enemy aircraft.

Corbetta smiled inside to think that to anyone watching from those windows, the arm in arm pair would have seemed to be a couple. She was grieving not being part of a couple as she once had been. These two were parallel universes unknown to one another, pulled together by the gravity of war. And so they walked speechless with only their footfalls breaking the silence. He realized that he had no idea where they were going.

At this particular moment, they were passing in front of a cozy little restaurant which was a reminder that man does not live on drinks alone. To call it a restaurant, however, almost seemed a bit of an exaggeration. It looked more like a gingerbread house snuggled into a row of small, trade cottages that one might expect in a children's story. To one side, there was a tiny bakery, to the other side, a cobbler. Like its neighbors, the establishment simply called Beatrice was situated a meter below street level so that walkers would have to peer down through the top of its ivy-covered lattice windows.

Presuming that the nurse would not accept his offer to take her to dinner, Corbetta banked on playing to her instincts of caring for others. "I don't know about you, but I'm starving. Can we take a moment to grab a quick bite to eat?"

"I beg your pardon, sir, but you're a sandwich short of a picnic if you think I'm going to fall for that."

"OK, you got me. But I really am peckered."

"Indeed, I would say so. Rather brash if you ask me," she fired back.

"Huh? What does being starved have to do with being brash?"

"You Yanks think you're being so courageous just to screw up enough nerve to talk to a woman."

"I don't know how much you had to drink, but all I was saying was that I was really hungry," protested the confused American.

Win paused and mulled things over in her mind, replaying the last couple remarks. Suddenly she burst out laughing. "Oh no! You said you were peckered. That means courageous. You meant to say that you were peckish! Oh, I am so sorry. You really were being quite peckered to try using local words like that."

Tony let out breath. "So now that that's out of the way, have I earned any points at all?"

Win appeared to give this serious thought, contorting her face into an expression of serious consternation.

Corbetta persisted, "C'mon, you need to get something in you, too. Besides, one of those ruffians back there slipped me a five quid for our troubles. I figure that's part yours. So this is not a date, alright?"

"Well," said the reluctant brunette, "I do suppose I owe you a little consideration at that, don't I?".

Only when they walked down the steps were they able to see that only one other couple was dining in the restaurant. It almost looked like a private meal in someone's home. The dignified pair, each with snow white hair, talked quietly with their privacy guarded by a surrounding sentry of six or seven empty tables. With no servers in sight, the place might have looked closed for the night. However, every empty table had a single lit candle which cast a warm intimacy to the oaken room.

It occurred to Win that for a non-date, this was already feeling a little too intimate. The G.I. and the nurse took a table in the corner, opposite the other guests. It was five minutes before a waiter emerged to check on the first couple when he noticed the newcomers.

By the white apron tied round his protruding girth, the middle-aged server may also have been the chef. The apron played the role of a cummerbund over a tuxedoed shirt and bow tie so that the man might also have been the owner himself. He had brought a pitcher of water to refill the glasses at the first table. But when he realized that he had missed the new guests, he seemed to change his mind and his destination in mid-stride. As he approached the officer's table, he noticed that there were no glasses there. So, he turned toward the back room to fetch two more. But on that maneuver, he realized that the first table did have water glasses which still needed refilling. He darted to that table with great apologies and began pouring the lady's glass when he turned to beg the other couple's patience.

That distraction caused him to miss the lady's glass but not her blouse with the freezing stream of water. His effort to dry the mess by dabbing a cloth at her rather ample bosom did not help the matter. The woman's initial shock from water and waiter was quickly replaced with her gracious dismissal and her husband's amusement at the Punch 'n Judy slapstick. The poor server offered to pay for their dinner, but the gallant couple would hear nothing of it. They settled for the offer of a complimentary sherry, more to calm the waiter's nerves than their own.

All of this served to take the officer and the nurse's attention off themselves. They watched the vaudeville as they shared a cocktail of muted giggles and restrained smiles. Their first bond had been established.

Once the first table had been secured, the waiter hurried over. "I do beg your kind pardon. I simply did not hear you come in. Business is a little slow these days and, I'm afraid, so is my vigilance." He nervously cleared his throat. "And my coordination at times." He nervously stroked his toothbrush mustache since that was the only place the fur could have been ruffled on his entire head. Trying to reclaim the dignity of a proprietor, he straightened up and smoothed out the apron. "Besides first rate entertainment, is there something else I can bring you?"

"The lady and I will be having supper, I believe," said the Yank.

"Simply biscuits and tea, then?" asked the waiter.

"No, I said supper," said the American.

"I think the gentleman means *dinner*," clarified the lady.

"Ah yes, a Yank are we. Leftenant, no less."

"Guilty as charged."

"I'm afraid I'm still a little new to the uniforms you Yanks wear. Infantry is it?"

"No, sir, those are crossed cannon. Field Artillery."

"That shoulder patch there?"

"Red Bull. 34th Division."

As a newly briefed officer "in theater", Tony remembered the warnings about people who seemed a little too curious about military minutia. "You'll have to excuse me, but aren't we a little past the name, rank and serial number for the typical dining interrogation?"

The proprietor burst out in laughter. "Of course. I do beg your pardon. Simply idle curiosity. You Yanks are still a bit of a novelty around here, you see. Allow me to bring you menus. Would you care for water?"

"In a glass would be fine," said the soldier.

The server appeared lost for a moment until Corbetta gave a wink to the man who got the joke and said, "I shall certainly do my very best, sir."

And so the evening began. Totally ignorant about local cuisine, the gentleman asked the lady to order for them. "That might seem a bit cheeky of me," advised Win. "Your first lesson in British cuisine is that it always is the gentleman who does the ordering."

"Fine with me. I'll do the talking if you want. Just tell me what to say," said her escort. "I don't usually stand on protocol."

"But Britain does," she said.

When he mentioned that he was in the mood for a steak, she recommended something on the menu that was called

Scotch Fillet. A prawn cocktail with scones suited her lighter appetite. So, he placed the order, and this time he would be the one who provided the entertainment for the server.

Slowly, Win was beginning to reclaim even a little bit of control after the assault on her dignity. "I do owe you an explanation for all that I have put you through this afternoon," she began.

"Begging the lady's pardon, but you owe me nothing," said Corbetta. "And besides, I have no idea what it is that you've supposedly put me through."

"How I treated you with such brusqueness at hospital, and was so downright rude to you at the pub," said Win. "How I got myself totally bladdered and could hardly walk a straight line home. How I got myself into a situation where you almost got the ten bells kicked out of you. And then I practically made you beg to take me to dinner."

"I say, you really are a Mrs. Scrooge, you are," mocked the American in a poor attempt at Britspeak.

"Don't you bloody Yanks ever get serious about anything?" Win said.

Tony put hand to chin and searched the ceiling. "I would say that we just met three who were very serious about you."

The nurse exhaled a mild exasperation. "There you go again. I'm trying to be serious here. It's not easy to apologize and . . ."

". . . and I'm just trying to make it a little easier," finished the soldier. "You obviously had a tough day at the hospital and it sure didn't get any easier. I'm just trying to get you to cut yourself a little slack, that's all."

"Cut myself what?"

"An American thing: you should be good to yourself."

At that, the nurse went silent. Her gaze descended to the tabletop and tears began to well up. Quickly, she opened her purse and withdrew a tissue to dab her tears and blow her nose. "Please forgive me. I'm not always such a mess."

"I think I'm the one who needs to apologize, Nurse Ensfield."

Swallowing back her tears, she said, "I think we've been through enough today for you to call me Win. All my friends do." She was surprised to hear herself let someone get so close so fast.

"I'm honored you think of me as a friend . . . Win. But I guess I'm a little new on the job. I didn't mean to step on your toes there and make you cry."

"No, you didn't. In fact, that's what this whole day has been about, why I acted the way I did at hospital, the pub scene which is not me at all. And now my tears here. Poor you just stumbled into my shambles of a life. I should be wearing one of those demolition signs: 'Unexploded Bomb – Keep Out.'"

"Now you've really got my interest," said the Yank. "I don't want to pry, though."

Win blinked out a faint smile. "You're not prying at all, Leftenant."

"I thought you said we were past all that . . . Win. The name is Tony."

"Alright then . . . Tony. I still don't do well when a man shows interest in me. I guess these kinds of things take a while to get over."

"I'm sorry?" said the soldier.

"I lost my husband almost two years ago."

Tony broke eye contact. "I am so sorry. And I just opened a wound, didn't I? Please forgive me. I don't want to make you have to talk about it."

"No, that's perfectly fine. In fact, it's probably exactly what I need. I've been keeping myself at a distance from just about everybody so that I wouldn't have to deal with it. That's what I was trying to do with you. And we probably wouldn't be talking, either, if I hadn't fallen into you."

There was a long silence.

The waiter returned with the water. But even if he had spilled it again, he could not have distracted them from their conversation. Perhaps that is why he took such pains to be so quiet and took so long to fill each glass so carefully.

"How was he lost, Win?"

"Battle of Britain. He was a fighter pilot. And that's about all there is."

"How long had you been married?"

"About two years. Roger had just been assigned to fly one of the first Hurricanes. Based just outside London. So he was up and at it all the time."

Tony said, "He and his pals did one heck of a job kicking Hitler back across the Channel."

Win slowly shook her head, "Funny . . ."

"Hmm?" said Tony.

"I've been his widow now almost as long as I was his wife. I was always so terrified of losing him. But he always came back. And then he didn't."

Tony was at a loss to know what to say. "Where the devil is that water?"

As if on cue, the server-owner-washer-chef was at their table. "Is everything to your satisfaction?"

"I was just wondering when you were getting around to that . . ." Tony stopped in mid-sentence when he noticed the water that seemed to have miraculously appeared. "Fine. Everything is just fine. Thank you."

The couple became intimate friends over the two hours it took the waiter to serve a relatively simple meal. But his bumbling inefficiency served their needs as well as it served his.

Their late evening stroll was ended way too soon when she simply said, "Here."

They had arrived. "Thank you for walking me home, knight in shining armor."

"You're still a little wobbly there. Let me walk you to your door."

"Tony, it is awfully noble of you to walk me to my door. But I have to warn you that it's three flights up."

"Do you think I would dare tarnish my honor by allowing you to do what I refused to do? By all means, lead on fair maiden."

On the way up, he did wonder why they called something flat that you had to climb three stories to reach. When they got to her door, she fumbled in her purse for the keys and then faced her rescuer with what little semblance of proper decorum she could muster. She held out her hand, "Thank you for a lovely evening, for seeing me safely home, Leftenant. I suppose I owe you back at hospital."

"Why, certainly. I haven't noticed my back pain in the last three hours. You do seem to have the right effect on me. I may have to return for further treatments since yours are so effective."

"Well, good night then," concluded the nurse as she turned the key, entered the flat and closed the door upon the soldier in waiting.

When her alarm went off, she awoke with the jolt of someone having kept her senses on high alert all night long. At this early hour, it was still dark outside and Win wondered if she had just flopped down for an hour or so. The hands of the clock confessed the truth that she really had been in bed a good five hours. Yet, she was still fully clothed and had even slept with her shoes on. No wonder she felt like she hadn't really slept. But the wrinkled clothes and disheveled hair said otherwise.

It must have been that horrible dream that had drained her rest. Even after the lovely dinner with her gallant protector, she had fallen asleep still feeling so violated, so threatened all throughout her long, fitful night. She vaguely recalled awakening again and again throughout the night every time she thought she heard some noise outside her door.

How close she had come to being assaulted on the way home. She felt equal measures of fear and shame. Instead of anger at the sailors, she chastised herself for having been so foolish, drinking alone to the point of visible wobbliness and then walking home alone, right before dark! How could she tell anybody of the terror that she had brought upon herself?

And now she would have to do that walk all over again. Today, her shift was rotated to the morning hours. She would again have to walk the same streets alone in the dark to get to hospital by seven. As she washed up, she planned how to protect herself this time. First off, she would walk down the middle of the street wherever she could.

She applied her base makeup as she refined her strategy. She figured that when traffic forced her off the street, she would walk as far away as possible from buildings, trees and hedges.

But what if figures came near her? She applied the eyeliner and decided that if anyone seemed too close for comfort, she would cross to the other side of the street, preferably near safer appearing people.

The hot water kettle began to whistle for tea and she interrupted her mirror-work for a moment. How would she protect herself if someone did reach for her? She filled the steeper with tea leaves and her eyes fell on a large butcher knife on the counter. That was it, that is what she would use. She would hide that under her coat.

But on second thought, this was totally ridiculous. "I'd probably wind up stabbing myself. Besides, I don't know anything about using a knife. Imagine that Excalibur falling onto the floor at work. She took her first sip of tea and quietly chuckled at the thought of trying to explain to Sally why a blade was sticking into the top of her shoe!

One more sip and then she was back to the mirror to crimp her eyelashes, when she thought of a better way to protect herself. Eyes! That's it! She planned to go for an assailant's eyes if necessary. "All that, so that I can make it to hospital to fix people's injuries."

She silently reprimanded herself. "Well, enough of this." She donned her light blue sweater, switched off the lights, turned the lock, opened the door and screamed bloody murder when a body fell through the doorway. Her heart almost stopped when the body came to life and scrambled to its feet like an embarrassed cat.

As she reared back to hit him, he blocked her swing, holding her hand in mid-air. "Win, it's me – Tony! Don't scream, it's OK."

"You almost scared me to death! What is the matter with you?! Are you stalking me?! I could tear your eyes out!"

The lieutenant started to laugh when she fired back, "Oh, funny, is it? You think this is funny?"

"No, no, no," was all he could say to try to get a word in edgewise. "I'm laughing because, obviously, I didn't have to wreck my back sleeping out here."

"What are you blathering about?!"

"I was, uh, kind of sleeping guard outside your door in case those morons had followed us."

"Sleeping guard?!"

"Well, it was supposed to be standing guard, but when nothing happened, I just decided to take the load off my feet for a bit and . . . well, the next thing I know, I was falling at your feet, me Laigh-dee," he said, trying to sound like a British noble.

"You do look horrid. I would invite you in to freshen up a bit, but I'm off to hospital for the early shift."

"Want company?"

CHAPTER 15

UNCLE HERO

13 July 1942
The Hartenstein family table
Plauen, Germany

By the time he arrived home on leave after his second patrol, Werner Hartenstein was something of a local hero. Newspaper accounts of his heroism on the high seas preceded him. Only yesterday, the front page of the local paper displayed photos of Admiral Dönitz awarding him the German Cross in Gold.

Twelve-year-old Hildi braved the questions that all the curious adults were reticent to ask. "Onkel Werner, what is it like to be under the sea?"

"Well, let me see, now," said the hero. "It's like having to be indoors all the time. So, I like to have my boat on top of the water whenever I can."

His older sister, Thea Irena, had her own questions. "For the life of me, Wernie, I shall never know why on earth you had to go join the Navy. We could not have lived further from the sea!

We don't even have anyone in the family who has ever been in the Navy."

Werner returned playful fire. "Ah now, Thea, it was you yourself who sent me into the Navy."

"I did no such thing!" she said.

Now, Hildi's six-year-old brother got into the game. "Auntie made you go into the Navy?"

"Well, in a way," the sailor said.

Charlotte could not resist baiting both of her older siblings. "Do tell, Captain Nemo."

"See? Even now you call me Captain Nemo," said Werner. "It was my elder sister who read me books when I was too little to read. Do you remember my favorite, Thea?"

Thea feigned exasperation. "Oh, really!"

Oma Selma, the matriarch of the little family, said, "Oh, but it's true."

"Mutti, not you, too!" said the eldest.

"Absolutely! You read him *Twenty Thousand Leagues Under the Sea*. He made you read it again and again until he had most of it memorized," recalled Selma.

"And how many times did I have to repair the kitchen chairs from nearly sinking, Captain Nemo of the submarine *Nautilus*?" Opa Willie asked.

Six-year-old Rudi said, "I don't get it. How can you sink a chair?"

The captain's mother said, "You see, when Onkel Werner was your age, your Auntie Thea was such a good big sister that she read him lots of books. One of them was about a sea captain named Captain Nemo. He had a submarine called the *Nautilus* that travelled all around the world, twenty thousand leagues, under the sea. Onkel Werner liked that story so much that he decided to do the same thing. Now he himself is a captain under the sea."

One question just led to another. "What is twenty thousand leagues?" asked Rudi.

Werner nodded to his elder sister as if to defer to her authority of position. "Thea?"

She accepted the responsibility a little begrudgingly. "Well, OK."

Thea's younger brother rested his chin on his hands to give mock rapt attention. Thea cleared her throat to pronounce the answer. "Twenty thousand leagues is how deep the submarine was in the ocean. Very, very deep."

"Oh, very deep indeed," the U-boat commander said with a very seriously authoritative voice. "Over ninety-six thousand kilometers deep!"

Rudi's and Hildi's eyes almost popped out of their heads.

Thea blushed in embarrassment as the adults tried to stifle their chuckles. Brother now saved sister from drowning in humiliation. "I think my big sister meant to say that twenty thousand leagues is three times around the earth. Is that right, elder sister?"

"Oh, yes!" Thea said. "The title means that Captain Nemo sailed the *Nautilus* under the sea three times around the world."

Hildi's next question was obvious. "How deep can you go in your U-boat, Onkel?"

"Well, let's just say that underwater boats can't go much deeper than, oh let's see, maybe two hundred meters. That's way, way less than even one league."

Rudi was lost in wonder. "So, have you gone all around the world?"

"Well, not really," said the hero. "I've probably been half way around the world."

"Where have you gone?" Hildi asked.

The family celebrity pondered a judicious non-answer. "You know, it doesn't seem fair. Everyone gets to know where Captain Nemo went. But I can't tell anyone where Captain Hartenstein went. It has to be a secret because I'm in the Navy and they make me promise not to tell."

Now a little boy's real question. "Have you killed any bad guys?"

"Now, Rudi," grandfather said. "We don't ask a question like that."

The little boy looked down with embarrassment.

To rescue the little guy's feelings, Opa countered with an offer. "But I'll tell you something that probably no one else here knows. Come here and I'll whisper it to you, so you can be the first one to know. Then you can tell everyone else. Come over here."

The little guy perked right up with excitement. The old man whispered the secret knowledge to the little man. "Really?!" was the boy's surprised response.

"Yes, yes, of course. Now you tell the rest of us what Onkel Werner's name means."

"Werner means 'Defending Warrior,'" said the proud little nephew.

The little niece was star struck. "Oh, I get it! That's what you do! You are a warrior who defends us."

The Werner Hartenstein glimer peeked through just a little. "Well, let's just say that I do my best."

"But, Opa, when he was just a baby, how did you and Oma know that that's what Onkel would do?" the little boy asked.

Opa pondered. "Well now, let me teach you a new word, Rudi. 'Mystery.'"

"What does 'mystery' mean?"

The sage lowered his head, eye to eye with his grandson. "I don't know."

"Then why did you say that word when you don't know what it means, Opa?"

"Rudi, the word 'mystery' means 'I don't know.' Some things in life even grown-ups don't know. There are lots of mysteries."

"Like what?"

"Like why we chose to name a baby 'Defending Warrior.' We just thought it sounded nice. Right, Oma?"

She just raised her eyebrows. "If you say so, Opa."

Charlotte had an idea to occupy the kids while the ladies visited in the kitchen. "Mutti, do we still have that book around? I wonder if Hildi would like to start reading about Captain Nemo to Rudi."

The kids jumped at the idea and Opa William said, "Werner, why don't you and I go into the other room to visit a bit."

CHAPTER 16

MOONWATCH

14 July 1942
New Zealand 2ⁿᵈ Division, 6ᵗʰ Field Regiment, Beer Battery
Western Edge of Ruweisat Ridge
16 km south of El Alamein, Egypt
Operation Bacon, last line of defense for the Suez Canal
2240 hours

"**B**omber's moon tonight, Sir," said the cannoneer gun chief.

Mention of the moon instantly took 1ˢᵗ Lt. Corbetta somewhere else in his thoughts. Somewhere like London. With someone like a nurse by the name of Win Ensfield. That was the last time he had seen a moon like this one. They had seen it together on one of those escort walks that he had used as the excuse to see her every chance he got. In fact, such a moon had illuminated the night of their last stroll, before he had to disappear, without warning, the very next day.

Knowing how terrified Win was of losing those she cared about, Corbetta had been in his own private agony at the thought of having done this again to her. But it had never been his intention to get so involved with someone. He knew that his London stay would be a short one. He castigated himself for being so stupid as to have made an advance on a girl who was hurting so much. His heart had tricked his head into thinking that he could control anything.

But he really punched himself out because of the truth. He had not been stupid at all. He had simply been dishonest. With Win. With himself. He knew well enough what he was playing with. His conscience twisted a mocking whisper of the Old Bard, "If to thine own self thou be false, then to no other man canst thou be true."

How many letters had he written to Win since then? Each letter was another plea: reminding her that, at their first dinner, he had said that he too might be forced one day to suddenly disappear like Roger; trying to explain about orders beyond his control; begging her forgiveness; speaking of coming together again as soon as possible. But he had written those letters knowing that he could never send them until after this mission had been completed. So not only was she cut by his abandonment, but by no word of explanation of any kind.

The sergeant tried once more to knock on the door of the lieutenant's mind. "Do you Yanks have that expression?"

Corbetta snapped back to the here and now. "Pardon me, Sarge?"

"Bomber's moon – you know that one, Sir?"

"Ah, not sure. I think our fly boys use that sometimes."

"Yeah, well, 'spose we nicked it from them, all right. Means a stonkin' bright moon what lights up everything on the ground. Makes real good hunting for our forward observers, it does."

"That's probably why they've got us all standing at attention," said the American.

"Begging Leftenant's pardon, Sir, but what brings a nice young Yank like you into this flea-bitten sandbox?" asked Sgt. Ainsworth.

"Just observing, Sergeant, in case Uncle Sam wants to come and play."

"Uncle Sammy's sent you here to watch the likes of us?"

"Hey, nobody's played in the sandbox longer than you guys. Figure you must know what you're doing."

"Truth is, Sir, we just got here ourselves a couple weeks ago. 'Course, Queen's artillery's been digging up this real estate a whole lot longer than that."

The American just nodded his head.

"So how did you pull the short straw to wind up here with us?"

"I'm not entirely sure myself," said the Yank. "I think it all started back on 21 June when your pals got pasted over in Tobruk."

"Blimey! That's what bought our ticket here, too. Twenty-five thousand of them, Sir. Surrendered. Me kid brother might be among 'em."

"I'm sorry to hear that, Sergeant. I understand your boys put up a real fight."

"Yeah, and all for a ditch." He was referring to Britain's struggle to hang on to the Suez Canal, only ninety miles to the east, which was one of the most vital chokepoints. Whoever controlled that also shortened time and distance by half a hemisphere. "That why you're here, Sir?"

"Well, I'm told that Tobruk fell while your Winston was visiting our Franklin. 'Spose they figured that North Africa here would be as good a place as any for us to get our feet wet. Or at least full of sand, anyway. My unit had just arrived in Northern Ireland when all this came down. So a bunch of us were hustled across the stream to London to begin coordinating our stuff with your stuff. Then we were sent down here for finishing school to learn from you blokes. Then we'll wing our way back to our units to get them ready to join you."

The gun field phone clackered awake and the gun chief picked it up. "Gun 4." As he waited for the rest of the information, the sergeant clued in his guest observer. "Alert order, Sir." Then to the rest of his crew he called out, "On your feet ladies! Time to go to work."

He was answered by a chorus of curses, gripes and groans. Morale was just fine.

"Thanks for the company, Sarge. I'm heading up to the CP to watch this thing develop," Corbetta called out. The observer hustled up to the Command Post which was the nerve center for the firing battery. There he could listen in to the forward observers who were the ones eyeballing the enemy. They would be the ones calling in the fire. In this same tent, he could observe how the Kiwis converted the forward observer's request into actual up and down, left and right settings for the artillery pieces.

The subaltern, the lieutenant in charge of the plotting operation, called over to his radio/telephone operator. "Billy, prep guns for target Fox Niner Two."

"Yes, Sir." He picked up the phone without needing to crank out the ring alert because he had already prepped the guns to stand by for orders. "All guns, set for Tare Fox Niner Two, high explosive, impact fuse, fire for effect and continued firing at will on my command. Report when ready."

Corbetta was not the only observer. A war correspondent was feverishly taking notes when he abruptly stopped in total confusion. Corbetta had nothing specific to do, so he tried to interpret some of it for the reporter. "'Tare' is the military name for the letter 'T' which in this case stands for target. 'Fox' stands for the letter F. They are about to open fire on Target number F ninety-two."

"But how do they know where target number F ninety-two is?" asked the writer.

The American artillery officer explained the basics of a surprise attack using pre-planned points on the ground. "A few hours ago, they fired a few rounds at some spot on the ground. On each gun, they recorded the settings which had dropped the rounds on that spot. They gave that spot a target number. So later, when the enemy approaches that spot, the forward observer simply tells them to set their guns to that target number. They ordered a fire for effect which means that they are going to drop as much steel as they can, all at once, without giving the enemy a warning of what's coming."

"So what's the hold up?" asked the visitor. "Why are they waiting?"

"Well, the forward observer is waiting for the target to move into position. He called this in early so that the various commanders could get their artillery batteries all organized. That way, they could all fire at the same exact moment. Gun crews sometimes stand by and wait for quite some time before the actual fire order is given."

Leftenant Baxter kept glued to the phone that was connected to Divison headquarters which would give the command for all the batteries to open fire at the same time. After ten minutes, he told Billy to make sure the guns were still awake and ready. Billy spoke into his phone, "Gun check."

As the guns called in, Billy repeated, "Gun One, check. Gun Three, check. Gun Four, check. Gun Two? I say again, Gun Two? Bobby, throw something at Hedgewick and tell him to get his ears on." Ten seconds later, "Well, thank you very much for joining the war, Gun Two. Stay awake down there. Stand by."

Everything went quiet in the tent, and the four gun crews were on full alert by their weapons. Each minute that ticked by pulled the bowstring back tighter and tighter. The phone from higher command clackered in Baxter's left ear. "Billy, stand by."

Instinctively, Billy relayed the same command to the guns, "Stand by. Stand by. Stand by."

As Baxter waited for the command, he raised his free hand in the air with three fingers extended and locked eyes with his telephone man who readied the guns to fire at the same moment. "Fire on my three. One, two, three …"

Baxter dropped his hand and said, "Fire!"

Billy relayed, "Fire! Fire! Fire!"

The guns fired almost as one and the night exploded into four belches of hell-fire. The skies lit up as battery upon battery spread out over a dozen kilometers joined the chorus of chaos.

The war correspondent jotted what would have been his finest headline: "This is where the gods make thunder." And that became the headline for the soldiers' anxious families back home.

The Battle of Ruweisat Ridge had begun. It also ended at that precise instant for the lucky ones of Mussolini's 17 Motorised Division Pavia, 6th Armored Battalion. In the twinkling of an eye that outran their nervous systems, twenty-three sons, husbands, brothers, histories, emotions, dreams and faiths were instantly turned into poorly butchered meat that now hung off gun barrels and sizzled on hot armor. The ones who were not so lucky writhed in sand-caked agony with missing arms and trailing intestines. Before it was over, no fewer than two thousand others would be captured from the Italian Brescia' and Pavia' Divisions.

From the hailstorm of high explosive shrapnel, the armored column had nowhere to run, no shelter in which to take cover in the barren sand flats. They had no idea where the fire was coming from. They could not pinpoint the Royal guns to silence them. And even if they could have located their tormentors, even the forward elements of the 21st Panzer Division could not reach them with their shorter range tank barrels.

His Majesty's fire planners had chosen this killing field a good two kilometers short of their own maximum range. This ensured that they could still reach out and touch any retreating elements. The forward observers had waited until the Italians' leading elements had passed by the aiming point. The column was cut in half, fracturing the Italians' command and control of their longer range guns in the rear.

After the initial salvo, the guns of Beer Battery fell out of cadence and now fired in a disorganized popcorn effect which kept the ground constantly shaking. In the battery area, the sweet smell of burned gunpowder was the incense offered up. An eerie moonlight washed through the thickening fog of artillery smoke. The guns pounded, pounded, pounded away with apparent impunity.

The bomber's moon began to set and so did the fortune of the Kiwi gunners. The night, which they had chosen to surprise the enemy, was now about to surprise them. Eighteen tanks of the 15th Panzer Division's 8th Regiment suddenly pounced on them from the darkness.

The first shots scored a direct hit on Gun 1, setting off its stacked projectiles and disintegrating the entire gun crew. From the command post, Captain Lester grabbed the gun phone and screamed, "Direct Fire! Direct Fire!" Immediately, the artillerymen cranked down their barrels from the high angle indirect fire settings so that the gun barrels were level to the ground.

Another blast detonated Sgt. Ainsworth's Gun 4.

The remaining crews frantically picked up the heavy stabilizing legs of the guns and tried to turn the barrels towards the advancing marauders. Breech blocks were slammed open and gun chiefs looked down the barrels to spot a panzer. Running towards Gun 2, the American officer could hear the gun chief trying to get his men to aim the howitzer further to the left by yelling, "Trail right, trail right! Hold it! Load!"

A projectile was loaded into the breech which was banged shut and the gunner pulled the lanyard. The cannon belched a fury of fire, and a Panzer immediately exploded with its turret flying through the air.

At that very instant, Corbetta saw the command post itself go up in a geyser of flame. The next tank round converted the steel and soldiers of Gun 3 into a thousand pieces of bone and metal fragments. That was the last thing he saw, or heard, or felt, or thought, or remembered.

CHAPTER 17

SWEDE HOLLOW

The dense woods of rolling bluffs and the grass-carpeted meadows soaked up the steamy summer air. Even in the sequestered delirium of Corbetta's coma, the heat was intense and the humidity oppressive in little Swede Hollow.

Funny, thought the young hardware clerk. Those crazy Swedes love sweating it out like this when it's twenty below outside. That first wave of immigrants who had moved up the Bluff liked to cook themselves in little outdoor closets called saunas and then roll around in the snow. These days, Swede Hollow, just east of downtown St. Paul, Minnesota, might be more accurately called "Little Italy." First the Swedes, then the Irish and now the Italians. Port of entry for every immigrant wave floating in on the Mississippi down below the Hollow. That's how a neighborhood with a Swedish name got a hardware store with an an Italian name like Corbetta's. Next to the pub, which was the business that the Irish found most important, this hardware store was the only other shop in the poorest eighteen acres of all St. Paul. Unless you count the little Catholic church that Father John Ireland once planted a bit further downstream in Connemara Patch.

In Corbetta's comatose wonderland, the air inside the hardware store was heavy. Swede Hollow was still not electrified, so no fans existed. Fortunately, the Hollow sat on high bluffs that captured the breezes which sometimes were channeled up from the river valley. But those breezes could be a mixed blessing because the Hollow also had no plumbing. Halfway down the bluff, many shanty owners used the down-flowing Phalen Creek as their personal sewer.

Like the sewer solution, everything in poor Swede Hollow had to be 'do it yourself.' That is why a hardware store became the second most important business to develop. Someday, son would take over the store from pa. Right now, though, the twenty-year-old heir apparent was stocking shelves when he heard the front door ring in a customer.

"Howdy, Miss. Can I help you find something?" asked the proprietor.

"Oh, how I wish you could," said the young woman in a British accent. The young man on the ladder instantly recognized the voice and his heart almost thumped him off balance.

"Well, give me a try," said the older man. "Haven't seen you before. New in town?" Like a caged bird, the laddered worker clung to his perch, listening to the conversation. How was he going to act in front of this woman?

"Actually, yes. I'm a nurse from London on loan to the United States. Part of the Lend Lease program. Currently, I'm stationed at the Port of St. Paul."

"Everyone around here calls me Walt. I own the tavern here and run it with my son over there. Would you like a pint of bitters to cool things down a bit?"

"Thank you, no. That son of yours is what I was looking for."

"We're running a special on him today. Hey son, come over here and let me introduce you to someone."

"I think we've already met, Pa."

"Well then, I can see that you two have some catching up to do."

"I'll make sure she gets home in one piece, Pa. Wherever that is."

The bartender, Walt, slammed down two pints of bitters next to the boxes of nails. In a heavy British accent of his own he counseled, "An officer and gentleman you are, me friend." He leaned forward and looked the younger man dead straight in the eye. "Remember that, son."

The young man remembered him saying something like this before his very first date: "Remember son, your first responsibility tonight is to take care of that young lady. If you don't, I will. Then I'll take care of you. Understand?"

In a phantasmic world where nothing is too strange to knit together, the couple sat under the counter and drank their drafts while they sorted out the nuts and bolts of things. "We'll be safe from the war under here," he assured his date.

The nurse got right down to business. "So, why did you leave me?"

"I had to fight the gophers here. They're everywhere. By the way, that washer there goes in this pile."

"But you didn't even say good-bye."

A gigantic battleship steamed down Swede Hollow's only street, the dirt trail outside the front windows of the hardware store. The visiting nurse gathered her skirt together before rising. "I have to go. My ship is leaving."

"So, you're going to leave me like I left you?"

"I have to finish rolling bandages at hospital. Besides, I'm not leaving you like you left me. I'm saying good-bye. Good-bye."

But by the time she finished putting Tony and other things in their places, the battleship had moved on. That didn't stop her from walking right out the door.

The young man called out after her, "Hey, wait! Don't leave me! I love you. Please, don't go. I'm not kidding, this sunburn really hurts, ma'am!"

But she could not see him and his eyes remained closed.

CHAPTER 18

POLAR BEAR

20 August 1942
Lorient, France

Things were quiet at the U-boat pens of Lorient, France. On purpose. At 2330 hours the crew of *U-156* filed aboard quietly so that no hostile observers could detect activity. At 0200 the moon had set, and nothing was illuminated on the pier. At 0230 hours, one of Germany's most deadly killers silently slipped out of its concrete covered pen and, without running lights, was slowly piloted out to sea for its fourth war patrol.

The men of *U-156* had the stored energy of compressed springs after six weeks of being landlocked while the boat was repaired, refitted and replenished. To add to their impatience, the men had been sequestered for the last five days so that no unfriendly eyes could detect plans for their departure. Most had been visiting families and sweethearts. But once he had said his goodbyes, each man began to recharge his own batteries with each step closer to the waiting sub pen.

On their last patrol, they had sent twelve ships to the darkest depths. They had that taste in their mouths now, and they could hardly wait to get some more.

Captain and Executive Officer stood together in the conning tower. "She is all yours, Gert," said the mentor.

This fifth war patrol would be trolling new waters in several ways. For the first time, Captain and boat would navigate the South Atlantic. For the first time, the Executive Officer would assume operational command for the start of a patrol. For the first time, Hartenstein would be commanding an entire wolf pack, even though he had never even operated *in* a wolf pack.

That is why he was surprised, honored and even a little intimated to be given command of wolf pack *Eisbar*. He had only served in U-boats for the last sixteen months and this was his first wolfpack. Even so, Hartenstein was already one of the Führer's top U-boat drivers. He had quickly become a triple ace with seventeen kills during the same period when sixty-six sister boats had been lost.

Eisbar was a top secret flotilla of seven of Germany's fastest, long range U-boats en route to observe Allied shipping activity in the vicinity of Cape Town. They would be the tip of the scissors to snip the Allies' jugular that ran between the extremities of all eastern theaters of operation and the heart of Britain. So critical was this operation that even the name of the wolf pack was designed to deceive. Should the existence of this operation be discovered, its Polar Bear name would mislead enemy intelligence efforts to search for something in the North Atlantic where U-boat wolf packs had already been so effective.

Executive Officer Mannesman ably assumed control of the boat's harbor egress while Hartenstein travelled back in memory to that terrifying moment six years ago when he had been summoned to the headquarters of Commodore Dönitz,

Führer der Unterseeboote in Berlin. Hartenstein had expected a firing squad, not the chance to train for the U-boats.

Hartenstein considered how his fears and his future both had followed the same trajectory from one late night visit with an old pastor; a pastor who had also been a decorated U-boat commander in the last war; a pastor who just happened to have once been senior officer to a young ensign named Karl Dönitz.

"And now here I am, doing the same thing under that same Dönitz."

And what of that old pastor? What had become of Martin Niemöller? It could cost one's very life to even wonder. But Hartenstein could never shake Niemöller's story about the event that had eventually driven him to the pulpit. He offered up a silent prayer. "God speed to you, Pastor Oberleutnant zür See."

The serenity of these first hours contrasted the horrible deaths occurring this very moment at sea, on land, in the air, on all sides of the world, and all sides of this war. On this particular day, Luftwaffe bombers had carried out raids on the south coast of England at Portsmouth. Two hundred and fifty miles west of the Faroe Islands off Iceland, a supply U-boat was caught on the surface and destroyed by a U.S Catalina Flying boat. On this same day at Guadalcanal, Japanese Colonel Ichki and his seven hundred attacking troops were surprised by vastly superior U.S. Marine defenses at Henderson Field.

But here in the conning tower there was a warm breeze on the face, splashing waves for the ears and protective darkness for the eyes. 0300 hours and all was well, if not in the world, then at least on this bridge, in this boat, on this sea, and under this sea. Hartenstein hoped that somewhere out there, some ship was working hard to make its accidental appointment with *156*. God willing, there was more than one ship out there on a schedule unknown to both hunter and prey.

God willing? thought Hartenstein. Can he even say that? Think that? These kinds of questions were not philosophical. They were very personal. And the questions were very old. At about the same time that Jules Verne was getting a young boy to think of underwater boats, Pastor Achterhof was getting him to read another book which also planted ideas. The first book sent the boy on course to become a U-boat captain. The second book set the same boy on course to become a lawyer in the world of rights and wrongs, consequences and redemptions. However, dutifully reading his Bible had been raising more questions these days than it had answered in past days.

His thoughts were interrupted when Mannesman called down to increase all engines full speed ahead. The wind picked up as the boat answered the command. The bow dug into the gentle swells and pitched up a spray of water. Nothing like a cold shower to realize that it was a little late to be asking those kinds of questions, the captain thought to himself. On the next furlough, he would have to find some time to sit down with his old teacher.

"Beautiful night, Sir," said Mannesman.

His captain responded with an absent-minded nod, "Hmm."

The assistant followed up, "Everything all right, Sir?"

"Things look just fine, Henry. Steady as she goes."

"Steady as she goes. Aye, Sir."

CHAPTER 19

RECOVERY

22 August 1942
RMS Laconia
Off the coast of Kenya, south of Mombasa

T he corpsman commented, "He's been going on like that now for three days. All he talks about is something called a sweet hollow or something like that."

"Well, that may be a good sign that he's finally starting to wake up," hoped the supervising nurse. "He's been totally under for what, the better part of three weeks or so?"

"Almost, ma'am."

Wounded allied personnel on the eastern end of the Mediterranean could not return to Europe via the most direct transit westward, across that dangerously embattled sea. All ships had to circumnavigate Africa, traveling southward along its east coast around the tip to Cape Town and then north toward Freetown, up the west coast of Africa. Of course, Lieutenant Corbetta had no idea that he was even on a ship.

The delirious patient slowly struggled to flutter open his eyelids. The nurse was reminded of the trembling struggle of a newly awakening butterfly trying to emerge from its chrysalis.

With her tube of lipstick clutched in her hand, she touched his hand, brushed back his hair, and bent close to his ear. "Welcome back, soldier," she said quietly. Those three words were the lullaby to his twilight confusions. His faint smile bundled him off to better dreams.

Over the last week, the patient was awakening more and more often. The efforts of his brain to orient itself to the present began to replace its dream walks in the past. But even when Corbetta was awake, he seemed to have left behind parts of his past.

23 August 1942
RMS Laconia
Off the coast of Mozambique, north of Nacala

The *Laconia* steamed into the third week of August off the coast of Mozambique. It had taken the nurse all that time to get over her shock. What had made her run was now the very thing into which she had collided. The clouds were beginning to gather for her because the fog was beginning to lift in the mind of the healing Yank.

She could see that he still did not recognize her. But how much longer would his amnesia delay the decision she would have to make about *them*? For the second time in as many years, she found herself having to deal with a relationship all by herself. She had been given little choice in her future with Roger. But she did have choices with Tony.

Dear Diary,

What if Tony does not come to recognize me on his own? Should I be trying to awaken his memories? And what if I succeed? What then? I'm not even sure that he wants to remember us. After all, he just up and disappeared with not so much as a fair-thee-well. He knew what it means for me to lose people I depend upon. He knew it and walked out of my life anyway. Even if he were to want to pick up again, I don't know that I want to. I am still so angry with him. I don't know if I can risk it again. How much more of this can I take?

Her heart as heavy as her eyelids, Win exchanged pen for pillow with the thought that maybe she should open her heart to something that could hear better than a diary. She fell asleep in the middle of prayer.

Somewhere in the middle of the night, sleeping memories were being resuscitated by a change in the sea air. The salty scent of the last three weeks now took on a distinctly sweeter fragrance brushing memories across her mind, sending her back to childhood days in church. The bored little girl would sometimes entertain herself in a way that no one could forbid. All she did was close her eyes and try to figure out, simply by the holy stink of their noxious perfumes, which ladies were sashaying past her.

When the nurse awoke in the morning, not only did her nose have a surprise, but so did her ears. There was a ruckus in the air unlike anything Win had ever heard. It sounded like a mob of ducks that had swallowed their quackers. "Quack" came out more like bass notes of "uh uh . . . uh uh uh uh."

She stopped a passing sailor in the corridor. "What in heaven's name is all this racket?"

"That would be your boobies, ma'am," blurted the young man who choked to realize, too late, what he had just said.

"I beg your pardon?"

He couldn't recover fast enough. "I mean, it's the birds. They're called boobies. Hundreds of em, ma'am. All over the ship. Be careful of your step, ma'am – the sound isn't the worst part. Must go, ma'am," he said as fast as he could make his escape.

When she went topside to see for herself, crew mates told her that these were flocks of dive bombing booby birds that were sort of crash landing all over the ship. Until now, *Laconia* had been so far out to sea that only rare, silent sentries would feather by from time to time.

Now the ship was within sight of land to starboard and the waters were the lighter shade of shallows. Coastal flotsam slid past the ship.

Nurse Ensfield hurried to find the Officer of the Deck and complained, "Mister James, no one told me that we were about to dock. I have not had time to see to my patients yet, and I have not prepared an inventory of necessary medical supplies to be replenished."

"Beggin' lady's pardon, ma'am, but we have no intention of landing until we reach Durban in a few days."

"But I can plainly see that we are nearing land, sir."

"We are simply *near* land, not nearing land. Captain's orders are for us to hug the coast until we clear this narrower bottleneck of the Mozambique Channel. The Admiralty has strongly advised all civilian ships to stay as far away as possible from Madagascar. Jap subs."

"You mean German," said Win.

"No ma'am. I mean Japanese. If you can believe it, they paddled all this way west from Malaysia just to say hello. The Jerrys are trying to cut us off in the north at Suez, where we set out from. The Nips want to cut us off in the south right about here."

This made little sense to Win. "But aren't we far enough away from Madagascar?"

"Over four hundred clicks, ma'am, which don't mean a whole lot when they got subs out there what can travel sixteen thousand kilometers on a tank of petrol."

"Japanese subs? Out here?!"

"Indeed, ma'am. Right here in this channel. Those buggers have already beat up one of the Queen's battleships and sunk another twenty-five merchants just like us. We're just about to pass through the deepest natural port this side of Africa. Lots of room for a Jap sub to sneak around in."

Win Ensfield grew silent.

"Not to worry yourself overly much, ma'am. We haven't really had any trouble like that for a couple weeks now. Just taking precautions is all."

Win Ensfield had heard that before. She just couldn't recall where. It almost seemed like something from a long time ago.

27 August 1942
H.M.S. Laconia
North of Durban

"C'mon, it's up and at 'em Yank," said Nurse Ensfield. "You've been laying down on the job long enough," she said as she gave him a wink.

The bedridden boarder was taken off guard. "What are you talking about?"

"I'm talking about getting you vertical again."

"I don't know if I'm ready. Still feeling a little woozy and all."

"That's natural to feel a little light headed, and also a little nervous. That's why I'm here. Let me lead, soldier."

The patient's mouth was starting to come around a little faster than his legs. "Well, I can't exactly say that my dance card is quite filled up."

"One step at a time," said his minder. "Let's keep this first trip just over to the wall and back."

The lieutenant tried to mask his anxiety and pain by keeping up the banter. "Well, I suppose it's the best offer I've had in a while." Sweat was beading up all over his face. As she propped him up, he tried to cooperate with trembling arms.

"Speaking about trips, ma'am, know where we are?"

"Well, we've been cruising off the eastern coast of Africa for the better part of a month now," said Nurse Ensfield. "We're heading for Cape Town, but they say we need to join up with a convoy first for a little protection. Should be pulling into Durban sometime this afternoon. The coastline there is supposed to really be something to see. Might give you something to look forward to after a little R&R from our trip to the wall."

The soldier look confused."You make it sound like a big deal."

"Your body will do the convincing, not me, love."

She was right. If he were not so shaky and nauseated, he would have felt foolish at being so winded after just a few steps. The pride may have hurt more than the body. He had no choice but to let his nursemaid tuck him back into bed.

No sooner had he laid down than she was back at him again, this time with a wheelchair. "Up for a ride, love?"

"I thought you said I needed a little rest," protested the groggy patient.

"And so you have, chap. You've been out now for five hours, sleeping like a baby, you have." Tony didn't even recall being propped into bed.

"They say we'll be coming into Durban in the next half hour or so," said his medical tour guide. "Thought you might enjoy your first fresh air and get in some sightseeing, as well."

No sooner had Ensfield secured them on the starboard topside than they heard the thundering approach of what sounded like the largest thing ever to have flown in the sky. There seemed to be no end to how loud this terror could bellow. Even this soldier with artillery ears had to cover his before the bones inside rattled themselves apart. When the sky suddenly darkened, both of them felt like diving into the sea. A massive flying boat lumbered overhead just off the deck.

"Now that's what I call a welcome back to the world!" said the nurse.

But there was no response at all from her charge. His eyes were wide open and he stared motionlessly toward the coast.

"Leftenant?" No response. She touched him on the shoulder and repeated his name. Suddenly, he startled and came back to life.

"Pardon?"

"You were gone there for a minute, soldier. Thought I'd lost you again."

He looked a little sheepish. "Something about loud noises, I guess."

"As you've been sleeping your way to recovery over the last few days, we've noticed that you've had problems with the thunder. Where did you go there when that flying boat went overhead?"

No answer. Just that stare again. "Don't slip away on me again, Yank. If you don't want to talk about it, that's OK. I won't pry. Promise."

"Don't mean to be rude, ma'am. I'm just . . . I don't know. Seem to have trouble remembering some things very clearly."

Win was grateful that the passing coastline provided an immediate opportunity to change the subject. "Oh my, look at that!" she exclaimed as the Durban skyline passed into view. Tall skyscrapers were springing up all along the advancing coast. "Have you ever seen such tall buildings all at once?"

"As a matter of fact, that's the sort of thing I last saw when I left the States," said the soldier. "Hmm, seems like just about everything reminds me of something."

Ensfield commiserated, "Makes sense when you're far away from home."

"Naw, it's more than that, more than just having a memory. It's like everything I see or hear moves me right back to the thing it reminds me of. Like, I'm right there again for a moment. Like the loud sound of that plane. It didn't just remind me of the guns. It was like I was really there again, right in the middle of that tank assault. You asked me where I had gone. It's like I really was gone for a moment, 'cause I really wasn't here, 'cause I really was there. Like, I could have been wounded again, and I would have started bleeding right here in front of you all over again."

This was the most that Win had ever heard her patient speak at one time. When she didn't say anything, Lieutenant Corbetta resigned himself to saying, "Talk too much. You must think I'm nuts or something. That's it. Maybe I am nuts."

"Not at all, Mr. Corbetta. That hard head of yours took one go of a beating, and it's just getting back on its feet, is all."

"But even you remind me of something I once knew really well. I can't place it. It's like I've known you before. When I hear your voice, the way you talk, my memory wants to take me back somewhere that I really liked, some place important. Think it'll ever come back?"

Part of her desperately hoped so. Some other part hoped not. This time it was the nurse who went somewhere in silence. She gazed into waters where so many other stories had passed.

CHAPTER 20

SACRIFICE

27 August 1942
2000 hours
H.M.S. Clan Macwhirter, bridge
250 miles southwest of Madeira, Portugal

After months of swimming alone, the steamer had eventually just managed to make the rendezvous with convoy *SL 119* at the harbor capitol of Sierra Leone, midway up the Atlantic seaboard of west Africa. In U-boat infested killing waters, the lonely sojourner had finally been able to join up for protection in numbers for the last leg of its northward journey to Liverpool. That was yesterday. Today there was no convoy at all, at least not for the H.M.S *Clan Macwhirter*. After racing for so long, the aging, seven thousand ton merchant seemed to have run out of breath. It simply could not keep up with the others which had to leave her behind.

H.M.S. *Clan Macwhirter* was schlepping a non-military shipment from Bombay: two thousand tons of manganese ore, thirty-five hundred tons of linseed and twenty-two hundred tons of pig iron. As though blazing the homeward trail for the

Laconia, she had recently passed through Cape Town en route to Freetown.

Superstitious sailors do not always weave their fatalistic fantasies out of whole cloth. Master Roderick Sutherland knew that the odds of surviving this last leg were chancy. Already, in just the first four years of this war, the Clan lines had lost seventeen merchants to enemy action, eight in this year alone, almost all to unseen, submerged predators. On the bridge, only the young helmsman and the Master kept watch. In the descending darkness, there was nothing to see, except in the mind's eye. All non-essential crew were working down below where there was light. It was a silent watch for the young sailor who spoke only when spoken to. The captain kept his fears to himself.

Able Seaman Hartwick practiced what he had once been told: God gave a helmsman two eyes, one to keep on the waters outside and one to keep on the gyrocompass inside. He wished he had a third eye to monitor the captain.

The patriarch of the ship considered how the seaman was barely older than his eldest grandson. He studied the young man's taught neck muscles. He knew what was tying the lad in knots. "Steady as she goes, sailor."

"Steady, aye, Sir."

"And steady as *you* go, young man."

"Sir?"

"I remember the first time I took the wheel on my own, Tommy. You never feel ready. You rise to the occasion just like the old lady herself does on each swell."

"Yes, Sir."

The young seaman felt a little more permission to speak. "Sir?"

"What is it, lad?"

"I thought they said that a fleet always travels no faster than its slowest ship."

"That's what they say, they do."

"But they left us behind."

"That's cause they're not a fleet, my boy. They're a convoy. A convoy's about mutual protection."

"But they left us to fend for ourselves."

"That they did, for sure. That's because the welfare of the many outweighs the one. What we're doing is protecting all the rest of them by not holding them back. Those are the accepted rules of convoy tactics. If one should get torpedoed, the others bug out of harm's way."

"Beggin' Captain's pardon, Sir. What chance have we got, sitting all alone?"

"This your first convoy, young man?"

"Aye, Sir."

"Well, Mr. Hartwick, I figure we've got at least two things goin' for us, if you don't count prayer, that is. First off, what do you think is harder for a U-boat to spot, a whole convoy of smoke or a little dinghy like us? And if they did spot us both, which do you think would make a better snack?"

"You said there were two things, Sir?"

The Master did not answer as he submerged deep into his own thoughts. His eyes looked down as he counted off each finger: *Macnaughton, Ferguson, Macfadyen, Mactaggart, Mactavish, Ross.* "Aye, six of them, Tommy. But not a one until *Macquarrie.*"

For the first time, the young steersman looked over to his mentor. "Sir, I'm not at all sure I understand."

"That's the other thing working for us, lad. *Macquarrie's* the only one of us to have gone down in these waters this year. To be sure, six others have been sunk, but not in these parts.

And as for these waters, eleven of our sisters have taken the big drink here, but not one this year, not here, except for the *Macquarrie*. You, my boy, are steering us through lucky waters, at least for the Clan Lines."

Tommy's forehead rested its wrinkled confusion, as he proclaimed with long sought confidence, "Aye, Sir!"

The Master had given the boy the gift of a little peace of mind. What Sutherland received was a feeling that he could have even a tiny measure of control over anything in this deep darkness. The young helmsman shifted his weight to assume the stance of one who felt more like the master of his fate. The captain of his ship knew otherwise.

27 August 1942
U-156, Control Room
2210 hours

"Ah, little lamb, lost alone in the woods," mused the leader of the wolf pack. "Hmm, no other smoke to be seen. I make her out to be a lagger," said Werner Hartenstein. "Too old or infirm to keep up with the rest."

At this time of the day, most land living people typically began to settle down for a night of rest. But in this control room, it was far more than business as usual. The scent of blood was in the air for this nocturnal predator. All hands were facing their respective machines and every hand was on one lever or another valve. The only words were curt reports about dials and settings. In the stalking run, conversation was permitted only among officers.

"Sir, we could plot her course and extrapolate a back vector along which we might locate her convoy," offered his Executive Officer. "If we leave this old gal alone, she won't tip off the others and we might bag a few more."

The Captain instinctively gave serious thought to any suggestion, which is why his senior staff always felt free to offer suggestions. They also knew that their commander had a mind of his own. He never allowed his open-mindedness to compromise his command authority. What he would make of suggestions was anyone's guess.

"Indeed. Reverse plot a vector of possible convoy location and relay same to Merten and the rest." Karl-Friedrich Merten commanded *U-68*, closest of the five trailing boats of the wolf pack.

Then the captain seemed to change his mind when he announced, "Prepare tubes two and four."

Hartenstein's second-in-command would never think of questioning his commander in front of the men. But before he could restrain himself, his eyes snapped up from the chart to Hartenstein in a look of confusion. Hadn't the Captain just ordered a search for the mother convoy? The captain answered the query by commanding his Third Watch Officer, "Mr. Fischer, please prepare the firing solution for a two-shot spread amidships on this sacrificial lamb."

Hartenstein's gambit was that by attacking the *Clan Macwhirter* so far south of its northbound parent convoy, the main body might drop its guard. Hopefully, the main convoy would think that the danger of U-boats had passed them by. The rest of the southbound wolf pack further north would intercept them for one big surprise.

27 August 1942
HMS City of Cardiff
2215 hours

Half a day's passage further ahead of the *Clan Macwhirter*, the *City of Cardiff* now held the vulnerable tail position of Convoy *SL 119*. Master Robert Leonard Stewart was among the last of the convoy to see the *Macwhirter* as it gradually fell behind and out of sight. Radio silence was maintained to avoid giving away their position to the ever-vigilant ears of underwater prowlers. Because the trailing vessel was the prey most likely to be picked off by a predator, Stewart had posted a frequently rotated watch on the fantail to keep a lookout for stalking U-boats.

For the last two hours, the Master himself had been on the bridge, personally scanning the forward, starboard, and portside seas for signs of periscopes when news arrived.

The intercom phone buzzed and was answered by the junior Officer of the Deck. He verified the accuracy of the message, signed off, replaced the handset and pivoted to face the skipper. "Urgent message from fantail watch, Sir!"

Stewart was waiting for this. How long could his luck hold before being spotted?

"U-boat spotted?" asked the Master, trying to suppress his anxious gaze for an answer.

"Not exactly, Sir. Well, maybe. At least further back."

The Captain's curiosity ran out of patience. "Spit it out, sailor! You're not making any sense!"

"Sir, fantail reports multiple massive explosions lighting up the sky beyond the horizon."

The First Mate had just gotten the words out of his mouth when an Able Seaman rushed through the bridge door and smartly snapped a note to the commander.

"Urgent radio for Captain. S.S.S. received *Macwhirter*," said the Able Seaman, in a tone that was serious and hushed against the machinery in the room.

"Did she have time to give her location?" asked Stewart.

"Aye, Sir: 31° 3'13.94"N   20°52'15.83"W."

"Good girl. She bought us some time."

CHAPTER 21

CAPE TOWN

28 August 1942
RMS Laconia
1 day east of and approaching Cape Town

For her part, Win needed to come to some new terms with her late husband. The winds were shifting so that the one hundred and ten pound young woman had to lean into the gusts to keep her balance. For his part, the gruff bulldog known as Captain Rudolph Sharp was steaming full speed ahead in the opposite direction on this same deck of regrets. The stocky, two hundred and fifty pound ship's Master was not focused on what lay ahead. He was driven by what lay behind, the always pursuing ghosts of four thousand men he had lost on his last command. The two survivors each walked their ghosts on a deck stroll collision course.

The two pasts collided into one another at full speed. His clipboard clattered to the deck and the ever-serving nurse immediately scrambled together the papers that were beginning to blow away.

"Oh, dear me, Sir! Please forgive my clumsiness! It was all my fault. I was not paying the least bit of attention. My mind was totally someplace else."

She quickly came to attention to offer him his property. Though not particularly tall, his five foot eleven frame nevertheless seemed to tower above her best show of five-two. He accepted her offer with a barely perceptible bow and one imperious word of reply: "Ma'am."

His face betrayed no expression nor word of explanation whatsoever. He was indeed the Master and just stood there awaiting further explanation from his vassal.

Win tried to fill the massive vacuum between them: she a mere nurse, he the lord high almighty of their fates at sea.

She did not know if he would accept her hand of apology, so she reached out once more with words.

"Please forgive my rudeness. My name is Win Ensfield. I'm a nurse here looking after a recuperating Yank. My first time on a boat. At least, on a big boat. I have of course been on little boats, like row boats and such. But not on a . . ."

"Ship."

"I, I, um, I … beg your pardon?"

"This is called a ship, madam."

"Of course, I did know that. I'm just a little flustered, bumping into one of the ship's officers and all."

Bowing ever so slightly again, he said, "Captain Rudolph Sharp, commanding. Very pleased to meet you, ma'am."

"Oh, I do apologize! I had no idea that you were the Captain!" Now it was Win who grew quiet as she cast her eyes around, as if looking for an escape.

"Perfectly acceptable, Miss Ensfield, is it? In fact, rather refreshing to be bashed about like a normal person for a change, rather than everyone keeping their distance from the Captain."

Win was finally recovering her composure enough to be properly embarrassed. "I do hope you'll excuse my prattling about. I don't usually act so school-girlish."

"Well then, could you accept forgiveness in the form of dinner tonight at the Captain's Table?"

Win was taken off guard. She caught herself beginning to stammer once again. "I . . . I don't quite know what to say. I usually dine with my patient who . . ."

"By all means. I would be honored if our American friend would also be my guest. In the interests of shipboard comportment, one of my senior officers will also be joining us, if that is agreeable with you, Miss Ensfield."

"I . . . I mean we would be greatly honored to accept your gracious invitation, Captain."

"I'll have an Able Seaman fetch you at six bells then."

Nurse Ensfield arrived at Lieutenant Corbetta's cabin a half hour early to help him pull everything together. She rapped at the door, cracked it open and called in, "Is the dashing young officer proper for an evening deck stroll?"

He called back, "You mean deck *roll*, don't you, fair maiden?"

The nurse was noticing how Tony's plucky personality was beginning to come around. Ever so subtly, he was transforming from patient to pursuer. "Unless you have any other ideas."

"Well, I was hoping that I could make the trek vertically with maybe a little assistance."

"You mean like a sky hook," said Ensfield.

"No really, I'm serious. I think I can do it. I want to walk into that Officer's Mess like the officer I am. You know . . . with a little dignity?"

"You are a stubborn one, you are," the nurse said.

"And I think you just like pushing people around," said the lieutenant as Win wheeled him down the starboard deck. "I'm just getting tired of not being able to do a single thing on my own. I can't even walk to the can without someone holding me up. And even that takes the wind out of me."

"You make it sound like you've been struggling with a permanent disability your whole life. You do realize, don't you, that you've only been awake for a month now? Your feet have been on the floor for all of three weeks, and that on a rolling ship."

"But . . ."

"Which is exactly where you're going to land. If you don't injure yourself by taking things too fast, you will be walking more and more with each day. I know you can already see the improvement in just this last week."

There was a pause in the rapid repartee. "Yeah, I gotta think about that. You have a point. I'll be a good boy."

"To tell the truth, Leftenant, you really have been one of my star patients."

"Yeah, sure. I'll bet you say that to everyone with a hole in his head."

"I'm trying to be serious. Of all the patients I've cared for, you have shown more improvement and spirit than most."

"You keep calling me a patient."

"Excuse me?"

"A patient. Is that still all I am to you?"

"I'm quite sure I don't know what you mean."

He looked down and paused. "I apologize, ma'am. I'm afraid I got a little out of line there." Emotional confusion replaced words in the awkward space between Win and Tony. Each silently wrestled between desire and duty.

He was the wounded one. She was the caregiver. She took the initiative to reach out. "Leftenant, mister, uh . . ."

"Naw, that's OK. I was out of place. Let's just drop it. But call me Tony."

"The longer we leave this unfinished, Tony, the harder it will become for us."

Tony could come up with no response other than to hang his head, which Win took as tacit permission to continue.

"Tony, I don't think I was being completely honest with you just now. I do think I know what you were trying to say. And I'm flattered. You were not out of line at all. It happens all the time that patients develop feelings for their nurses. We spend a lot of time together in some very close and emotional situations. It's the most natural thing in the world to confuse closeness for other things."

"What other things?" said the hopeful patient.

"Well, that's something only you yourself are able to know." More silence followed. She brightened up and changed the topic. "Well, Mr. Corbetta, we have only ten minutes or so to appear before his royal majesty. What say we roll along and pick up this conversation afterwards?"

"You're the driver, ma'am. Lead on."

An Able Seaman intercepted them and brought them to the entrance of the Captain's Mess where they were met by the Senior First Officer. "Captain's pardon, ma'am. He begs your indulgence for another ten minutes or so while he attends to a small matter. He has extended me the privilege of welcoming you to his table."

He bowed to Win, "Senior First Officer J.H. Walker at your service." The wheelchair bound officer was a bit peeved that the Senior First Officer totally ignored him and spoke only to his handler.

His irritation only increased when the officer again spoke over him to Tony's nanny. "Would the lady like some assistance in securing some extra space for the wheelchair at the table?"

Tony answered the question himself. "The Wheelchair will find a way to do just fine by itself, thank you."

Walker came to attention and tipped a nod of acknowledgement to 'The Wheelchair,' cleared his throat and then glanced up to Win, as if verifying the acceptability of The Wheelchair's answer.

"Is there anything else?" Tony asked the officer.

"Not at all, Sir. Very fine, Sir. Thank you, Sir." As if to make amends, the Senior First Officer now spoke directly to the Lieutenant. "I would consider it an honor if you, Sir, would allow me to join you and the lady for a sherry as we await the arrival of Captain Sharp. Would sherry be acceptable to you and the lady, Sir?"

"Miss Ensfield?" Tony asked his companion.

"A spot of sherry would be exquisite, thank you," said The Lady.

Tony nodded at Walker who left to fetch the aperitif. As Win parked her date, she bent close to his ear and said, "A bit testy are we?"

As if mocking her style, Corbetta whispered an overly affected innocence, "I'm quite sure I have no idea what you mean."

"I think you do. We agreed to continue our conversation after the dinner, not during the dinner. I'll jam your spokes good if you don't behave yourself."

Tony feigned obedience. "Yes, Mom."

She snapped his earlobe with her fingers and it carried a bit of a sting. "I said yes!" Mercifully, the host returned with some pain killer in the form of brandy infused wine.

"I hope I didn't keep you waiting too long," Walker said as he first handed a sherry to the lady, then one to Tony. The host came to attention, held up his glass, bowed toward Win and toasted, "His Majesty, King George the Sixth." Then he bowed toward the ally and concluded the toast, "President Franklin Delano Roosevelt. Cheers." The guests replied, "Cheers," and all took their first sip.

Tony slowly pushed his wheelchair back from the table. Nobody said anything as he shakily hoisted himself out of the chair to stand on his own two feet. He steadied himself, smoothed out his clothes, stood erect, looked Walker straight in the eye, and saluted. "First Lieutenant Tony Corbetta, U.S. Field Artillery."

Walker returned the salute. "Artillery you say? Don't you artillery Yanks go by something the likes of the Red Britches or such?"

Tony said, "Red Legs, to be exact."

The Brit paused to consider what he may have just done. "Well, I do seem to have dropped yet another clanger."

"I'm afraid I missed that one," said Corbetta.

"I mean, I'm afraid I have, how do you say it, stuck my boot down my throat, is it?"

Tony burst out laughing, "The expression is, 'stuck my foot in my mouth.' And, no, you haven't. You've just given me the best laugh I've had in a long, long while! No offense taken in the least." Grinning with glee, the soldier thrust out his hand to a new comrade.

Walker strongly grasped the hand, "My honor, Sir. Again, the Captain asks me to beg your indulgence. He expects to be here straight away."

"Well, it's not like I'm going anywhere," quipped the Yank. "Come to think of it, I guess we are going somewhere. Even sitting still, we're traveling . . . how fast?"

"Oh, normally the old Cunard here could be making fifteen knots or so."

"What's that to a landlubber like me?" asked the artillery officer.

"Make that about twenty-five, twenty-eight kilometers per hour."

"OK, I should have said an American landlubber."

"Oh dear, I'm afraid I'm not that good with Yank stuff . . . let's see." After a few seconds of mental figuring, he lit up with a discovery. "By Geoffrey, you know, I do believe it comes out to about the same thing, knots and miles. So that would make it also about fifteen or sixteen miles per hour, what."

"You said that this is what the ship usually can do. What do you mean 'usually'?"

"Well, at the moment, we're picking up a bit of speed. Kind of like a tail wind, you might say."

Tony chewed on that for a moment. "But since we're heading west, aren't we heading *into* the wind?"

"Not bad there, old son. Not many would think of that."

"Artillery habit, I guess. Always figuring wind direction and other weather things that affect the trajectory of our rounds. So how is it that we have a tail wind when we're heading into the wind?"

"In fact, you're dead right, Sir," explained Walker.

"Could I ask you to call me Tony?"

"If you'll make it Johnny, with no references, please, to the blessed libation in the presence of Little Winston."

"Little Winston?" asked the American.

"Oh, that's our term of endearment for Captain Sharp," said the Brit. "He likes to think he's all the Scotch we need. Some people think he bears a bit of a resemblance in appearance and a total likeness in command bearing to the PM."

Tony was trying to keep up. "PM?"

"Prime Minister," Walker said as he seemed to look around for hiding Winstons.

"OK … Johnny. So, what gives, that we should be gaining speed when we're heading *into* the wind?"

Walker was enjoying conversation with someone who was interested and able to follow what he was saying. "It's not actually the wind that's pushing us along, but a really strong westward current called the Agulhas. If the opposing wind isn't too strong, the Agulhas could give us as much as a five knot – excuse me, Yank, five miles per hour lead. So right now, we're probably making close to twenty."

"Sounds like pretty smooth sailing then," said the Lieutenant.

"Except that it often isn't," said the First Mate. "Especially in these waters."

Win's eyes immediately snapped up to lock on to Walker's. "I'm sorry?" She seemed to have heard more than he had said. "We're in some sort of danger?"

"Oh, not to worry. Rather routine, if not a bit exciting at times."

Just then, the deck door opened and gusting winds announced the Master of the *Laconia*. Walker immediately came to attention. "Sir, may I present to you our guests for the evening? Miss Win Ensfield and 1ˢᵗ Leftenant Tony Corbetta, may I introduce to you the Master of the ship, Captain Rudolph Sharp."

Captain Sharp this time gave a deeper bow as he took Win's hand. "I have already had the honor of making this one's acquaintance."

Then he stood erect and extended his hand to Tony. "Leftenant Corbetta, it is a privilege to meet you. Please be seated, by all means." He unfolded his napkin, snapped it open and smoothed it across his lap in one efficient move. He tipped his head to Ensfield and said, "Please do not allow me to interrupt your conversation. I'm sure my able colleague here has entertained you quite adequately."

"Yes, indeed," said Win. "He was just explaining the precarious nature of the waters in this area."

Now it was Sharp who locked eyes on Walker, but with a focus of totally serious concentration. "Did he, now."

The two seamen carried on an extended nonverbal conversation in the two seconds that sounded like silence to the others.

The Senior First Officer got the message that he would be well advised to explain himself. "Point of fact, Sir, I was just telling the lady that these waters are *not* in fact all that dangerous, even though they can be a bit bouncy."

"I see." Sharpe kept looking at his Executive Officer. "Mr. Walker is quite right, of course. I'm sure that he was about to explain why the seas tend to be a bit more active in these areas."

"Yes, Sir," confirmed Walker. "I was just about to get to that. Right now, we're approaching Cape Agulha. This is approximately where the warmer Indian Ocean collides with the colder Atlantic waters coming up from Antarctica. That keeps things pretty hoppy out around here."

Win said, "That wouldn't be much trouble for a ship as big as ours, would it?"

Walker shot a quick glance at the Captain before suddenly remembering the correct answer to calm anxious guests. "No. No, not at all. Not usually."

Win cocked her head, awaiting a fuller clarification. "Not usually, you say?"

The Captain took command of the sinking conversation. "I think Mr. Walker was simply alluding to the fact that sometimes the waves can cause even a ship as large as ours to bounce around a bit. In such cases, we sometimes ask passengers to remain in their cabins for their own safety. In more active weather, we have been known to have passengers don their flotation devices as prudent precaution. That is all." He looked directly at his second-in-command. "Is that not correct, Mr. Walker?" he said.

"Certainly, Sir." Walker looked about for a moment. "Uh, Leftenent, from where exactly in the States do you hail?"

"Me? I'm just a Midwestern kid," Tony answered.

"I'm afraid you have me there, old chap," said Walker. "Midwestern, you say?"

"Kind of refers to the middle of the U.S. - at least the northern middle, I guess. I come from the furthest northern state called Minnesota, right on the border with Canada. We're on the furthest western shore of the Great Lakes."

Captain Sharp's attention seemed to have wandered away from the conversation. He stared at the far end of the table as he sipped his sherry. "Your mum and dad?"

"My folks own a little hardware store in the capital city called St. Paul."

"I beg your pardon, Sir," said the Master. "Hardware store? I'm afraid I am at a loss on that one."

"Um, it's a small neighborhood store that sells all kinds of things for repair at home like nails, glue, hammers . . . that sort of thing," said Tony.

"I wonder if this is what we call a 'DIY,'" Win said.

"Now I'm the one who's lost, which is nothing new these days," said the Yank.

This time it was Walker who jumped in for the rescue. "Of course you don't understand. DIY stands for 'do it yourself' shop. In St. Peter, you say?"

"No, St. Paul. A little area called Swede Hollow."

"Ah yes," said the Master of the *Laconia*. He finished his sherry, excused himself and wished everyone a pleasant evening.

Win was taken aback. After Sharp exited she asked, "Was there something wrong?"

"Please excuse the old man," apologized the Senior First Officer. "He has had a tough go of it since the *Lancastria*."

"Surely you don't mean that massive sinking in the Dunkirk operation a couple years ago?" asked Win.

"One and the same. Lost over four thousand men."

"What did that have to do with him?" asked Tony. "Did he lose someone on it?"

"Lost everyone on it, including a young Swedish expat he had taken a fatherly interest in," Walker said. "Old Winston was the Captain. I don't think he ever forgave himself for surviving."

"Oh, my Lord," said Win. "They say that was the worst maritime disaster in British history."

"Without a doubt," said Walker.

Tony reflected, "I remember something about the ship being overloaded which is what caused the huge loss of life."

"Also true," said Walker. "Some blamed Sharp for that. It hurt him all the more. I think he was the first one to blame himself. He won't tell anyone this, but the truth is that he warned them about the overloading."

"Warned who?" asked Corbetta.

"High command. But they were in a bit of a sticky wicket themselves. We were all desperate to get our lads off that French coast to Dunkirk any way we could. Weren't a whole lot of options."

"Sounds like you've done your homework," said Tony.

Walker looked downward and said with a quieter voice, "Didn't have to."

As though knowing the conversation needed a distraction, two stewards quickly entered with the first course. All conversation paused while the items were distributed and arranged among the diners.

After the stewards left, five very long seconds were filled with silence. Johnny Walker stared through the table. Suddenly, Win remembered that she needed to become very busy polishing and then very precisely re-positioning each and every utensil. Tony kept watch on Johnny's eyes. "You were there."

Johnny raised his eyes to Tony's. "Still am."

Tony raised his sherry and the others followed suit. "The *Lancastria*." Win and Johnny answered, "The *Lancastria*."

After allowing the sherry to settle, Johnny took a deep breath and exhaled a fresh start to the conversation. "Yes, indeed. That is why Captain always gets a little preoccupied when we push through these kinds of waters."

"Are there threats of German attack in this area?" asked Tony.

"Not particularly of late, no. It's the waters themselves. They call this 'The Graveyard of Ships.'"

To overcome her anxiety, Win tried to make light. "Ooooo, that sounds spooky, it does. Probably even has its own ghost stories, too."

Walker did not return the playfulness. "As a matter of fact, it does."

"Really," said Win. "I thought you were saying that there was nothing to worry about."

The British officer cleared his throat again. "Well, the sea gives rise to all kinds of superstitious legends and such. You may not have heard of something called The Legend of *Waratah.*"

"I feel like we should all be in our jammies around a campfire out in the woods," said Tony. "Go on, make this a good one."

"In point of fact, Tony, the *Waratah* really isn't made up at all. Big girl she was, called 'Australia's *Titanic.*' Almost the exact size as we are, sailing our exact route from Durban to Cape Town to England. And even this same exact time of the year, back in O-nine, I think it was."

"So what happened to her?" asked Win.

"That's just it," said Johnny. "No one knows. Simply disappeared."

Tony was listening carefully. "What do you mean, *simply* disappeared?"

"Just what I said. Not one sign of her, said the Brit. Not one body, not one piece of debris, not an oil slick. Not even a distress call. All souls lost. Except maybe one."

"*Maybe* one?" asked Tony.

"Well, they say that a week or so after its disappearance, there was supposed to have been some poor old chap wandering along a beach, looking like a drowned rat. Story goes, when they found him, he was just stumbling and mumbling, '*Waratah*. Big Wave! *Waratah*. Big Wave!'"

"So there was a survivor?" said the nurse.

"If he was the real thing," said Walker. "Supposedly, they just locked him up in a looney bin. But the legend has one other little twist, as they say."

Win had become engrossed in the tale. "Oh, do tell!"

Walker did not appreciate being mocked. "I'm not making this up, ma'am. A few days earlier, before the old gal had pushed off from Durban, one of the passengers, an engineer if I'm not mistaken, he refused to continue on because he claimed to have had some weird dream."

"Oh sure, about someone coming up from the grave or something," Tony said.

"Well, there again, you're not too far off," said Walker. "Mind you, this was maybe a week before the ship vanished. Apparently, he had a kind of vision where some ghoulish character waves a bloody sword and moaning, '*Waratah*! *Waratah*!' They say that the engineer refused to board and created quite a disturbance, trying to convince others to turn back as well. Of course, none of this would have been remembered if the ship hadn't blinked out after all."

"Do you yourself actually believe this?" asked Win.

"Well, we old seas dogs kind of have a reputation for these kinds of stories. But on a holdover in Durban a while back, I once did a little checking. Turns out there really was a *Waratah* and it apparently really did vanish when the weather was not a problem. Thing is, it is a well-known fact that big ships do just disappear in these parts from time to time."

"Oh, now you're really making me feel a whole lot better," said Win. "Disappearance due to what?"

"Well," the host said, "there has always been a lot of talk about super huge waves that just pop up out of nowhere."

"Super waves?" said Win.

"Waves that rise up maybe two, three, four times larger than all the others. So if you're running say, three meter seas, a monster could rise up as high as six to twelve meters." Then he interpreted for Tony, "Uh, make that twenty to forty feet for you, old boy."

Tony tried to imagine. "Hmm, tall as a four-story building. But how could a wave that is only twenty to forty feet high overcome a huge ship like this that's so much taller?"

Walker instantly replied, "Taking it by surprise and hitting it broadside. I've had waves just sneak up in the dark when you can't see them."

The conversation was interrupted by the same young Able Seamen who had escorted them to the Captain's Mess. "Begging the officer's pardon, Sir. Captain would like to see you on the bridge immediately, Sir."

"Thank you, Mac," replied the officer. As the seaman departed, Walker excused himself. "My most sincere apologies. Please enjoy another sherry. I shan't be long."

Walker's promise to return shortly seemed less certain when the Captain's stewards quickly entered with all the rest of the evening fare. "Hmm, looks like our friend is expecting to be delayed a bit longer than he had hoped," said Tony.

Win looked pensive. "It is strange," she said.

"How so?"

"The stewards brought all courses at once. That is quite out of the ordinary for a formal dine in."

"Why is that important?" asked the hungry American. His culinary etiquette was more along the lines of the 'bring it on' variety.

"Well, this all does not look so much like we are going to have to wait, as much as we are going to have to wolf it all down quickly. As if they're making sure that we get fed in a hurry."

As she stared thoughtfully into her cup, Win was reading the tea leaves perfectly. The Agulhas current was speeding the *Laconia* westward straight into sharply rising opposing eastward winds. Night engulfed the world. The seas were developing an attitude and heaven was answering with its own tantrum. Most passengers inside were still unaware of the developing danger.

Win and Tony were left together in the same thoughts. For several seconds, their mutual silence accentuated both the noise of the weather and the increasing motion of the cabin. The mouth-watering fragrances of the dinner fare were replaced by some stale smell of impending danger. If their mouths had gone dry, their palms had not.

The haunting creaking of the ship's joints was thankfully interrupted by the hatch suddenly slamming open and then shut. The ever vigilant Able Seaman entered and quickly walked to the table. "Captain's pardon, Sir, ma'am, but he has ordered all passengers immediately to their cabins to don life preservers and brace themselves for sudden movements of the ship."

Win went pale. "Are we in some kind of danger?"

"Probably not, ma'am. Just routine precautions. These rough seas can bounce us around a bit. Captain has asked me to see you to your cabins."

Tony was unaware of the major disturbances in atmospheric pressure that were bringing the wheelhouse to maximum alert. But he was picking up a similar effect on Win's face. The plucky Yank tried to ease things a bit by making light of this.

"That's the last time I'll ever enjoy a five-course meal all at once." He put his hand to his mouth and said, "I just hope I don't see this one again."

Win did not seem to hear him. This time, it was her turn to be lost somewhere else, somewhere long, long ago. She reached into her handbag and retrieved her ever present tube of lipstick.

Tony kept it up. "You Brits choose a heck of a time to freshen your make-up."

Win did not seem to hear.

The trip back to Tony's cabin reminded him of the old game of trying to pat his head while rubbing his tummy at the same time. While the ship traveled one direction, Win and Tony were trying make their way the opposite direction. At the same time, the waves raised them up and then dropped them back down again. With all this, the ship also danced in another plane while it rolled port to starboard and then back again. To add to this excitement, gusting winds changed direction moment to moment.

Win remained speechless all the way as she dutifully pushed the wheelchair through one gale spray after another. As always, Tony tried again to make a joke of things. "Don't let go of me, Win!"

Both of them were totally fluffed by a blanket of sea foam. She yelled back at him, "What did you say?"

"I said, 'Don't let go of me!' I don't swim well with wheels!"

"No, not that. What did you call me just then?" she yelled above the wind.

"Sorry, Nurse Ensfield. I called you Win," Tony bellowed back.

"No, you didn't – you called me Lyn. Why would you call me that?"

"You heard it wrong. I said 'Win.' I don't even know anyone named Lyn."

When they finally made their way back into his stateroom, Tony was curious. "So what was the big deal about the name?"

"I have no idea. Maybe I was afraid that you might be getting back some sort of memory problems, confusing my name for a similar sounding name. Those things can happen now and again with head injuries. I'm a nurse. I notice things like that."

She stopped in her tracks with a sudden thought. "No, wait! No, it, it was something else. It was like *I* was having some sort of flashback." She tried to collect her composure and shook her head at herself, "Oh my goodness! I'm so embarrassed." She cleared her throat, "Nurses always forget that sometimes we are the ones who need help."

"So now you're the one having memory problems? That's interesting."

The ship's emergency klaxon began sounding over the howling winds.

"What's that?" said Win.

"Apparently, ma'am, you seem to have set off my alarms," said the wise-crack.

"I'm not kidding, Tony! What is going on?" said Win.

It was the wounded soldier who now took command. "I don't know, but we've got to get those life preservers on now!"

"Oh no," said Win. "Mine is in my cabin!"

"Check the stowage bin there," Tony said. Win lifted the lid and found only one life vest. In two lunging steps, she towered over Tony to wrestle him into the vest.

"Oh no, you don't!" Tony said.

"That's all right, I'll get mine on next," said Win.

"Win, I know that there was only one in there."

"You are the patient, and you happen to be in a wheelchair, mister. Now stop arguing and cooperate with me."

"Knock off the nurse thing." Suddenly the coy kidder took on a voice of a no-nonsense, command presence. She snapped her head toward him when he said, "Put on that life vest. Now."

She paused just a moment to recognize an almost forgotten feeling of security, of someone else putting her first, taking care of her. Maybe even loving her to death. As she struggled into the vest, she smiled. "You said it again."

"Say what?"

"You called me Lyn."

The collision klaxon continued to blare as the bridge personnel prepared to meet an approaching sixty-foot wall of black water. The First Mate relayed the Master's commands for full power, trying to head the *Laconia* ninety degrees to port in order to meet the rising monster, bow first. She was only thirty degrees into the maneuver before being totally submerged by the crashing cascade of hundreds of thousands of tons of water.

Tony was thrown into the bulkhead, though the wheelchair took the brunt of the impact. Win became a human missile and crashed into him. He had no way of knowing how much later he awoke to hear her sobbing like a little girl, "Mummy! Don't go! Mummy! I love you! Mummy! Mummy!"

He also didn't know how many of his bones were shattered. He didn't care. He stroked her tear-wet face. "It's OK. I'm here. I'm not going anywhere. And neither are you."

Somehow, it was not the words she heard, but the deep voice of a man who was holding her. Different words came back to her: *"Lady, we've got to get the child off this ship! We're going down, and there's room for one child in the only lifeboat that we can get to!"*

Tony held her even tighter which made her scream. Every word he said snapped up the memory of another rescuing man who long ago had yelled, *"Here, hand her to me! We'll get her in the boat, ma'am!"*

"Mummy! Mummy! Mummy! Mummy!" It took this second time of hearing the same phrase that finally made him realize that Win was being trapped in another memory. He grabbed Win by the life jacket and roughly pulled her up to face him only inches away. Putting on his command voice, the lieutenant bellowed in her face, "Nurse Ensfield! Snap out of it! Snap out of it, Ensfield!"

Just like that, the screaming stopped and Win's eyes began to focus on his. "Tony?"

She was back. Tony rearranged his grip into an embrace and pulled her into his hold. "I think you had some kind of bad flashback. Things are really OK, Win."

The comforting words soaked through her terrified memories. She relaxed quietly into safe arms. Then the lights went out. For the ship. For Tony. For Win.

DAVE GARWICK

CHAPTER 22

TRAP

1 September 1942
U-156 submerged 30 meters
North and seaward off Gabon, Africa
2334 hours

Few people had even heard the name of Gabon. But a year before America joined the dance of war, Gen. Charles de Gaulle had led his Free French forces into battle there. His successful campaign liberated Gabon's capitol and all French Equatorial Africa from Hitler's French puppets, known as the Vichy. The first big player to fall in the four-day Battle of Gabon had been the Vichy submarine *Poncelet.*

Though the land had now been liberated for almost two years, the sea off Gabon had not. Through these waters, Allied shipping beat a straight line from the southern tip of Africa to the goal line of English ports. Though the Vichy had been expelled from the land, their Axis masters still freely prowled the maritime hunting grounds. Even as it decayed on the coastal seabed, the ghost of *Poncelet* haunted its revenge further out to sea.

Six hundred miles to the west off Africa's western dent, the leader of the Polar Bear wolf pack paced back and forth, waiting for some unsuspecting prey to cross his path.

"I'm beginning to wonder, Henry, if perhaps our last kill may have spooked off others for a while," said the Captain to his First Watch Officer. The subordinate's name was Gert, but for some forgotten reason, the tradition had developed that senior U-boat officers sometimes referred to their juniors as Henry. That term generally signaled a more approachable stance on the part of the senior. Taking that as a cue of permission, Kapitänleutnant Gert-Fritjof Mannesmann said, "Or maybe they have just shifted routes to avoid the danger area?"

"Suggestions, Henry?" asked Hartenstein.

"Perhaps, Sir, we might want to run a back and forth east-west pattern to intersect whichever longitude they may be following."

Werner Hartenstein reflected on the suggestion. "Not bad, Mr. Mannesmann, not bad at all. Normally, I would follow your suggestion." He paused in further contemplation.

"Sir?" said the protégé. "Would you like me to plot a course correction?"

"Not at this time, Gert. Our mission is to move the pack as soon as possible into a reconnaissance pattern off Cape Town. Anything we happen to pick off along the way is extra. Cape Town is our target this time. We hold steady on a direct southern course."

"Ya wohl," was the obedient reply, especially in front of the men. After a ten-minute delay to avoid any untoward appearances, the junior quietly asked, "Sir, may I speak with you in the mess?"

"Certainly, Herr Mannesman." Hartenstein ordered his second watch officer, "Herr Silvester, you have the conn."

The corridor was not much more than a catwalk which the crew had nicknamed "Main Street." Not that there were any other streets. Main Street led to everything, including the dining space which was the only place a person could hold a conversation with more than himself. In typical galley humor the men called it "The Maxim", after one of Berlin's finest culinary venues. The U-boat version boasted private dining for a party of four, so eating was an endless rotation of sailors coming and going for brief, no-talking shifts at the feeding trough.

Since everything had to serve multiple purposes to conserve space, "The Maxim" also served as the Ward Room when officers needed to talk in privacy. In this case, it meant displacing the four unfortunate sailors who were in the middle of their meal.

"Gentlemen," said Hartenstein, "could Mr. Mannesman and I interrupt your meal for just a moment?"

The men accepted the polite request as an order to leave.

"We shall not be long. Your coffee will not get cold and the Maxim's Head Chef here will compensate your trouble with an extra serving of . . . well, something. Right, Heinzie?" he said to the cook.

"As you say, Sir," was the only answer that a less than enthusiastic Heinz Dengler could cook up.

When the last diner had cleared the table, it was the commander's place to open the discussion in a subdued voice. "Mr. Mannesman? With four hungry sailors waiting to reclaim their meal, I imagine we should get right down to the matter at hand."

"Yes, Sir. I know that I'm not saying anything here that you do not already know. I'm concerned that the men are hungry for something more than food," said Hartenstein's apprentice, who was taking pains to not appear disrespectful.

With four crewmen hungrily waiting just a few feet away, the captain reminded Mannesman, "Let's keep our voices down, Henry."

Gert-Fritjof continued in an urgently strained whisper. "Captain, as you know, it has been fifteen days since our last kill. And right before that, it had been twenty-one days without action. This is something the men are not used to. Our typical pattern has been to bag something every three or four days."

"The men did seem a little too excited about getting that last mouse yesterday."

Mannesman either missed or skipped the fatalistic humor. "I think the men are losing their edge, Sir. I am seeing irritability, overhearing some whispered sarcasms about wasting time, about returning to base full of fish and fish tales."

"Ideas, Mr. Mannesman?" the skipper whispered, as he privately entertained a few thoughts of his own.

"That is why I recommended heading south toward Cape Town by running back and forth down east-west rungs of a ladder. We would have a much better chance of intercepting northbound merchant traffic. The men need the taste of a kill, Sir."

"I appreciate your concern, Gert. You know what they say about these new IXC's: the curse of this beautiful can is all the things we can't."

The understudy was not sure he fully grasped what the captain was trying to say. "Sir?"

"The crew might assume that serving on the most advanced boat promises a level of action that does not materialize during the longer range patrols that this boat is designed for. Unfulfilled expectations can all too quickly sour into disappointment."

"Do you think, Sir, that perhaps that explanation might help the men's patience?"

"Perhaps so. Keep us on course for Cape Town, Mr. Mannesman, and I will address the men in a few hours." The commander of the boat wanted to delay the announcement so that there would be no question about the decision being solely his.

Hartenstein stood and resumed his normal voice. "Gentlemen, thank you for your kind patience," he called out to the waiting diners.

To give the officers privacy, the undisputed and almost sovereign king of the galley had banished himself to busyness in the pantry. As if the cook had not been subjected to enough indignity, Hartenstein tried to mollify him by the affectionate appellation. "Smutje, would you be so kind as to re-warm their coffee and maybe find some little extra goodie for their trouble?" As for his own trouble, Smutjie simply grunted an obedient acknowledgment that was not much warmer than the ersatz coffee.

CHAPTER 23

THE CALM BEFORE

4 September 1942
Laconia
290 nautical miles southwest off coast of Namibia

The better part of four days had been required to calm both the *Laconia* and its passengers. The rogue wave was long since gone, but not its signature on steel and souls. Tony had sustained a broken leg, but Win had suffered a concussion. Only now did Win wake up enough for much in the way of conversation.

"So how does it feel to have the shoe on the other foot?" said the patient who now was nurse to the nurse.

She looked down at the cast on his leg. "I might as well wear it since you won't be needing it for a while."

He returned the serve. "Now I am afraid that the concussion has affected you."

"I really can't remember much of what happened," said Win. "There was a ship's klaxon as you were helping me on with my vest. The next thing I know, I'm waking up in your arms."

The lieutenant smiled, "Yeah, something like that."

"Wait a minute, soldier, you were helping me get my vest *on*, right?"

"I beg your humble pardon, ma'am. You are speaking to an officer and a gentleman."

Not that many years ago, yet a whole world away, this very ship had been a top-of-the-line-luxury ocean liner. Win and Tony were toying with each other on a deck that once had been where other couples had flirted in much happier times.

She smiled. "Of course. I do know that. And I do mean that. I remember this much, how you made me wear the only floatation vest just before the lights went out."

"Well, don't make too big a deal out of it," said the tease. "My plan was for that vest to do double duty. That's why you woke up in my arms. I was hanging on to you for flotation."

The Yank always had to make a joke out of a serious matter. So the nurse decided to give him a dose of his own medicine. "Just be careful with damsels in distress. You could be hanging yourself in ways that you hadn't planned, love."

"Love" took the cue and cut the funny stuff. His tone changed. "I know that you're the one with the concussion, Win. But, well, I really don't know how to say this."

"Tony?" It didn't escape his attention that she had just used his first name. Was this some kind of signal? Even such a little thing could trigger low voltage excitement.

Tony said, "Well, I don't really know what to say 'cause . . . well, I know that things really are all mixed up in my head. I mean, that's why I'm in this condition. I mean, it is my condition."

"Of course it is. But that's not your fault," Win said.

"I guess not, but I don't want it to be my fault for screwing up everything else."

"How do you mean?" Win asked.

"Well, I know this might sound crazy, but for a long time now, I've been feeling like I've known you before. Known you really well."

There it was. Now what? What was she supposed to do? Had he opened a door that she was supposed to go through? He didn't exactly say that he remembered her. Was his fragile mind ready for the shock of whom she really was? Of what they once had been?

All of these thoughts reverberated in her mind so quickly that the man across the table did not even notice a pause in the conversation. "But, Tony . . ."

"No," he cut her off. "I've got to say the whole thing. It's not just like something in the past. I feel the same thing now. And it's like you know it, too. I can feel it."

Win suddenly felt a light-headed spin of mild panic as though she were a double agent, whose cover may or may not have just been blown. She didn't know how to react, because she couldn't be sure what to react to. She thought to herself, "Am I being that transparent? Or is this just so obvious?"

Tony noticed something change in Win's eyes. "Are you all right?"

She recovered. "I don't know. Maybe a touch of seasickness. I'm fine. You were saying, love?"

Corbetta tried to pick up where he had left off. "What I'm trying to say is that I don't think we're really strangers. I'm not just your patient. Almost nothing fits together in my busted head. But this is the one thing that does feel like it makes some sense. Like we've found each other again, but either you don't know it or you're keeping something from me."

Win's blood pressure was returning to normal as it became clear that her cover had not been lost. But Tony really was picking up on something. One of his phrases was echoing back and forth: *"You're keeping something from me."* The real problem was that it was from herself that she was keeping something. When people said that nurses make the worst patients, she had never taken it personally. Since she was twelve years old, she had decided to stop being a patient, and rather be a person who tends to the needs of others. Until now.

She still wasn't sure that she was ready to be exposed, so she did what came naturally. She asked about his needs. "So, what are some of the things you think you remember?" she asked.

"I don't know, just little fragments of things . . . meeting you at the hospital, walking you home, having a quiet, romantic dinner in a quaint little spot. Most of all, what I remember is the feelings we had for each other. And there is this weird little thing where I slept outside your apartment or something. And your smell."

"I do beg your pardon?"

"No, I mean your perfume or something. You're not wearing that fragrance right now, but I think you've worn it a couple other times around me. I recognize it. This might sound funny, 'cause I'm not good with words, especially about girl things like jewelry and perfume. But it reminds me of the way Kool-Aid smelled."

"I have no idea what in the world you're talking about," she said.

Tony was frustrated that, when it came to food, it would probably be easier talking to a German. At least you wouldn't constantly make the mistake of assuming that you were both speaking the same language. "You know, Kool-Aid!"

"Never heard of it," Win said.

Tony slowed down his speech as if Win needed help following along. "When it was hot, in the summer, our moms would mix, a packet of this fruit flavored powder, in cold water."

Win feigned insult at his plodding rate of speech. "I'm not a blathering idiot, you sod! We've got something like that, and we call it Squash."

"Well, at least I'm not saying that you smell like a vegetable," Tony said with a smirk. "It's a little fruity, maybe with some kind of spice. I don't think I've ever known anyone else who has worn it except when we were together back then. When you've worn it around here, I feel just like I felt back then with you. It almost sends me into a trance."

Win was looking down and struggling with her lower lip, deep in thought. She looked up at him and then back down in hesitancy. "Tony, back in your cabin, before we were at Captain's Table, I told you that I hadn't been completely honest with you."

"Yeah, that you were flattered that I was having some kind of school boy crush on his teacher, or something like that."

Win said, "I didn't mean to insult you. But I don't think that I was being completely honest at that moment either. There is more. Something more I have to tell you."

Win paused and seemed to shift gears. She looked down and then looked around as if looking for a way out. "Umm, that's what I was starting to talk to you about. The things you are remembering," she said. "Like your feeling that you and I had once been together."

The man who was looking for answers did not answer, but locked his attention on every word she was saying.

"Tony, I know exactly what you're remembering." That much was true enough. She was now approaching the moment of no return.

"You do?" he asked.

Win took a half-step closer to the line. "I do. We did in fact know each other."

"I knew it!" he proclaimed. All of a sudden, the air was filled with no words. "And?" he asked.

She split the difference again and took another half step toward the line, but only a half-step. "Yes, and I do know what you are feeling."

She stepped right up to the line, adding, "What we are feeling."

"You've known all along and haven't said a word?" Tony's eyes narrowed. "You would have left me alone in my memories if I hadn't said something?"

Now Win crossed the point of no return. "Tony, we did know each other a few months ago, just as you are remembering. When we first met, I was still having a hard time with the loss of my husband, Roger. Do you remember?"

"Not all that much," said Corbetta. "Things are still a bit hazy."

"Well, I had just started to let you in to my life when you left me, too. Just up and disappeared. No goodbye. No letter."

Tony was totally helpless without a clue as to what he apparently had done, and why he had done it. Win blew her nose and sniffed back the last tears. "Well anyway, that is why I left my position at hospital and hopped this tub as a TANS. Figured if you could do it, then so could I."

"You went to war to get a tan?"

"No, that was your game, Yank."

"My game? I have no idea what you're talking about."

Of course he didn't.

"Well, that was how we first crossed paths, how you first walked through the doors at Bart's."

"There you go again. Suntans, Bart's. Not a clue what on earth you're talking about."

"OK. Back up. Not suntan, but TANS. I said that I signed on here for a TANS spot. TANS stands for Territorial Army Nursing Service. It's kind of like you. You're an officer with your Home Guard."

"National Guard," he corrected.

"Right, forgot. Well, TANS is sort of like that. We're civilian nurses who are part of the reserves for nurses. Regular active duty nurses are QA's, Queen Anne's. We're TANS. So, I just put in a request for temporary TANS duty.

"As for suntans and you Mr. Corbetta, you walked your sorry hide into St. Bartholomew's Hospital – we call it Bart's – because of a rather nasty case of sunburn. A self-inflicted injury, to be sure, which your own superiors do not look all too kindly upon. Which is why you came begging to us. And which you tried to use as an excuse to keep coming back for further attention from nurses. Somehow or other, and I will never understand how you managed this, your sunburn always got worse on my shift. That is how we made repeated acquaintance."

"Yeah, funny how things happen," said Corbetta.

"So I came here to escape," said Win. "And here you are! Or, what was left of you. I almost wanted to jump overboard. But then, when you started to come to, you didn't recognize me. I didn't know what to think. Should I try to bring you back to me or just leave things alone? I don't know how many times I can take it: finding someone, losing him, finding another, losing you, finding you again."

"But then, why have you decided to let me in on all of this now?" Tony asked.

"Because your memories are awakening. And so are my feelings. Your brain is beginning to heal. I got to thinking that maybe it's time for the rest of me to do the same thing."

"So is it?" he asked.

"I don't really know," she said. "That is what this conversation is all about, isn't it?"

"Let me tell you what I think," said Tony. "But you need to come very close to hear this one. Close enough for me to whisper it to you."

Hesitantly, she walked over to him and bent down as though to receive a whisper. He took in the Win-balm of her hair and makeup that no other woman on earth would have. He gently placed a kiss next to her ear where his lips rested to feel the heat of her skin. The incredibly soft heat. She did not pull away, but rather gently moved her cheek over his lips as she turned toward him. They shared a tentative kiss and parted for a moment to verify permission in each other's eyes. She took his face in her hands as he braced himself on the arms of the wheelchair to push up toward her. This kiss lasted much, much longer. Nurse and patient had touched each other so many times before, but never as man and woman who were both in need of the healing touch.

PART IV
ATTACK

CHAPTER 24

BETTER LATE THAN NEVER

7 September 1942
Topeka Army Air Field, Topeka Kansas

None of the crew wanted to heft the heavy duffels across the airfield, only to be told that they needed to report to the opposite corner of the base. Repeated radio requests only got "Wait one."

The crew had already nicknamed the base "Wait One Field." Their four officers had hoofed it toward the nearest building to get some answers. The rest of the new crew had stretched out on the tarmac. They tried to make themselves comfortable in the wing shadows, as their only hope of relief from the grilling Kansas sun.

"You know what they call you when you get nailed in combat?" asked Dingle. That name had gotten him nothing but teasing all his life. But he rose to the occasion. When he joined the crew as radio man, he was naturally nicknamed Jingle. Lieutenant Harden always loved to say it: "Give 'em a jingle, Dingle."

"Killed in action?" asked Tiny Tim, the ball gunner. Tiny is what he was, because men chosen as bubble gunner on the belly of the plane usually had to be rather small in order to fit in such a small space.

"Hey, give the kid a kewpie doll!" said Hennessey.

"Right. Killed in action," said the de facto morale officer. "So, you know what they call you when you die of boredom?"

For once there was a pause in the wise-crack ping pong. Total silence. They were actually thinking. "OK, Einstein, what do they call you when you die of boredom?" said the tail gunner, Otto Miller.

"Killed INaction," said Jingle.

The youngest member of the crew was also the most unassuming. Waist gunner Pfc. Frankie Sawyer said, "Yeah, you already told us."

"No, you don't get it. Killed INaction. One word. Inaction. You're killed from inaction, from nothing happening at all. You're Killed INaction," said the crewman who was in charge of communication.

Silence once again.

"Jingle, did those earphones short-circuit what was between 'em again?" said Hennessey.

Everyone laughed this time. "Now that's funny!" said the nose gunner, Cpl. Sal Spinoza, whose nickname was "Nosey".

The rest of the squadron to which they were assigned as replacements had left the States two months earlier. By the time the main unit had reached station in British Palestine it had lost three planes, though not one to hostile action. The Liberator, for all its heft, range and firepower, was a notorious nightmare to pilots and mechanics alike. Many pilots called it the "Flying Brick" because it had to be manhandled with such strength that pilots were recognizable by their over-sized arm muscles. The vast majority of "Flying Coffins" that went down did so because of mechanical failures. Entire tail sections had been known to fall off in mid-air. Fragile wings sometimes detached from any sort of hit whatsoever.

Accordingly, replacement aircraft and crews were routinely in the process of being assembled. This crew was one of those. But everyone knew that the war was going to be over quickly. Combat or bust. It was the nature of untested crews to itch for action. Soon enough, Messerschmitts and ack-ack would be only too happy to scratch both the craving and the crew.

Two weeks ago, at Gowan Field outside Boise, Idaho, the entire crew was assembled by the time this brand new B-24 was ready. This upgrade from the B-17 had only been introduced a year ago and already the Brit's had a name for it. They called it the Liberator, and that is exactly what its new crew hoped it would do for them, so that they could finally get into combat.

They had flown back-to-back flights day after day over the Pacific Northwest in order for ship and crew to get to know each other. Then they camped out for a couple days of further refitting at Bruning Field, Nebraska. Then they were temporarily assigned to Mountain Home, Idaho, as an Instructor crew.

Finally, crew and Liberator had been liberated. And here they were, in all their glory, fighting the war. In Topeka, Kansas. Supposedly, this was to be their last stop to stage for overseas duty. Two hours later, they were still grumbling about all the waiting when the crew's officers arrived from their recon mission.

The pilot, First Lieutenant Jimmy Harden, addressed his crack outfit that was laid out all over their duffels. No one stirred in the baking heat. In fact, no one showed any sign of awareness that their commanding officer (CO) had just arrived.

The short, slender, boyish looking twenty-five-year-old pilot was younger than some of his men. Especially to compensate for his physical stature, he had developed a natural command wisdom. He knew when to let things ride. He silently inspected his laid out heroes. "At ease, gentlemen." The other three officers looked quizzically at each other.

One of the duffel bags spoke up. "Beggin' Lieutenant's pardon, Sir, but we already kind of figured that one out?"

"Right. So I see. But would it be too much to ask you aerial warriors to kind of sit up just a little, so's I know which of you are not already dead?" He was definitely tuned in to their wave length. They were going to get along just fine.

At thirty-two years of age, Hennessey was "Pop" to the outfit. "C'mon guys, let's sit up and give the CO some attention." They slowly roused themselves to various lounge recliner angles.

"I know it's hot as a griddle out here, you're starved and thirsty and nobody has a clue what's going on," said the commander. "Turns out we're one of their first customers. This base just opened for business a week or so ago. They don't have a clue what to do with us. Lieutenant Milberg here has some info about getting us settled in."

The navigator took the cue. "Yeah, they're going to send out a three-quarter or something to pick us up with our gear and take us to our brand new, just-built quarters. They'll leave the wheels with us as our limo. And if we're all good boys and girls, the CO here will take us all in to beautiful downtown Topeka for the evening. Right, Dick?"

"Yup," said the co-pilot. That was the moment that the crew nicknamed him "Yakkey."

Now the crew started to wake up.

"Sir?" asked Frankie. "When are we ever gonna get going? Seems like no one knows what to do with us. Rest of the squadron's been in action for most of two months and we just keep marking time. Everything's going to be over with by the time we're ready."

"Glad you asked, Private," said Harden. "We'll spend a couple days here getting briefed, pick up some clothes and equipment and then we're off to sunny Florida for our overseas take-off point. We'll make a brief stop in Puerto Rico, then fly down to Brazil and then we're off over the wide blue Atlantic. That all should be in about a week or so. We could be picking splinters out of our back sides within the month. How does that make you feel?"

"Like a pain in the ass, Sir?" said Jingle.

"When it does, remember the Good Book," said the tail gunner. "Turn the other cheek."

Harden played along. "Guess a *tail* gunner should know, huh Dick?"

"Guess so," was the co-pilot's reply. Two words this time.

Tiny Tim said, "It's just that with all the waiting, we're going squirrelly crazy, L.T." Enlisted men often referred to lieutenants by the rank's abbreviation. They had abbreviations for almost everything, such as SNAFU: "situation normal, all fouled up." Or something close to it.

"And that brings me to my last point," said the pilot. "We found a nose artist over there at the hangar. He can paint the name of our beauty here right on both sides of the nose while we're monkeying around. All we gotta do is name her."

"How do we decide that?" asked the crew engineer, Hennessey.

"You don't. I do," said Harden. "That's why pilots get paid the big bucks. If your pilot's a decent guy like me, he might ask you sad sacks for some ideas."

Hennessey had a commentary for that as well. "Oh, this oughta be a whole lot of fun."

"Yeah, that's kind of what I expected," said the pilot. "So I decided to name her after the attitude of you joy boys. We're going to call her the *Bitch and Ditch*."

This snapped up everyone's head in what was the closest to attention they had ever been. No one was laughing.

Harden could hardly hold it in. Seems he had finally gotten them at their own game. "Just kidding. Believe it or not, I really have been listening to you guys. What is the thing you sweethearts have been grumbling about the most, non-stop?"

After a silence, the shy belly gunner said, "About how we're having to wait all the time?"

"Exactly, Corporal. I figure you guys have named her. Meet your new gal. I present to you, *Better Late Than Never*."

CHAPTER 25

DANCE

11 September 1942
Bridge of Laconia
Northwesterly course parallel to coast off Gabon, Africa
0103 hours

These were the hours when massive ships disappeared without a trace. Especially those unlucky enough to have to travel alone. But *HMS Laconia* was not alone. In the atmospheric ink, predators lurked where sky and ocean mixed without a horizon. Tonight, even the moon abandoned its post so that not one passing soul would ever be witness to the death throes of a vessel. By first light, even floating evidence would saturate and sink out of sight.

Something was up. Sixty-two minutes ago, the radio room had shocked First Officer Clucas out of his wandering imaginations with an intercom alert. Some urgent message had just come through from Home Office in London. Commanding the bridge, Benjamin Clucas had been pacing the deck now for the better part of an hour, waiting to find out what was so all-fired important in that message.

Bridge Bellboy, Victor Pells, was gasping for breath when he burst on to the bridge.

"Oh, then you didn't fall overboard, after all," said the agitated Officer of the Deck.

"Begging your pardon, Sir?" asked the terrified boy.

"Do you realize that it took less than a second for that message to get from London to this ship, and then took the better part of an hour for you to get it to me from the signal office?"

"Sorry, Sir, but Sparks had to decode it, Sir."

"And that took an hour? It was a short message!"

The sixteen-year old tried to hide his trembling, which had nothing to do with the cold. "Yes, Sir."

"Well, what in the name of everything holy took Sparks so long to get this back to me?"

"Well, Sir, he kept rechecking the message to make sure he got it right, because he said it didn't make much sense, especially if we were going to have to be waking the Master."

"Waking the Captain?!" said the officer.

When the lad stood silent awaiting the next blast, Clucas could still hear his own bellowing echo in the silence. It was then he noticed the frail courage of a young boy standing his ground awaiting the inevitable volley. The deck commander took a deep breath as he looked down and searched the floor for his next words.

Addressing the brave young man with the respect he had just earned, Clucas said, "I apologize, Mr. Pells. You did not deserve that. I must be wound a bit tighter than I realized. Let me see that message."

A little more confidently, Pells handed it over.

The officer unfolded the paper and furrowed his eyebrows as he took in the data. "Is Sparks sure that he got this right, Victor?"

"Three times, Sir."

Clucas took two strides to the charting table to plot the contents of the message. "Something's not right."

"Sir?"

"I hate to do this to you, sailor. You do, indeed, have to rouse the Captain, after all."

Having dodged one blast, the youngster was not eager to face another. He swallowed hard, "Yes, Sir."

"There's only one problem. The Master should be summoned by someone with rank."

"Sir?"

"You have your first orders, Acting Ordinary Seaman Pells. You've earned it, lad."

In the ten minutes that it took for the ship's skipper to appear, Clucas had hot tea ready for the captain. Master Roger Sharp lumbered onto the bridge and accepted the mug without a word. It would never have occurred to "Little Winston" to offer a word of thanks to any subordinate. Newly-minted Acting Ordinary Seaman Pells, nowhere to be seen, had either been sent on other errands or he had been run over by the captain.

Master Roger Sharp ordered the helmsman, "Mr. Steel, let's make that course change as directed by Home Office."

The captain's shadow was at his elbow with the question that was on everyone's mind. The second-in-command had learned mysterious ways of knowing when the master of the ship was afoot in the middle of the night. Sharp was not the least bit surprised when Senior First Officer Johnny Walker appeared out of nowhere but right where he was expected to be, right on the Captain's heels. "Any thoughts, Sir, on what they could possibly be thinking? They're vectoring us off our direct course for home and turning us further out to sea."

Sharp said, "This may have to do with our special cargo."

"The prisoners, Sir?" asked Walker.

"Aye, all eighteen-hundred of the miserable wretches," said the Captain. "Our course correction extrapolates to America and Canada, does it not?"

"And this does seem to be where we are sending more and more of these lost souls," added Walker.

"So, to avoid making this my last voyage with the Company, and with your kind permission gentlemen, let us comply with the mysterious ways of Cunard-On-High, and make it so, shall we?" said Captain Roger Sharp. "Change course to heading three one zero."

As if obeying her master's voice, the massive vessel turned twenty-three degrees to port and sailed northwest to its unknown destination. She transmitted a short burst notification of compliance to London. And to other listening ears.

September 11, 1942
U-156 surfaced
Southeasterly course
1400 miles west and parallel off coast of Gabon, Africa
0200 hours

The two officers stood side by side, each scanning a different quarter of the horizonless black void. Third Watch Officer,

Max Fischer, turned up his collar to the bracing breeze in their perch atop the conning tower.

"What I would give for just one drag off a smoke," said the junior officer.

Only under the cover of darkness could the U-boat dare come to the surface for a breath of fresh air. Long, claustrophobic hours of submerged secrecy could now be interrupted by a cautious openness. Hatches were opened so that fresh air could fumigate the guts of the mechanical predator. Men coughed a bit as their lungs strained to handle a richer concentration of oxygen. Nothing a bit of smoking couldn't eventually take care of.

Hartenstein had his mind on other things. "Nothing since Hacker picked up that last burst?"

"Not a sound, Sir."

A little after midnight, a brief transmission from the tracked target had been picked up by the senior radio operator, Oberbootman Erich Hacker. That transmission had come from a target on its relatively constant northbound course, parallel to the western coast of Africa. By coordinating with one of the other boats in the wolfpack, triangulation had fixed a precise location of the target. There were two tantalizing things about its position. It was trapped about halfway between *U-156* and the coast. Also, it was moving northward right into the jaws of the southbound hunter.

"Any thoughts yet, Sir, about turning to intercept its course?"

"In time, Mr. Fischer, in time. She's just a bit too south yet. That radio burst intrigues me though. So short, so late in the night. She's about to do something." The commander went as silent as the radio transmissions themselves. The conversation was closed. These would be his last words for the next three hours.

The starving shark trolled on the surface where it could travel faster, since the darkness provided safe concealment for surface operations. In the absence of conversation, only the hull waves had a voice as the twelve-hundred-ton weapon split the surface at a speed of fifteen knots.

The young lieutenant normally would not have risked disturbing his superior with unnecessary talk. But after three hours of silent rocking side to side in a salty breeze, his was a contemplative curiosity in these relaxed hours of a new day. "Sir, can a target be too small for us to bother with?" The question roused Hartenstein from his own depths. "Say again, Max."

"I was only wondering, Sir, if perhaps the target might be too insignificant? This one is traveling alone. If she were a worthy prize, I would expect her to be in company of a convoy."

"True enough, Henry," commented Hartenstein. "But her zigzag pattern suggests that she considers herself fair game for some reason." He was referring to the evasive practice that larger ships used to make themselves a more difficult target. In this case, the irony was that the *Laconia*'s efforts were attracting the very attention it was trying to avoid.

The cloud cover made everything pitch black. The only color at all was the white of the agitated waves which outlined the black hull in the black water. "Fourteen days without even a nibble," said Hartenstein.

"A lot like fishing sometimes," said the junior officer. "Sometimes makes you wonder if there are any fish left at all."

"And that is exactly why it is like fishing," said the skipper. In the monotony of the changeless darkness, the sea captain drifted back in memory to his first days on water. He was a little boy learning to fish with his father. The memories were better than the experience itself. He smiled to himself to recall how absolutely boring the whole thing had been to him. The underwhelmed little fisherman had to sit quietly in a boat for what seemed like hours upon hours with not a single bite.

He recalled saying, "Vater, why don't we move somewhere else where there are fish?"

"There are plenty of fish where we are, but now we have scared them off again by your talking," would come the reply.

And so, the long wait would have to start all over again as the first lesson for a young U-boat commander in training. He remembered thinking how boring it must be to be a grown up. How could they sit and do absolutely nothing for hours, like in church? Strangely, the only sermon that he could ever remember paying attention to was the pastor talking about fishing. A boring sermon about a boring thing.

The pastor said that most of the apostles Jesus chose were fishermen. He said that even these fishermen sometimes had to wait all night long without catching anything. Finally, for the first time, the boy was hearing a sermon that made some sense. But then the pastor said that Jesus told the apostles, "Come, follow Me, and I will make you fishers of men." He recalled thinking how this was the dumbest thing he had ever heard. It had taken twenty-five years to finally make some sense.

"Pardon me, Sir?" asked the Watch Officer.

Hartenstein was snapped back to the present. "What is that, Max?"

"You said something that I couldn't quite catch. Something about fishing and men."

The captain searched his thoughts and smiled faintly. *"Come, follow Me and I will make you fishers of men.* Jesus said that. You said that what we're doing is a lot like fishing. But I think it is a lot harder when you are fishing for men, don't you agree?"

"I never thought about it like that, Sir. But yes, now that you mention it, by all means."

Below deck in the control room, the radioman leaned in closer to the console. He tuned the dial locator back and forth as he strained to listen for another faint transmission from the target. His supervisor, Second Watch Officer Silvester Peters, was reminded of hunting forays with his beloved German Short Haired Pointer. "So, what have we got here, Schatzi?"

"Sir?" queried the confused operator.

"You remind me of the pointing stance of my hunting dog when he gets the scent. What are you picking up, Ludwig?"

"New transmission, Sir," answered the Funkmaat. He jotted coordinates on a slip of paper that he tore off and smartly snapped to the officer.

Peters immediately took one step to the plotting table and determined the new location of the target. He then grabbed the intercom to signal Hartenstein who was topside in the conning tower. "Possible course correction on that target, Sir."

Hartenstein left Fischer on the bridge and immediately dropped through the hatch to personally inspect the plotting table. Sure enough, since its last transmission at midnight, the target had inexplicably turned seaward on a northwesterly course. "Perhaps the time has come for us to finally meet each other," said the hunter to the prey.

CHAPTER 26

SEPTEMBER 12TH

12 September 1942
Laconia
518 nautical miles SW of Monrovia
Northwesterly course, bearing 310 degrees
0925 hours

"**Y**eah, well just 'cause you've seen me as my nurse, don't think you know everything about me," said Tony.

The game was on and it was Win's serve. "Oh, really. Like what, for instance?"

It was breakfast. Patient and nurse had become so much more than patient and nurse. The last days had been an endless discovery of each about the other: their homes, their families, their favorite foods, the places each had been and the places each wanted to visit. Like so many new romances, they both felt like they had all things in common. Endless and animated conversations lived late into each night. Each was convinced that life could be happy and complete simply by being together and sharing everything, every day.

Tony had to think for a moment. "Well, books for instance. Bet you don't know what I read."

"Didn't know *that* you read."

Tony said, "Pardon me?"

"Well, you're a bloke," she said.

"Like Shakespeare was, you mean."

"Got me, Yank. It's just that I don't see a lot of chaps carrying 'round a book."

"I've always had one," Tony said.

"How come I've never seen it?"

"I lost it when I lost my uniform. It was a pocket-sized New Testament that my dad carried in the last war. I kept it in my left breast pocket just like he did. You know, sort of over the heart."

"That's really sweet," said Win. "I didn't know you were the religious type."

"I'm not really," Tony said. "There've always been stories about a Bible stopping a bullet. It's kind of superstition, I guess. But then, I've always kind of thought that way about religion anyway. It's all superstition."

"Well," said his new interest. "I think we've probably discovered at least one thing that we're different on."

Tony filled the next few seconds by considering whether or not he wanted to pursue that remark. "Well, to tell you the truth, I haven't really read it all that much."

"Not that much, huh?" said Win.

"Well, hardly at all."

She rested her chin on her folded hands and feigned a look of great concern. "*Hardly* at all."

"Ok. Not at all."

Her eyes never left the target. "But you hoped it would save your life anyway."

He looked up at his grand inquisitor. "You are not going to let this go, are you?"

"Just trying to learn what a Yank means by superstition is all. And now I know a whole lot more about you than I did one cup earlier," the nurse said. "So, what do you like to read?"

"Well, I seem to have this attraction to British women."

Win mulled that one over. "Mrs. Shakespeare, then?"

"Not unless her pen name was Agatha Christie."

"Oh, that's simply delightful! She's my all-time favorite! What's your favorite book of hers?"

Tony really had to search his memory. "Well, it had been that one about a killer on a train, or something like that." Win did not take the bait. "But since I just about got myself blown up in Egypt back there, I've been thinking a lot about her last novel."

"You mean *Death on the Nile!*"

"That's the one. When I read it a couple years ago, I found myself wondering what it would be like to live in Egypt. Instead, I almost found out what it would be like to be dead in Egypt."

"Shows you need to be careful what you wish for, Yank."

"Does that go as well with who I wish for?"

"And whom, gallant sir, might that be?"

"I think her name is Win."

Win broke eye contact and looked down. "I, I think not."

Tony was a little taken off guard. He wasn't sure how to respond. "I fear you have me at a disadvantage, ma'am."

"I fear that you are more right than you know," she said. "I have a confession to make. I've been misleading you about who I really am."

"Ah, a good mystery! Jacqueline de Bellefort, I presume?" he said, referring to the heroine in Christie's latest work.

Like romantic Bolero dancers, Win and Tony faced off with playful challenge. "Oh my, sir, you do know your Christie," said Win, his own femme fatale. "But don't be so sure that you really know either of us women of dangerous mystery, Mr. Corbetta. Or should I say, Detective Poirot?"

Tony played along. "Perhaps, my dear lady. But it is the lovelorn woman who can be the deadliest suspect."

As soon as he said it, Tony knew he had just played way out of bounds. Win gulped in a gasp and looked down. She nodded and smiled ever so faintly. "Lovelorn. Indeed."

Tony scrambled to recover. "I . . . I didn't mean . . ."

"And what is it that this lovelorn woman could possibly slay?" she quietly asked.

Tony could see himself crashing and burning just like Win's first love. The only answer he could think of was two words: "My heart."

She stared into her lap and only shed three tears. Then two more. Tony risked shattering more than the silence. "Win?"

She sniffed back her tears, but could not bring herself to make eye contact. "My real name is Lyn."

This time, Tony kept his mouth shut.

Lyn kept looking down. "At least they say that's what I was named at birth. I was adopted after my mum and dad were killed. I was never told much about how that happened. I guess I couldn't say my name right when I was a wee one and Lyn came out Win. That's what I've always been called."

Tony tried to lighten her up with a little comedic melodrama. "I knew it! Tricked by a two-year-old-enemy agent with a false name."

Win might have laughed. Yet Lyn blinked back a faint smile. A tear escaped her troubled gaze. As she brought up a tissue to hide behind, Tony noticed a tremble in her fingers.

U-156 surfaced
566 nautical miles SW of Monrovia
Southeasterly course, bearing 115 degrees
0937 hours

"Yes, yes, yes," said the skipper. "There she is."

There is a line that separates earth from heaven. On that horizon balanced 2,732 souls within one tiny speck of smoke, at one fleeting, unfortunate moment when a U-boat skipper peered through his binoculars. A lesser eye might not have even noticed the aberration on the skyline. A different destiny might have awaited those who now did not know that they were about to cross that eternal line.

"Do you want me to order a submerged approach?" asked the First Watch Officer. He was conscious of risking detection on the surface during the daylight of a climbing sun. The target would have the sun at its back. Its observers would not be blinded and might spot an illuminated glint off the U-boat's mast.

"Not necessary, my cautious friend," said the more experienced Captain. "Too far away to spot us so close to the surface. We need the speed to close for identification before the sun backlights us. Order full speed ahead."

"Aye, Sir. Full speed ahead."

Because prey and predator were quickly closing, the surface sprint was brief. Hartenstein ordered the boat to slow the approach and submerge at 1145 hours. He personally took periscope controls.

The old salt could hardly believe his eyes. There before him was by far the largest target they had ever happened upon. At 19,600 tons, this prize was more than twice the size of the next largest meal that the predator had ever consumed. And this prey was all alone.

By 1330 hours he could identify his target as a liner of some sort. But he would need to get closer to determine if the vessel had armaments which would make her a bona fide military target. By running submerged, the U-boat sacrificed more than half its surface speed. The *Laconia* was moving twice as fast.

As he considered the approach on target that he wanted to make, he recalled what he had read just last night: *God made two great lights; the greater light to rule the day, and the lesser light to rule the night.* Right now, his job was to cooperate with those lights. He decided to make a rapid surface approach on the target's port side so that the high western sun would provide a blinding glare to any *Laconia* observer looking his direction.

As the U-boat closed the distance, the sun was dropping lower in the western sky and threatened to backlight the predator as an easily detected silhouette. As he submerged, Hartenstein had another problem, and this one transcended the concrete simplicities of complex trigonometry. The asymmetrical warfare between his heart and his head grew so loud that his assistant could hear him whisper to himself, "Can't quite tell if this beauty is armed or not."

Mannesman knew exactly what his skipper meant. If an otherwise civilian ship was in military service, it could be attacked without warning.

The truth is that *Laconia* was both. Exactly three years earlier, the civilian liner had been requisitioned by the British Admiralty and converted into an armed merchant cruiser. She had been fitted with eight six-inch guns and two three-inch high-angle guns. These were covered under huge tarpaulins to disguise the size and shape of what was hidden.

Every U-boat carried photo catalogues and detailed descriptions of every major vessel afloat. Each officer was specially trained to know what to look for. All that was needed was to get close enough to see. The submerged *156* edged closer at 2000 hours, just as the crew of the *Laconia* began its pre-dark, top-side routines. One of those duties involved uncovering the weaponry, checking it and re-covering it for the night. That is when the hunter saw what it needed to see.

RMS Laconia
2°09'S - 17°43'W
2150 hours

Tony snapped the lighter closed as he sucked the cigarette into a brief bright, orange flare. His tongue maneuvered a tiny strand of tobacco until he could bip it out his pursed lips. He didn't even notice the guy who sidled up next to him at the railing. "So how many seconds?"

Tony was taken off guard by this intrusion from the world. "Huh?

"How many seconds did it take?"

"For what?"

"For it to hit the water."

Tony didn't even look up at the stranger and didn't really try all that hard to participate. "Don't have the foggiest idea what you're talking about, pal."

For the better part of an hour, Tony had been leaning on the bridge rail, staring off into the monotonous ocean, far away in his thoughts. He really was not looking for company. He vaguely registered the fact that something was extending into his space. He looked down at what was reaching toward him. It was some guy's open hand.

"Bugs Nealy," said the stranger who wasn't put off by Tony's distance.

Tony shifted his gaze from the guy's open hand to the guy's open face. The guy's name was the first thing that made sense. He had two huge eyes that wanted to pop out of their sockets. Tony couldn't help but smile as he grasped the handshake and introduced himself.

"So how long *did* it take to hit?" repeated the curious, new friend.

"You've still got me," said Tony. "How long did what take to hit what?"

"Whatever you were spitting out your mouth."

Tony searched his memory until he recalled lighting up the smoke. "Oh, I don't know. Guess I had a piece of tobacco on the tip of my tongue."

"That'll kill ya," said Nealy.

"No worse than the slop they're trying to push by these same lips at every so-called meal. Besides, I hardly ever smoke," said Corbetta.

"Nah, I mean lighting up after dark," said Nealy. "They say those sneaky U-boats can spot a hot flash on a fruit fly at a thousand yards."

Tony gave a courtesy chuckle. "Yeah. Right."

"Anyway," continued the bug, "When I was a kid, we'd lean over a bridge and drop a gob of spit over the edge and count how many seconds it would take to hit the water."

Corbetta suddenly came back to life. "No kidding? We did the same thing back at our neighborhood bridge over Phalen Creek. But the best thing was when some twig was passing by and we'd try to hit it." He paused to chuckle over one particular memory. "This one kid was a fatso we called Tubby and he always had the best luck 'cause he was always hocking back some snot from a cold. Always had a cold. But his bomb had the best heft so the wind couldn't blow it off target. That's when I decided to be a bomber pilot."

Corbetta's new friend asked, "So what's a bomber pilot doing on a cruise like this? Get shot down?"

"Nope." He pipped another tobacco strand over the side.

Bugs had no idea if Tony meant that he hadn't been a pilot or that he hadn't been shot down. He did get the message that the other guy didn't want to talk about it. So, he popped up his eyebrows, pursed his lips upward and turned away to gaze seaward and tried another way to keep a new friend. "So, you from around here?"

"Yeah," Tony said vacantly, staring out sea. "If you consider this the shore of my continent."

"Hey, me too! Knew we had something in common. Jersey myself. You?"

Tony couldn't help shaking his head at the good-humored persistence of this homely, well-meaning pest. "Other side of the tracks. Minnesota, specifically."

"No kiddin'! Had a guy in my outfit from some place out there. Strange name like Quiet Waters or something like that."

"Hmm . . . never heard of it." Then it dawned on Tony, "You mean Stillwater?"

"There you go! Know it?"

"Oh yeah, it's pretty well known. In fact, I grew up kind of in that general direction. On the Mississippi. Stillwater's on a big river right before it dumps into the Mississippi. My place is called Swede Hollow."

"Man, you guys really go in for the names, don't'cha?"

That remark took Tony off guard. It was the whole business of names that had driven him to the rail here. Win, Lyn, whatever. "Yeah, every kid gets one."

Bugs couldn't leave it alone. "No offense, but you sure don't look like no Swede to me."

"Italian. Real name is Antonio. My people kind of moved in after the Swedes moved out."

"Hey, we got a bunch of EYE tai's on this bucket. Maybe you got a relative on board."

Tony flared the orange tip again with a long drag. And that was the signal that he did not know he had sent.

U-156 submerged
2155 hours

Hartenstein stared through the periscope at his unsuspecting prey. He felt like the lioness he once read about that will crouch low to the ground and remain motionless for long, long minutes. It's powers of observation lock its target in an eternal, mysterious bond that will take its prey out of this world forever.

248

The living meal calmly goes about the moment-to-moment routine of its last supper, exactly as it always has done, but will never do again. But only the intruder knows this. Just before the serenity explodes into terror, the victim will sometimes interrupt what it's doing. It will look up in the direction of the stalker as though somehow aware that something is out there.

Hartenstein was almost mesmerized at the periscope and thought to himself, "But not this one. This one is not looking up at all. They are smoking on the decks, and portholes are not covered. Her course is unchanging. It hardly seems fair to come after an innocent fawn."

Mannesman was at his side as usual. "May I suggest, Sir, that fair is when one gets what one deserves. Survival of the fittest."

"Ah, spoken like a good son of the Reich, Henry," said Hartenstein. He slapped the periscope handles into place, calmly completing his sentence and theirs. "Prepare for surface torpedo attack."

Laconia
P.O.W. hold
2201 hours

Crewmembers of *U-156* were not the only ones below the water line. The German hunters didn't know it, but the ship they were stalking held almost two thousand of their own allies. These were Italian prisoners of war who had been taken at some battle near a place called Ruweisat Ridge in North Africa. Now they were in a hold beneath the water line of the *Laconia*.

To say that war is a stinking business is not a figure of speech to those who have smelled it. The Germans might have felt better about their own malodorous world if they had known what their Italian comrades were having to breathe. The heated, stinking humidity in the bowels of the *Laconia* produced an atmosphere in the prisoner hold that was almost too thick to inhale. Every breath taken was of air that had already been exhaled thousands of times by other diseased lungs.

The hold of the ocean liner had originally been designed to contain things that didn't need to breathe. Or see. Or think. Or feel. When the liner was converted for wartime service, the hold was reconfigured for things that were supposed to have been killed anyway, sometimes referred to as vermin by the people whom they themselves had tried to kill. So, not all of their Allied captors were overly committed to providing them first class accommodations.

The first amenity to be sacrificed was the amount of space into which the Italian prisoners were crammed. If the entire cargo hold had been one large area, then the prisoner accommodations might have become something approaching humane standards. But the hold had been divided into multiple water tight compartments so that a breech in one area would not flood the whole ship. Such were the marine engineering needs.

The human engineering needs ran in just the opposite direction. Civil engineering specified that the typical adult male required a minimum of one-and-a-half square feet of standing room. The Polish guards assigned to the POWs had their own way of determining how much space would be allotted per prisoner. The formula was quite simple. The Poles were short-handed and did not want the prisoners spread out. That meant stuffing as many victims as possible into the fewest number of compartments.

But it was not like the efficient space was totally without accommodations. Some of the Italians were lucky enough to find that precious foot-and-a-half of standing room. After all, not that much space had been sacrificed to the six "honey pots" for the six hundred men in each compartment. The resulting stench could have been a lot worse if the overflowing sewage buckets had not been emptied every twenty-four hours. There was even ingenious privacy to use the facilities: each prisoner hold was kept to the dim night-light illumination of only two hanging, bare, low-watt light bulbs that were never turned off.

The real problem, though, was ventilation which also helped in its own way. The heat, humidity, and oxygen depletion doped most of the prisoners into a somnolence on the constant edge of unconsciousness. Every group of military men, however, has one small group that always manages to have a constantly running game of some sort going on. If the group doesn't have playing cards, they gamble with dice. If they don't have dice, they'll run races with lice. If they don't have money to wager, then the default is cigarettes. If they don't have cigarettes, then they'll gamble the very buttons off their shirts. And that is exactly what was happening under one of the two dangling light bulbs.

Geno had just gambled away his earthly treasure of trading buttons. He didn't really miss them anyway, since this left his shirt hanging open for better ventilation. Nevertheless, he invoked the name of the patron saint of gamblers. "How in the name of Saint Cajetan can one man be so lucky?"

The victorious opponent, Vito, gathered up his fortunes but still did not consider himself all that fortunate. "Look around you, my friend. We're all in the same boat. How do you call this lucky?"

Geno had lost the game but he was not about to lose his optimism as well. "What's the problem? We're only centimeters from freedom."

"You are crazy!" said one of the onlookers, named Sal, whose bloody head-wrap left him only one serviceable eye. "What do you mean centimeters? More like five thousand kilometers!"

A soldier in an arm sling sat crumpled against a bulkhead and was one of the few who had not crowded around the gamblers. He never looked up, but spent his time picking up debris off the floor and flicking it with spring-loaded fingers. He was not about to let anything shine on the reign of his dark parade. "Oh, so you know our exact location?"

Roberto had also lost his share of buttons, but not the brass ones that held the ear flaps on top of his sweat-stained, tan field cap. He pushed it back on his black curly hair. "Sure, it's all that metal in his butt! Notice how his south end is always facing north?" A roar of laughter showed that not everybody had been dozing.

"No, it's all how you look at it," said Geno, the self-appointed morale officer. "We're only three kilometers from land: straight down, of course!" Another peel of laughter.

"So, what's this crap about centimeters?" said Sal.

"Right here," Geno said, as he tapped the steel hull. "Steel plating. On this side, us in this stinking toilet. On the other side, sunshine, cool breeze and a paddle for home."

"Or three kilometers to land, right?" said the victor, Vito.

"See, just centimeters and you've already got two choices!" said the optimist-in-chief.

Appreciative groans rumbled throughout the crowd.

"All you gotta do is picture it," said Geno. And then with mock bravado, "Are we not the sons of the world's greatest painters? Michelangelo? DaVinci? Pittore?"

Sal voiced everyone else's question. "Pittore?"

The glum finger flicker on the floor finally chipped in, "Don't ask."

One-eyed Sal persisted, "I'm asking. Who's Pittore?"

"Hey, no wonder you can't picture anything," said Geno. "You're looking at him. Geno Pittore, at your service!"

Eyes rolled, as one by one got the joke. Pittore meant painter in their native tongue.

"So why don't you paint us a way out of this dungeon?" said Vito the Unlucky.

Geno did not say a word as he looked around for something. He squatted down and gathered up all the detritus from the filthy floor. He spat into his hand to make a spittle that would open the eyes of men who had been blinded by despair. From such, he painted the most realistic door on the wall of the hull. It took a while to work in all the perspective. No one noticed how long. Time itself was changing.

Geno returned the challenge. "So, I make the door. But you have to walk through it, yes?"

All the moaning, chattering and snickering came to a reverential silence as the artist tapped the door. Something answered it, just as eyes began to open and men began to dream of going home.

Some of the more devout might have said that this is exactly where they went, though it wasn't dreams that made these wishes come true: it was a two-story long steel cylinder crammed with almost two tons of high explosives that slammed into the hull at fifty-five kilometers per hour. In torpedo time, every man was long dead even before Hartenstein knew by sound or geyser that his heavyweight final solution had run true. Far below the visible water line and faster than the speed of sound, a high-pressure shock wave, expanding at almost two kilometers a second, opened Geno's door. A super-heated gas bubble expanded, then collapsed, then re-expanded and then rammed through hull and men, all in under one second.

In her tiny stateroom, Lyn was again pouring out her heartbreak to the confidant that was her journal.

So now what? Do I want to go through all this again? In some ways, it's been easier to be alone. Ever since I let him touch my heart, I've been remembering things that I never knew I remembered. It was so hard to let Roger in. Then look what happened. Then I let a Yank get too close, and he disappears. Now he wants in. I want him. But everything that touches me goes away. Maybe better to end it myself. Now. On my own terms.

Her thoughts drifted off and her pen settled on the page. She was startled back to focus by a muffled noise that resonated deeply within her being. Her pen fell to the floor and slowly picked up momentum as it rolled toward the door, as if re-writing a frantic memory right there on the floor boards. Her eyes were wide and frozen as she stared at the door and awaited the sea to wash over her, yet one more time.

"Everybody out! Flotation devices on! Everybody to their evacuation station!"

Lyn had been here before. She could hear her mother's eternally young voice calm her, "Lyn, you are such a big help. We're going to be alright, love."

She looked down and noticed that somehow her life preserver was properly fixed and strapped to her torso. She opened the cabin door and then suddenly turned back into the room to search for her tube of lipstick. That had also fallen to the floor and rolled, uncapped, leaving blood-red streaks until it bumped into her pen.

Topside, when Tony recovered his senses and his feet, Bugs was gone. Mostly. Tony launched himself to find the one person he could not live without, whatever her name was. Passage lights were flickering as if the big ship itself were struggling to remain conscious. On crutches, he was racing, not only against time, but against the surge of panicked passengers who were trying to get out through the narrow hallway.

"Tony! Tony! Where are you going? What are you doing? Are you crazy? We've got to get out! The other way!" Like always, she was the one who found him.

Tony was almost out of breath and could hardly get the words out, "Thank God, it's you! I think we've been torpedoed! We've got to get to the boats. Follow me!"

The lights went out and there was a momentary hush in the narrow corridor, followed by a cacophony of screams. In panic for their lives, men lost control of the bowels of their mouths. Profanity spewed forth even in front of the women and children. The women were more articulate.

"Oh my God!"

"We're going to die!"

"Get out of my way!"

"Mommy!"

"Billy, where are you?"

"Help me find my baby!"

Twenty seconds later, the sister torpedo slammed into the number two hold, also filled with Italian prisoners. All compartments of the hold were now opened to the sea which began rushing into the underbelly of the vessel. The same impact that had sent cascading water to drive the prisoners back, also breeched one of the pen doors to give them a way out. The Polish guards who had been issued no ammunition were quickly overcome by the surge, first of desperate prisoners and then of the sea.

Lyn Ensfield was not the only one reliving a nightmare. On the bridge, Captain Sharp was in command of the uncontrollable. He relived his dress rehearsal aboard the ill-fated *Lancastria* nearly two years ago.

The Senior Third Officer scrambled into the command center. "Sir, your orders?"

"Mr. Buckingham, take whomever you need and deep six the ship's code and log books."

"Aye, Sir. Immediately."

The First Officer burst through the door. Sharp turned to the man who had gone through all of this with him two years ago. "Mr. Walker!"

"Sir!"

"Johnny, you know what to do."

"Aye, Sir. All compartments watertight."

"Good lad. Take command of lifeboats, debarking women and children first and then male passengers, followed by crew and then prisoners. In that order. Am I clear?"

"Aye, Sir! Right away, Sir!"

Walker left the command room while Buckingham grabbed the first Able Body Seaman who crossed his path. "Follow me, Seaman. We've got some sinking of our own to do!"

They did not have far to go since the chartroom was adjacent. Amid all the drama and confusion, Buckingham was somehow able to recall the combination to the safe. Since the documents were in weighted canvas bags, it took both men several trips to toss them overboard.

The young man was honored to be working side by side with an officer, almost as if they were mates. The officer even talked to him like a partner as each loaded the arms of the other.

"Glad these parcels are not locked, Sir," said the seaman.

"I beg your pardon, lad?"

"Well, the way I sees it, this way our poor sods got something to read down there in Davey Jones locker now, don't they, Sir?"

Buckingham just stared at the young man.

The sailor began to shrink at having taken liberties with a superior. "Beggin' Leftenant's pardon, Sir."

A Mona Lisa smile accompanied Buckingham's retort. "That's the way. Keep your pecker up, Mr. Goldthwaite."

"Aye, *Sir!*" said the forgiven sailor.

By 22:22 hours, the radio room was silent except for the clitter-chatter of key taps of three radiomen giving voice to the *Laconia*. It screamed out its peril to the world on the six hundred meter band:

SSS SSS 0434 SOUTH / 1125 WEST *LACONIA* TORPEDOED. SSS SSS 0434 SOUTH / 1125 WEST *LACONIA* TORPEDOED. SSS SSS 0434 SOUTH /1125 WEST *LACONIA* TORPEDOED.

When First Officer Johnny Walker arrived at the lifeboat stations, chaos was running amuck. By this time, the ship was already listing to starboard so that half of the boats could not be launched. Further down the line, a group of POW's was trying to swarm a lifeboat when shots rang out and several Italians fell to the deck.

Walker waded into the milling crowd and he could hear the confusion of some who wanted to climb to a higher deck to outrun the sea. Others were trying to work their way to a lower deck to lessen the height from which they might have to jump into the sea. Still others were looking for a boat to climb into.

Tony and Lyn were waving at him. "Johnny! Johnny! Over here!" Their signaling to each other was halted as everyone's attention was pulled in the direction of a rifle shot somewhere further left on the deck. Italian POW's were frantically trying to scramble aboard several of the lifeboats. A volley of three shots, then two, then five sounded now like a neighborhood of firecrackers. Several prisoners were falling to the blood-slicked deck. Every time a prisoner managed to scramble to the gunwale of a boat, he was skewered by a bayonet and then fell into the sea.

Walker yelled back, "Stay there, I'll come to you!" He took several minutes to push his way through the crowd. Each frantic person tried to haul him down with desperate questions of what to do, where to go, what had happened, what was going to happen. The congestion was hampered by all the suitcases and steam trunks and boxes and pets that people were trying to bring along.

"What can we do?" asked Lyn when Walker finally reached them. Once again the two were "we."

"I'm afraid there is only time to abandon ship. Captain's orders. Women and children first, I'm afraid, old son," he said to Tony.

Tony expected nothing less. "Of course, no need to explain."

The dying ship seemed to take another deep breath and briefly right itself, enabling the launching of more lifeboats.

"In fact, I could use the two of you to help with some crowd control," said the First Officer.

"Tell us what to do."

"Tony, I will need you to help keep discipline so that no man tries to board until I give the order. Can you do that?"

Tony nodded.

"Win, I'll need you by this first boat to help the women get aboard, especially if there are children. No luggage of any sort. I want you to be the last one on that thing. You got that?"

Walker then turned to the crowd and asked everyone to step back from the rail. He yelled out the boarding rules with the warning that no violations or exceptions would be tolerated.

"I'm not staying here to drown!" yelled a man who pushed forward right where Tony was trying to hold the line.

"Step back, sir," said Lieutenant Corbetta.

The man balled up his fist and cocked his swinging arm with the battle cry, "Ain't no rotten Yank telling me what to do!" Before he released the punch, Tony laid him out flat and cold with an upper cut to the man's bragging jaw.

Walker produced a pistol and fired into the air. "The next warning will not be so gentle! Women and children in the boat! Now!"

The shot seemed to snap many of the men to their more noble senses. One called out, "Here then, let's help these ladies into the boat!"

Men worked in teams. One man would get on all fours to become a step up for a lady in lengthy gowns. She then would be steadied by two other mates who would guide her up and over the gunwale into the lifeboat. Two others would work as a baggage team. One man would help a lady separate from her most treasured possessions and another man would carry things away. As soon as he left, another would take his place. Other men would witness this operation and form similar teams down the line alongside other boats.

When the lifeboat was nearly full and no other women were nearby, Lyn refused to board until Tony pushed through to her. "It's time, Lyn. Up you go now."

"No," she protested. "I'm needed here."

"We're all getting off this thing! Those women and children need a nurse with them. That is where you're needed. You know that."

Just then a man elbowed his way through the crowd. He was cradling a tiny girl who was crying for her mama. "Somehow she got separated from her mum. Somebody thinks the child's named Sally. You've got to take her!"

Lyn stood on top of luggage and strained to locate some frantic, searching parent. Tony had to yell to be heard above the chaos. "There's no time! Take her. We'll find her mom later. You've got to go now!"

Again, a man made himself into a step for Lyn who was helped into the boat by two others. The little girl was screaming louder, "Mummy! Mummy! I'm scared, Mummy!"

Lyn froze in place. It was all too familiar.

"Ma'am! Please take her! Now!" Deckhands began to free the ark from its holds. Lyn reached out and took hold of the fighting child just as the lifeboat began to jerk away. It descended by starts and stops as the hoisting gears seized and released. The side of the ark's shattering husk swayed and crashed against the steel mountain that was the dying ship.

Lyn looked up to see the hull rising almost beyond sight, filling the entire night, displacing the moon itself and every star of heaven. The only light was the pulsing red glow of the superstructure inferno. Hell was gutting the ship throughout and belching like a volcano through the decks high above her. Every time the lifeboat swung into the ship's side, the boat crunched like a hardboiled egg. The passengers screamed as splintering wood cracked and ripped throughout the boat.

The little girl buried her face into the nurse's coat. Lyn glanced over the side to see how much further they needed to descend. Had the child not been hiding her face, she would have screamed to have seen Lyn's blazing red eyes. The oil slick fires reflected off the windows to her soul. Liquid brimstone of floating oil slicks was waiting to consume them on the water's surface.

No sooner did the little shell settle on the sea than a massive series of explosions ejected flames skyward from the steel volcano. Huge pieces of machinery and two partially filled lifeboats fell from the sky and crashed into the water within fifteen meters of the stunned women and children. Gigantic geysers erupted from the splashes. Several huge swells overtook the lifeboat, lifting it high, capsizing it sideways, slamming it into the ship's hull and spilling out every victim into the icy waters.

Lyn tumbled over and over under the water. She hit her head hard on something. The last thing she recalled was seeing flames floating above her. That was the only way that she knew which direction was up. As she made her way to the inflamed surface, she was almost hit several times by people crashing all around her. The *Laconia* was settling deeper and men were now able to more safely spring off the decks into the water. Bodies were falling all around. Many were floating motionless. Some of them became flotation devices for others.

Every piece of flotsam was clung to by some desperate thrasher. One vastly overfilled lifeboat rocked back and forth as those inside did everything possible to repel others who were trying to climb aboard. Someone in the boat found an axe which he used to hack off the hands of anyone clinging alongside.

Others were paddling away from the ship as fast as possible.

"Swim away from the ship!"

"Get away from the ship!"

And so, Lyn began to paddle furiously. With both hands. Suddenly she realized that she was using two hands! Where was the child? Lyn stopped and looked. And turned. And looked. And turned around again. And looked. And called out again and again and again. She paddled around and around in circles. The only things that were not moving were things that were not living.

How could she have lost this little thing? Just moments ago, Lyn's arms had swaddled snug a terrified little soul that cried for her mummy. The nurse had promised, "It will be OK, love. You'll be with your mum soon."

That promise was now kept.

The frigid waters could not numb what hurt the most. She choked on a mouthful of diesel-slicked water as a small wake slapped her in the face and jolted her back to her sodden senses. Just that quickly, Lyn heard distant men calling out to her as she treaded water in place.

"That ship is sinking!"

"Get out of there, lady!"

"Don't let it suck you under!"

The brilliance of burning oil slicks dazed her night vision and she could not see the people who were calling out to her. Nevertheless, she dog paddled toward the voices that lay beyond the floating bonfires. The danger of the flames was overruled by the seduction of their warmth. The shivery ocean that saturated her clothing did not penetrate her awareness as much as the heat that came off the flames and warmed her face. The beacon of voices was suddenly extinguished and all that Lyn could hear for a moment was the sound of the burning oil patches.

Then the silence was split by what sounded like a choir from hell as a hundred voices rose in a crescendo of agonizing screams. As she paddled closer to the voices Lyn could hear a commotion of frenzied splashing among the clamor and shrieks.

"Here comes another one!"

"Get me up!"

"It's got my leg, it's got my leg!"

"God Almighty, save us!"

"Three more!"

All the agitated splashing sent ripple surges that pushed aside the patches of flame and parted a curtain of horrors. Lyn saw a bloody trap of jaws rise out of the foamy killing field and swallow someone whole. Neither man nor man-eater made a sound.

Other dorsal fins were slicing back and forth like serpent strafers scattering defenseless refugees in three dimensions of terror. Lyn felt sandpaper scrape her outer thigh and she screamed like all the rest.

"My Gawwww!" cried a woman who was thrashing a couple meters from her. Her last utterance in this realm gurgled short as she was jerked out of sight. For the first time since Lyn entered the frigid waters, she was enveloped in some kind of slippery warmth that rose from beneath her all the way up to her chin.

When she tasted the coppery water, she knew that she had been saved by the blood of another. Just that quickly, she also realized that this same blood was attracting even more sharks.

"Jesus Christ!" screamed the last watery words of a man less than a meter from her. More slippery warmth bathed her into a blessed resignation.

She also invoked His name. "Jesus, take me Home."

Something clamped tight around her upper torso and she found herself ejected out of the water. She shrieked in terror and flailed with every last impulse of draining energy. The more she struggled, the tighter she was pinned.

"Lyn! Lyn! Stop it! Stop struggling! It's me. It's Tony. Lyn, settle down! I'm going to lose you!"

She screamed even louder and Tony could hardly believe the raw strength of this woman. She was going to capsize the flotsam and drag them both under if this kept up another five seconds. For the second time in half an hour, Tony reared back and struck, but this time with a backhanded slap that was only meant to startle.

Lyn went limp and her soaked, dead weight almost accomplished the same disaster as her flailing. If he could not get her out of the water immediately, Tony knew that he soon would be struggling in a tug of war with a submerged opponent that would win. Even if it got only half the prize.

Slowly, it dawned on him that all was strangely quiet. There was no more screaming. No more splashing. No more fins. No more sharks. Except for one that had chased off all the others.

An almost inaudible thrumming was felt before it was clearly heard. A surf sound could be heard sloshing against something like a pier. A massive leviathan cleft the sea of survivors, separating groups one from another with a black force that squeezed new cries of terror with a hundred last breaths.

"Oh my God!"

"We're all dead!"

"Aiuto! Aiuto!"

Bridge of Laconia

The First Officer made his way back up to the bridge and found the ship's master alone. The Captain was staring out through jagged holes that had been the windows. Sharp did not even look at him. Walker knew where this was going. "It's just you and me, Sir."

Sharp stared straight through Johnny. "I see you have remembered your lines, young man."

"Sir?"

"We've been here before, haven't we, Johnny?"

Walker looked down. "Yes, Sir."

A long conversation took place in total silence. Then the master turned to his protégé and pronounced the benediction. "The ship is now yours, Mr. Walker. I stay here."

"Yes, Sir." There was no use and even less mercy in trying to change the resolve of Captain Rudolph Sharp. The First Officer came to attention and saluted.

Sharp returned the salute, "Dismissed."

Treading oil twenty minutes beyond the suction zone, First Officer Walker watched the bow of the *Laconia* ascend vertically and then slide below the surface. At 23:23 hours both ship and master laid down their lives together.

CHAPTER 27

FISHERS OF MEN

12 September 1942
U-156 surfaced
2345 hours

Under the cover of darkness from more than two miles away, *U-156* had fired its torpedoes from the surface. According to standard operating procedures, Hartenstein edged closer to the sinking victim in order to gather basic identifying information for German naval records. Eager crewmen with rifles at the ready strained against bow deck cables to see and hear what their work had wrought.

From the conning tower high above the deck, the captain could see hundreds of thrashing and screaming souls in the water. Despite the danger of disengaging the power train which would be needed if a sudden emergency should call for instant speed, he ordered, "All engines, stop. We can't hear a thing." The momentum from more than eleven hundred tons of mass kept all seventy-seven meters of the boat smoothly plowing through the field of debris, human and otherwise.

As junior officer, Leutnant zür See Max Fischer was in command of the bow party, the forward eyes of the trolling monster. As an officer, he had occasionally trained beside Italian officers. As such, he had picked up a few Italian words here and there. He was the first to recognize the Italian screams of "Aiuto." Into the closed-circuit deck phone he called up to Hartenstein who was overseeing operations from his aerie on the conning tower, "Sir, we have Italians in the water! Lots of them!"

The commander could not believe his ears. A storm of thoughts thundered inside his head, though he appeared totally silent. "Sir?" asked the deck officer.

"Repeat what you just said, Leutnant. And you better get this right." Addressing the young officer by rank and tone was an unmistakable double warning. Maybe if he could intimidate the man into not saying it again, the problem might go away.

"Kapitän, many people in the water are calling out 'Aiuto.' I think that's Italian for . . ."

"I know what it is!"

Except for being on the bow deck, the young officer did not know where he stood. Was it his turn to speak next? Agitating the commanding officer was not always the wisest career move.

The Captain's end of the line was still silent. Hartenstein was momentarily frozen like he never had been before. He had never prepared for something like this. All his mental rehearsal had been in preparation for what could happen to his men, not about what could happen to his victims. His mind did not race in terror. It just froze.

"Awaiting your orders. Sir."

The Captain was anything but silent in his mind. "My orders. It always comes down to my orders. We're in this spot *because* of my orders!"

In a resigned voice, he finally answered the deck officer, "Young Max, you know what to do."

Among the floundering Italians, there were also survivors for whom a U-boat was a deadly enemy. If they had heard Hartenstein's words, they would have known that they were done for. Throughout England and America, stories had floated about of U-boats machine-gunning survivors in the water. Everyone knew someone who knew someone who heard from someone about somebody else who had survived such a massacre. With all the surviving story tellers, apparently all the bloodthirsty machine gunners on all those U-boats apparently hadn't even been able to hit ducks in a barrel.

No such intention even crossed the mind of the young deck officer but to order, "All lines and flotation overboard! Get them out of the water." His youthful voice now rose to a booming command authority, "Now!"

Hartenstein leaned on the conning tower railing with his shoulders hunched. He thought to himself, "My God, what will happen in Berlin when I radio what I've done?" Only his own neck knew how faintly he shook his head when he looked down upon his thrashing carnage. In fact, it was that very neck he was thinking about. By sending that message, he would be sticking his neck out exactly the way nobles had once done on the chopping block. The prisoner did what he could to help the axe man execute his job cleanly, with one efficient move. Sticking out his neck is sometimes the last way for a condemned man to be the master of his own fate, even if he can't really be the captain of his soul.

It was time to radio High Command about what he had just done. Even under the best circumstances, sending messages was a risky thing. Talking got in the way of listening for threats. Signals could also be intercepted by enemy eavesdroppers who could triangulate the location of the sender. Therefore, transmissions were done only when absolutely necessary, in the shortest burst of time possible, and with a disciplined precision that was required when only one attempt could be risked. Therefore, right then and there in the conning tower, Hartenstein decided to write the message himself to High Command and then personally deliver it to only his most senior radio operator, Erich Hacker.

History books are full of people who have said that nothing focuses the mind like the gallows. What Hartenstein had just done, first with torpedoes and now with a radio transmission, could never be undone. From the moment he sent that message in the open for the whole world to hear, Hartenstein knew that he himself would need saving in some very deep water of his own.

Not that he was a particularly religious man, but for some reason Moses came to mind. He recalled someone saying that Moses and his people had actually been saved by deep water. It occurred to him that, right now, it was probably only the vast ocean that was keeping him from the infamously hair trigger rage of the Führer. But he also knew that furious fate could be patient. He reflected how the first time he had prepared for the Gestapo, it was because of Niemöller. Now they will almost certainly come for him, too. And again, it was because Niemöller was haunting him.

But even Hartenstein could have no way of knowing how the message he just sent had lit a fuse which would send shock waves through the highest reaches of the Third Reich, years beyond the war's end.

CHAPTER 28

GERMAN HIGH COMMAND

13 September 1942
Headquarters, Commander of Submarines
Avenue Maréchal Maunoury
Paris
0014 hours

"Sir!" The radio operator tore off a typed sheet and snapped it to the Officer of the Day, Kapitänleutnant Alfred Mueller. "Word from *Eisbar* leader, Sir." Especially for a stealth operation like this, it was understood that radio silence was absolutely critical. The naturally reduced radio traffic in the early morning hours would make any transmission that much more susceptible to prying ears. Even before the junior officer read the content of the message, he knew that it had to be extremely critical.

SUNK BY HARTENSTEIN BRITISH "LACONIA." GRID FF 7721 310 DEGREES. UNFORTUNATELY, WITH 1500 ITALIAN POWS. SO FAR 90 FISHED. 157 CUBIC

METERS (OF OIL). 19 EELS [TORPEDOES], TRADE WIND 3, REQUEST ORDERS.

"Fifteen hundred Italians in the water? By us?!" It was the responsibility of the duty officer to awaken the senior officer, if the situation demanded. *If* the situation demanded. That was always the issue. What might happen to him if the volatile Chief of Staff did not think the message warranted disturbing his precious sleep at this hour?

For a good ten seconds, indecision froze Mueller like a statue in front of his desk where he had been handed the message. To wake or not to wake his superior? Was *that* the question? Really? When thousands of people were fighting for their lives in a frigid night sea? In the half second that it took petty fear to reach the velocity of shame, Mueller was propelled in a high speed trajectory straight to the door of the untouchable, sleeping Chief of Staff.

Mueller straightened his uniform outside the door of Kapitän zür See Alfred Kittel. He rapped twice, stepped in, snapped on the dim watt light bulb, came to attention, and awaited his fate.

Kittel rolled over and said in a bellicose voice, "My God, what is it this time, Mueller?"

"Begging Captain's pardon, Sir. Urgent message from *Eisbar*, Sir. I think we may have a major disaster on our hands, unfolding as we speak. I thought it required your immediate attention. Sir."

With a digusted exhalation, the self-important superior-on-high deigned to let himself be bothered. "Very well, Mueller," he said, as he rubbed his eyes and fumbled for his glasses. In his fog, he could not recall where he had placed them. With a show exaggerated boredom he said, "Let's have it, then."

The lieutenant first retrieved the spectacles and handed them to Kittle, who just stared at him as though the unsolicited assistance was an act of presumptuous insubordination. He slowly stretched the flimsy wire spectacles from one ear to the next. Mueller remained at rigid attention, daring not to go one step further until asked. The spectacles made the superior's beady pupils dilate so large that Mueller could almost see people drowning in that blackness.

Kittel, who hadn't even been able to find his own glasses, now asserted his terrible power. "Well? Are you going to keep me awake all night or am I supposed to guess what's in the message!"

"Sir!" said the lieutenant as he snapped the message to his superior.

Kittel read the text and rocketed himself out of bed toward the open door, before he realized that his bare feet were out of uniform.

Mueller kept his thoughts to himself, his expressions off his face, and thereby also kept both his rank and his head on his shoulders. The senior officer plunked himself back down on his bunk to tug on the long black boots. "Stay here!" the master barked, who then hastily walked directly to the private quarters of Dönitz himself. In less than five minutes, the Commander of U-boat Operations was personally taking charge of the signal room. Mueller felt vindicated.

"Any further messages?" Dönitz asked Mueller.

"No, Sir!"

To the signal operator, Dönitz ordered, "Send to entire Eisbar pack:" ALL BOATS CONVERGE ON LEADER. ASSIST RESCUE ALL SURVIVORS. DO NOT ACKNOWLEDGE.

Kittel was ordered to awaken and assemble all staff officers in the ready room. Once again, Dönitz turned to the signal operator. "Prepare following message to Raeder:" LEAD *EISBAR* SINKS BRITISH TRANSPORT WITH 1500 ITALIAN POWS IN THE WATER. HAVE ORDERED ALL EISBAR BOATS TO ASSIST IN RESCUE.

Grand Admiral Erich Johann Albert Raeder was Commander-in-Chief of the Navy. In Berlin, he reported directly to non-other than the Führer himself. They were about the same height, but Raeder was thirteen years older than Hitler and bested his superior in professional stature. The Great Admiral projected the Olympian visage of his hereditary superiority.

The chaos at sea stirred a tidal wave of command decisions that washed over high command from Paris to Berlin. Careers could be sunk in the ensuing hours by this self- inflicted wound to the already fragile German-Italian alliance. Dönitz was in the cross hairs. So was every other commissioned officer in this debacle. Reader's signal room in Berlin was ignited as quickly as Dönitz's had been in Paris. Within ten minutes, Dönitz received affirmation of his actions to rescue.

Berlin's message concluded with one caveat: in no way, however, must the safety of any U-boat or the mission in progress be jeopardized.

Dönitz knew that his seaward transmissions were being monitored by High Command. He immediately relayed to the U-boats the cautionary proviso: MESSAGE *EISBAR*: LEADER TO REMAIN ON SPOT BUT READY TO SUBMERGE. REMAINING BOATS TO ASSIST WITHOUT INTERFERING ABILITY TO SUBMERGE. DO NOT ACKNOWLEDGE.

CHAPTER 29

MESSAGE IN THE CLEAR

13 September 1942
Deck of the U-156
0300 hours

Within thirty minutes of sending his message to Paris, Hartenstein was encouraged by Dönitz's permission to proceed with the rescue. From his conning tower, Hartenstein was regaining his command presence as he phoned below deck. "Mr. Mannesman, it seems we have a few friends out for a swim. Send all non-essential personnel top-side for survivor recovery. Have Gerhard report on deck to accommodate refugees. Fischer, I'm on my way down."

Everyone in the chain of command instinctively knew what to do. From the deck-side lieutenant and every sailor under his direction, to the commander of the boat, to his superior in Paris, all the way to the Navy's Commander in Chief in Berlin, it was instantaneously obvious: hundreds of confederates needed to be rescued on the spot.

Seamen scrambled to the lines as if a fish had been hooked. They were unprepared for what the sea gave up. The ocean was offering back the pollution of violence. Half an hour earlier, these same men had gleefully jumped up and down on deck, whooping and hollering with pride at the massive firework display which they had lit off over two miles away. They had vanquished the foe! Now they were trying to reverse the waves of death which they had so proudly accomplished.

As exhausted as all the swimmers were, the more able-bodied victims deferred the rescue flotation to those who were more injured. The first to be hoisted aboard was a charred man who opened one white eye and stared at his tormentors. The one he looked at was a young teenage sailor who doubled over and wretched on the deck. When the crewman lost his grip, the burned victim started to fall and three other sailors grabbed hold. Something of the man broke off.

By this time, a dozen other injured bodies had been lifted up over the side. As gently as the sailors tried to lift, even the gentlest handling was rewarded with screams and curses. Most of the yelling, however, was from the crewmen who themselves were screaming for assistance. Some of them were also throwing up. Here and there, a young sailor was standing motionless with a transfixed stare. Horror and gore were coming over the ropes and splashing onto the deck.

A senior crewman yelled at two younger ones who were on their knees trying to comfort a dying victim. "Off your knees and get over here! Everyone on the lines!"

Within two minutes, the commander of the boat was on the steel plated deck. As bad as he knew things were, his eyes were assaulted by what he could never have imagined. To Leutnant Fischer he demanded, "What in the world is all this?"

Hartenstein was gazing in disbelief at two women and one child who had just been fished out of the sea. "I didn't know these Italians included women and children!"

The soaked Leutnant corrected him. "The women and children are not Italian, Sir. They're British."

Hartenstein was again at a loss for words. Five seconds later, his head was still swiveling in all directions. The officer in charge of bad news added, "And, uh, it seems, Sir, that not all of the men are Italian either, Sir."

"Brits, too?"

"Perhaps, Sir, but that one over there is American. They just keep coming! We're going to run out of deck."

Oberleutnant Gerhard Franceschi emerged from the hatch and ran over to Hartenstein. "Sir! Reporting."

"I want all the women and children below deck in officers' quarters. Find out if there are any medical personnel among these people and get them attending to the most injured."

The shouts for help, the commands among the crew, the wailing of the injured and the fragile cries of children added to a growing din of compressed calamity. In that vast ocean, the undulating waves peacefully mocked the misery.

The U-boat had no medical personnel of its own. The three radio operators had to cover as medics when necessary. But, in their surfaced vulnerability to air attack, Hartenstein had to have his best radioman, Chief Petty Officer Erich Hacker, on vigilant listening for approaching threats.

Franceschi instinctively knew that his captain had more to say. He was still there awaiting further instructions when Hartenstein said, "Get both radio operators up here on medical, but I want Hacker's ears glued to the comm. Hacker does not leave those earphones under any circumstances. Do I make myself absolutely clear?" said the commander.

"Absolutely, Sir!" The junior officer saluted, spun on his heels and collided with a taller, soaked man who stood straight but not erect in his exhausted condition. Franceschi dodged around the man whose hair was matted and whose right cheek sported a bad, five-inch diagonal cut that was still oozing. He wore a British merchant officer's uniform. The man looked Hartenstein directly in the eye and slowly raised a salute. "Executive Officer J.H. Walker, *RMS Laconia* reporting, Sir."

Without any change of expression, Hartenstein just stared at his foe, keeping his eyes locked on the man for a full five seconds, before clicking his heels together, coming to full attention, and returning the salute. "Korvetankapitän Werner Hartenstein, *U-156*, commanding. At your service."

Hartenstein made a slight bow and dropped his salute, only then giving permission for the vanquished officer to lower his salute. "Executive Officer, you say. Where is your captain?"

"I am the senior officer, Sir. Captain Sharp went down with his ship."

"I am truly sorry to hear that," said Hartenstein. "It is neither my desire nor intention to cause the suffering and death of fellow warriors at sea. Unfortunate but necessary consequences. I'm certain you understand."

Walker bitterly remembered the last time he had heard that. That was exactly what the doctor had told his wife and him when little Sally passed. *'We did all we could. I'm certain you understand.'* Just like that. Just that simple. Nothing personal. No hard feelings. It was always his job to understand.

Walker stared right through the victor's eyes, but betrayed no reaction, as he tried to figure out what exactly he was supposed to understand. In defiant silence, the vanquished Brit kept his eyes locked on the German.

Hartenstein understood. He would not insult the beaten man by further intruding into the room of his private pain. "Of course. I do require you to surrender your ship's logs, Sir. I am sure there is no point in asking about ship's code books."

The Brit answered, "When it was clear that our ship was lost, Captain Sharp's first order was to dump all books over the side in weighted bags, Sir."

"Then all that remains will be for you to provide me with whatever information you can recall. I have no intention of forcing you to divulge information that is protected by the Geneva Convention. Basic identifying data of ship and passengers is all that we need at the moment."

"Yes, Sir."

It was 0550 before Hartenstein had time to get the information from his guest. Walker informed his host that the *Laconia* had been carrying upwards of five hundred passengers which included women and children as well as military personnel from maybe half a dozen Allied nations. Also, eighteen hundred Italian POWs.

Business concluded, the captain said to his junior officer, "Mr. Fischer! Please have Mr. Walker here escorted below decks for medical attention and dry clothing. Inform Mannesman that I will be in Signal."

The sheer immensity of it all was beginning to erode the facade of control which Hartenstein tried to project. He hoped that his show was convincing others more effectively than it was convincing him. There could be something like two thousand badly injured survivors to deal with. Even with the assistance of the four other boats in his wolf pack, how in the world could they begin to deal with these numbers? How many surface ships alone would be necessary for such a mission?

It was not just a matter of capacity. The order from Dönitz *commanded* him to be ready at all times to submerge in the event of increasingly likely air attack. Rescue of any kind, even for a single moment, made rapid diving impossible. Fifty-plus men, plus the mission at hand, plus the boat itself were jeopardized every single time the boat stopped on the surface for any reason at all.

Hartenstein knew of other boat commanders who had given aid to survivors at sea. But offering a little food and water and maybe a map to people in a lifeboat was one thing. Even bringing a few on board was daring. But hundreds? Thousands? How in the world could you do something like this without sealing your own fate? There was absolutely no way that an emergency dive would be possible. To continue this rescue would be nothing short of disobedience to a direct order, one probably from Hitler himself. And to what end? The destruction of the boat would also mean the destruction of the survivors themselves. The most logical option would be to get these people off the boat and as far away as possible.

This was the longest two-minute walk Hartenstein had ever taken. He made his way to the signal niche inside the cramped quarters of the boat. What he was about to do was the most insane thing he had ever fathomed. For all he knew, nothing on this scale had ever been done in the history of maritime warfare. Even if he got away with it, he could very well imagine himself being shot for treason. Shot, if he were lucky. Would Germany ever forgive him? Should it ever forgive him for sending its sons to the bottom in a guaranteed suicide mission, just to save an enemy who could never be saved anyway?

Chief Petty Officer Erich Hacker was, just as ordered, listening for signal traffic with intense vigilance. He was startled to look up and see his commander looming over him. "Sir!"

But Hartenstein was somewhere else in his thoughts and held up an index finger to ask the radioman to wait a moment. He had never before been in a situation like this where he was floating in a sea of hundreds of his own victims. He also had never floated between the devil of his duty to orders and the deep blue sea of duty to his conscience. He was recalling the late night clandestine visit with an old pastor in Berlin who had been a U-boat captain in the last war. In the late hours of that discussion, the old man had told him of a situation not unlike this one. That nightmare had gone on to haunt the old sailor the rest of his life, driving him straight into the pulpit, then into the jaws and right down the gullet of the Gestapo. God only knew where this Pastor Niemöller was right now, if he even *was* anymore. Hartenstein thought to himself, "*I could use that old salt beside me right about now*". He no sooner had that thought than he remembered his own pastor's advice: be careful what you pray for. If he wasn't careful, Hartenstein really might have Niemöller by his side after all: on a Gestapo scaffold.

Again the radio operator said, "Sir?"

Hartenstein was still doing the math.

Two thousand souls.

No room inside.

Not enough ships.

No more than one minute possible to make an emergency dive from air attack.

Can't leave them on the deck or anchored to the boat.

Suddenly, Hartenstein snapped out of his thoughts and commanded his ever-waiting senior radioman, "Mr. Hacker!"

"Sir!"

"Send message in the clear. Twenty-five-meter bandwidth. In English. Then repeat in ten minutes on the international six-hundred-meter bandwidth: IF ANY SHIP WILL ASSIST THE SHIPWRECKED *LACONIA* CREW, I WILL NOT ATTACK HER, PROVIDING I AM NOT ATTACKED BY SHIP OR AIR FORCE. I PICKED UP ONE HUNDRED AND NINETY-THREE MEN. 4 DEGREES - 52" SOUTH. 11 DEGREES - 26" WEST. GERMAN SUBMARINE."

13 September 1942
Royal Navy Base
Signal Operations
Freetown, Sierra Leone
0615 hours

When *U-156* spoke, everyone with powerful enough ears listened. Especially enemy eavesdroppers at a British listening post in Freetown.

Only the lowest ranking men got stuck with the dead-of-night watch. The young age of the freckle-faced radioman meant lack of experience. But that also brought a level of energy that his older mates too often sacrificed to the boredom of their assignment. Because nothing exciting ever happened in his little corner of the war, the young red-head liked to spice things up by trying to visualize the source and circumstance of messages as well as who was sending them. In other words, he paid attention and he thought. He called over to the Officer of the Day at the next desk in the officially sterile signals office. "Sir, curious follow-up just received on that earlier distress call from *RMS Laconia*," said Able Seaman Basil Haycox.

"Let's have it, then," said the leftenant in a tone of routine monotony.

The young operator tore off a sheet from his transcription pad. "Well, this message claims to be a bloody U-boat transmitting in the clear, asking Allied help in rescuing survivors of the *Laconia*."

Leftenant Brisbane uncrossed his legs from atop his desk and sat up. "How much sleep have you been getting lately, old Baz?"

"I know, Sir," agreed the signalman. "It sounds totally daft. I thought I heard it wrong, but it was rebroadcast on a second bandwidth as well."

The leftenant walked over to the receiving desk and reached out his hand. "Here. Let me read that."

The officer looked at his wristwatch. "When did we receive that first call from *Laconia*?"

Haycox thumbed through a short stack of messages. "It was 22:22 last night, Sir."

"Hmm, and some bugger's just got the word out now, has he?" reflected the duty officer. "Sounds like just about enough time for Jerry to gather the rest of his pack and set up an ambush for anyone coming to the rescue."

"Sir, I've got a brother in the Parachute Regiment and he says that Jerry snipers do something like that all the time," said the young seaman. "They shoot one of our blokes in the leg and then let the poor bastard scream his guts out till his mates can't stand it and come to rescue him. Then the sniper picks 'em off, one by one."

"That's the idea alright, Baz," said the officer.

"But, Sir, what if it's true?" said Basil. "Isn't it possible that this message is on the square?"

"Just about anything is possible, son," said the officer who was only six years older than his younger charge. "What we have to consider is what's probable. Would you be willing to bet your next pay that there is a U-boat commander out there decent enough and dumb enough to risk his neck for a bunch of Limeys?"

The signalman rushed to not contradict his superior. "Yes, Sir. I mean, no, Sir! Wouldn't bet a shilling on something like that. You're right, of course, Sir."

Brisbane said, "Remember when the *Devonshire* finally nailed the *Atlantis* last fall?"

"Sorry, Sir. Can't place it," said Haycox.

"Good story, this one," said the mentor. "*Atlantis* was a Kraut cruiser. They fixed her up to look like a merchant ship. Fact is, she could look like over twenty different types of merchant ships. But that blighter carried over a dozen heavy-duty guns, a load of torpedoes and mines and even a couple planes. So, she'd pretend to need help, in order to lure in other merchants and then blow 'em to pieces! Nailed over twenty ducks like this, as sweet as you please, before *Devonshire* punched her ticket a few months back."

"Blimey . . ." said the radio operator.

"Blimey for sure!" said the leftenant. "These Krauts are sneaky and they know what they're doing. Fighting fair ain't on their list."

"What would you like me to do with the message, Sir?"

"Just put it in the Intelligence basket," said the boss. "Let the big boys decide what to do with it. Mark it routine. They'll get around to it sometime."

No other receivers picked up Hartenstein's message-in-the-clear to the Allies. Except for Dönitz' U-boat headquarters in Paris. And Raeder's High Naval Command in Berlin. Words have still not been invented to describe Hitler's reaction.

DAVE GARWICK

CHAPTER 30

TRIAGE

13 September 1942
U-156
0455 hours

"**K**apitän? I have the British Executive Officer as you ordered," said Leutnant Fischer.

"Thank you, Mr. Fischer. Dismissed. Mr. Walker, was it?"

"Yes, Sir. And thank you for the dry clothes and medical attention."

"Of course. Speaking of medical attention, do you happen to know if there are any medical personnel among your people? I have only two radio operators who have some training in first aid. Your people have injuries far beyond what we are equipped to handle."

A dozen meters forward, four able seamen awkwardly wrestled another corpse overboard. The body vanished to make a splash as its last sound on earth. After three seconds, a frenzy of wet slaps ensured that the poor soul would not even have the dignity of being buried at sea. Ashes to ashes and dust to jaws.

Some say that mankind was born from the sea. Long ago, as the son of medical missionaries, this one had been baptized in the sea. Now he was returned to it.

The Captain said again, "Are there any doctors among your people?"

"That one you just tossed overboard," said Walker. Hartenstein looked perplexed and Walker answered his unspoken question. "He was our ship's surgeon."

"So, physician, heal thyself," whispered Hartenstein, almost as a salute to the fallen doctor. Victor turned toward victim. "Would there be any nurses among the women?"

"As a matter of fact, there was one nurse aboard ship, though I have no idea if she made it."

Johnny Walker tried picking his way among the tangled human debris, disarrayed on a deck that was almost the length of a football field. The only light was the periodic peek of the moon behind the passing cloud cover. Moving shadows on the faces of the huddled, shivering people made them all look alike. Walker couldn't even tell men from women.

"Miss Ensfield?" Walker called out as he tried to make his way. "Nurse Ensfield? Are you here?"

"Walker! Over here!" said a man. Ironically, Walker *was* the only walker on the crowded sleeping deck. He tried to be extra careful not to step on anyone who was already crunched in a space of just over a square meter. It was one of the standing zombies who moved toward Johnny. "Is that you, Corbetta?" asked Walker.

"Yeah, I've got Lyn with me. She's sitting on the deck. Kind of dazed, but I think she's probably OK. Trying to keep her warm."

Just then, without any warning, a commotion erupted across from them on the starboard side. Even with everyone crammed on top of each other, no one seemed to have been aware of anything developing. But that was specifically *because* they were packed like sardines. Nobody had any privacy or space, so each person made space for himself by psychologically walling off everything and everyone else. In fact, nothing at all had led up to the outburst. One man simply had inadvertently been jostled into another's sacred square foot of space. "I'll kill ya!" screamed the invaded man as he bent the dastardly trespasser backwards over the steel cable.

A friend of the pretzel pushed the aggressor. "Get off him!"

"Pull him off!" yelled another.

In a last effort to keep from being snapped backwards, the man on the cable desperately clawed at the eyes of his attacker. The newly one-eyed fighter released his grip in a scream of agony just as a referee rushed to break up the fight and tripped over a deck fixture. All three tumbled into the inky blackness.

"Men overboard!"

But there was nothing to toss, since everything had been used to rescue people coming in on the other side.

"Get 'em out of there!"

A scream. Then another scream. Splashing more than all three men could make together. Then total silence.

In the temporary quiet, a gentler man closer to Lyn was comforting a little boy. "Hey there, little man. Let's let mummy sleep a bit." Not one sound escaped from her vigilant little guardian. "Come on over here so she can rest. Come on, son.

Let me warm you up and I'll tell you a really good story, OK?" The man looked up at Corbetta and then to Walker and then faintly shook his head just one time.

Walker stood back a couple meters as Tony Corbetta leaned in close to the blank and haggard face of a devastated nurse. Lyn had been sitting by herself on the cold, wet deck with her legs drawn up tight to her chest.

"Lyn? Lyn, look at me," said Tony in a quiet voice.

Walker said, "I thought her name was Win."

"Long story, Johnny."

Lyn took no notice of the two men. She just stared down at the deck and rocked herself in tiny movements that were almost imperceptible.

Tony said again, "Lyn, what's the matter?"

She tilted her head, still looking down. She was trying to find something. She wrinkled up her face like a little girl who was complaining about eating her vegetables. In a tiny, dreamy voice she kept whispering something over and over again.

Tony looked back up to Walker who furrowed his brow and didn't have to say a word.

They could just make out the next thing: "Mummy? I'm so scared."

Tony unknowingly filled in the next line of the old script. "Lyn, we need your help."

She recognized that: a voice that made everything OK from so far, far away, but a voice heard only by her.

She tilted up her head inquisitively to look in Tony's eyes. Some key had unlocked some door. Lyn narrowed her eyes, trying to figure things out. Her expression said, "Who are you?" and then, slowly, she said, "I. Know. You." Her eyes cleared and her blink lasted just long enough to put the past in its place.

She recognized Tony. This time, her eyes closed in a serenity as she slowly wrapped her arms around him in a tight embrace.

"Are you back with us?" he asked.

"Hmm?"

"Are you back with us?"

"Um, I think so," was her hope.

"So, where were you?"

"I was ... a little girl. A ship. Like this one. Sinking. Fire. Everywhere. My mum. A lady, a stranger carried me."

Then she looked down at her empty arms. And her eyes reflected terror. Suddenly, Tony saw what he had not noticed. When Tony had intercepted Lyn in her thrashing, she had been without the little girl who had been handed off to her for safe keeping. The nurse doubled over in anguish, folding her arms tightly across her stomach where she had just taken a hit to the gut. She bent forward with each quiet sob for two lost little girls.

Five minutes passed as Tony kept watch over her. Johnny Walker stood watch over both of them. When she was wrung out of tears, she sniffed back fresh air, rubbed her arm across her eyes and blinked a tight smile at both men. Lyn took a deep breath, "I'll be OK."

Walker said his first word. "Should I tell our host that I've found a nurse to tend the hurt?"

"Of course," she answered. Leftenant Walker headed off, partly to give the two a little privacy.

Tony wasn't so sure about the nurse's condition. She had only just come around. "Lyn, maybe it's going to be too much for you."

The conversation continued in silence until she closed her eyes for a moment and shouldered into Tony's arms. The noise and the chaos all about them seemed to fade into the background for the longest sixty seconds. The fragile tendrils of her mind could not be shaken awake too suddenly.

Suddenly, the windows of her mind were thrown wide open. "Begging your pardon, ma'am," said Walker who had just returned. "The captain of the boat here is asking if you would be so kind as to meet with him as soon as you feel up to it."

"I think I'm fine, really." Nodding toward Tony, she added, "Can my orderly here accompany me?"

Walker guided the new medical team to be introduced to the captain of the boat. Even amidst all the carnage and chaos, the commander lightly clicked his heels together, came to a relaxed stand of attention and bowed, extending his hand to her. "Kapitänleutnant Werner Hartenstein at your service, ma'am."

Odd. The man who had just tried to kill them all was now saying that he was at her service.

"Pleased to . . ." Lyn cut short her automatic response and averted her eyes downward. "Captain."

An awkward silence was graciously ended by Hartenstein's gallant honesty. "Of course. I do understand. Please believe me when I say that I am truly saddened by the death and suffering that this horrible war has inflicted on us all. We all do what we must. But there is no reason to make it worse than it has to be, no? This is the world of both warriors and healers. For once, I am glad to be of service to a healer, ma'am."

Lyn looked up to his eyes and saw a man of integrity who seemed to be bleeding in his own way. "Thank you, Captain. I will do what I can."

"Am I correct in understanding that you are Miss Win Ensfield, a British Army nurse?"

"Everyone calls me Win but my actual name is Lyn. I do serve as a nurse with British military, but I am a temporary civilian volunteer."

Hartenstein pursed his lips and nodded in acknowledgment. Then he turned to Tony. "And you, Sir?"

"First Lieutenant Tony Corbetta . . ."

Hartenstein nodded with a slight smile. "Corbetta. Antonio Corbetta. Italian name."

"My grandfather immigrated from Sicily," said Tony.

"Ah, yes. The American officer," the captain said.

Lyn said, "He has been convalescing as my patient in route to hospital in Britain. Since we have worked together, he has graciously offered to serve as my orderly in my duties here."

Hartenstein faced Tony. "Thank you, Sir. I appreciate any assistance you may be able to offer. I must advise you, Lieutenant, that you are my prisoner of war. I will accord you the respect due a fellow officer, but I will not tolerate any hostile behavior of any kind. Are we clear?"

"By all means, Captain."

"Very well, then. Miss Ensfield, I need your assistance in sorting out the wounded. We have very little available space on this boat, especially below decks. First, I want women and children protected from the elements. Then I want the most seriously wounded Italian officers sent below."

The nurse said, "Captain, what you are asking me to do is to perform what we call triage. With all due respect, we typically offer the most intense service to those most seriously wounded, but who are most likely to survive."

"I believe that is what I just asked," the captain said.

"This would mean that we would be forced to leave on deck the most seriously wounded who are closest to death," she said.

Hartenstein kept his eyes locked on hers and showed no sign of what he was thinking. "Very well. Obviously so."

She had her own query. "One last question, Captain Hartenstein. What of non-officers who would be good candidates? May they also be sent below deck?"

The commander paused to think and then slowly nodded. "Only as space allows, after the others have been secured. Once we accommodate all those I mentioned, then we will do what we can. Now if you will excuse me, I must see to other matters." He clicked his heels, touched the tip of his hat in a nodding salute and resolutely moved off.

"Well, it seems we have our orders, Mr. Corbetta," said the nurse to her new orderly.

By 0530, the sky was beginning to lighten so that Lyn could assess at least the outward physical appearances of some of the injured. Tony followed along as she threaded her way among the two hundred deck-side castaways. Tony spent much of his time fetching crewmen to carry designated patients below deck.

Naturally, the triage nurse spent most of her time evaluating people who were lying or sitting down. She did not notice one spindly figure who was carefully threading his way toward her. Like everyone else, he looked like a drowned rat. But he had made an effort to plaster back his thinning hair and even tuck in his shirt. With great care, he apologized his way through the great unwashed masses. "Excuse me, please. I'm sorry. Didn't mean to step on you, sir. Please forgive me, sir. How clumsy of me."

Eventually, he excused himself all the way to Lyn. "Excuse me, ma'am, would you by chance be a nurse of some sort?"

Lyn was bending close over a charred figure, turning her head to place one ear close to what was left of the person's nose, while observing the chest for signs of breathing.

"Pardon me?" begged the thin man.

Lyn let out a breath of discouragement with a dismissive tilt of her head. "May I help you?"

The plaintiff man read her manner as a rebuff. "Oh, I don't mean to be in the way. I can see you're busy."

"Not at all," said Lyn. "I didn't mean to put you off. Quite frankly, it is rather pleasant to help someone who can talk. What can I do for you?"

"Strange, but I'm not at all sure."

"What seems to be the problem?"

"I don't mean to interfere with all you have to do here, but I'm reasonably certain that I may be dying."

"May I ask where you have been injured, sir?"

"Well, that's just it. I'm not aware of any out and out injuries. But I have the strangest sensation."

"Show me where it hurts, please."

He looked downward and shrugged. "I know this must sound daft." Behind him, where the man couldn't see, Tony rolled his eyes and made a crazy gesture for Lyn to see. "But I don't think I have a specific pain, you see, but a building sense that something in me is about to come loose."

"Where? Inside your abdomen? In your head?"

The man's eyes grew vacant and seemed to stare through Lyn who said, "Sir, maybe you need to sit down."

The gentleman did not take up her offer. There really was no place to sit, not that he actually looked around for a spot. He did not respond in any way. Except to drop dead.

DAVE GARWICK

CHAPTER 31

OF NIGHTMARES AND MEMORIES

14 September 1942
Headquarters, Commander of Submarines
Avenue Maréchal Maunoury
Paris
0455 hours

For over thirty hours, Dönitz's command staff hardly slept. They had to respond to the constant requests for updates from Naval High Command in Berlin, four hundred and fifty miles away. At the same time, they were trying to oversee a rescue operation at sea over thirty-five hundred miles in the opposite direction. They were the men in the middle.

Naval High Command in Berlin was keeping up a constant volley of demands for updates.

Updates from 156?

How many Italians rescued?

How long to be exposed on surface?

Closest friendly assets?

Dönitz and his staff were themselves desperate to know what was going on. But even they had to deny their curiosity in the interests of radio discipline. It was imperative in these lonely, middle-of-the-night hours that signal traffic be neither greater nor lesser than normal. Otherwise, enemy intelligence would know that Hartenstein's message in the clear had been from a virtual sitting duck. He imagined every single ship and plane of American and British forces racing against each other to bag an entire wolfpack.

What was the point of granting permission to rescue the Italians if Hartenstein was going to paint a target on himself and get them all sent to the bottom anyway? Hartenstein became the horizon that no one could see beyond. Berlin was demanding Hartenstein's head on a platter. Dönitz considered that the platter might have to be large enough to accommodate his own head, and maybe a few others as well. The Führer was not known for moderation when he felt betrayed. So now what? Suspend the rescue operation and put them all back in the water? And thereby deliberately sacrifice the Italians as well?

This was very likely going to be a drawn-out affair. Last night, Dönitz had instructed his chief of staff to see to it that only half of his senior officers were on duty at any given time. He himself tried to close his eyes for a few short hours. But he worked harder in sleep than he did on his feet.

Every single time he closed his eyes, he again was the young Third Watch Officer in another war, listening to Leutnant Niemöller who was looking through the scope and saying, *"I only see a few lifeboats in the water, Sir. Looks like a destroyer changing course to close for a rescue."*

Dönitz could close his eyes, but not his mind. He threw off the covers, sat on the edge of his bed and lay back down again. The dreamland cinema commenced right where it had left off. He could see his commander of unblessed memory reply, *"Well, let's tuck in a little closer to make sure that our little swimmers don't get fished out."*

This time, Dönitz rolled out of bed, stood up and paced back and forth half a dozen times to completely rouse himself awake and extricate himself from this tortured dream. The problem was that this was not a dream. It was a memory. Standing still, he closed his eyes. A dream might fade, but not the memory of Leutnant Niemöller clarifying the command. *"Sir? What are we proposing to do with those men in the water?"*

Dönitz was back in his first U-boat. *"What we are going to do, Leutnant, is to keep them from coming back another day,"* explains Kapitänleutnant Forstmann.

"Up periscope." The clack of the control handle means business as the skipper rotates the periscope to the left and then to the right. In a barely audible thought he says, *"Yes, yes, yes, that's a good destroyer. To the rescue!"* The captain raises his voice, *"But let's get her attention to chase us instead, my boys."*

Then a soft bump is heard from the outside on the raised periscope. Then another. And another. No one asks. Everyone seems to know what is making the sound. Non-human debris would sound louder, sharper.

Forstmann keeps looking through the viewfinder. *"Here we are. Come and get us! Here she comes. Dive! Dive! Thirty degrees right rudder. Full speed. Brace for depth charges."*

Between the shards of memories, Dönitz had been trying to get some sleep. There was very little that could be done, back out in the wardroom. But on his bed, in the vault of his memories, there was much that needed to be undone. But how could an old man undo what had been done a world war ago on a boat called *U-39?*

Maybe that is why the next *U-39* had become the very first U-boat to be sunk in this war, already three years ago. Depth charges had forced it to the surface in the very middle of three destroyers. But those enemy warships had immediately ceased firing when they realized that the German crew was abandoning ship. Not one single casualty. The mercy shown to the new *U-39* only magnified the treachery of the old *U-39* on which young Dönitz had served. And it magnified the shame of the much older Dönitz who now served as commander of all U-boats. And it turned up the volume on the replays that went on and on and on and on.

Dönitz stepped smartly into the command center. His entire senior staff and their subordinates snapped to attention as Chief of Staff Kapitän zür See Peder Altenbach announced, "Good morning, Admiral!"

Dönitz nodded and then in a routine voice asked, "Why is everyone assembled, Peder?"

In response to the question, the Chief of Staff nervously glanced toward the more senior officers who were beginning to gather. Commander U-boats West intercepted the question. "With your kind permission," interjected Kapitän zür See Johann Wiedenhoef.

"I'm listening," said Dönitz in a routine manner.

"Herr Vizeadmiral, I must advise you, Sir, that our *Eisbar* situation is becoming problematic."

Herr Vizeadmiral liked to use the fewest words to make the sharpest jab. "You don't say."

As if Wiedenhoef's statement were some agreed upon signal, the senior advisors all arrayed themselves before their commander. All seven of them. Dönitz couldn't help thinking of these seven as a week of bad news.

The fourth man in line was his strategics chief who spoke up. "Sir, we feel we can best serve you by expressing our serious reservations about this rescue effort."

Not entirely to himself, Dönitz said, "Ah yes, 'Wednesday's child is full of woe.'"

"Sir?" asked a confused Motschenbacher.

"Never mind, Rudolph," said Dönitz. "What are these reservations you speak of?"

"Admiral, please forgive the impertinence of any appearance that any of us would presume to question your esteemed judgment, but . . ."

"Mr. Motschenbacher, please forego the traditional groveling. You men are my advisors. I expect you to advise me and to advise me honestly."

"Thank you, Sir," said Wiedenhoef. He straightened up and cleared his throat. "We are unanimous, Sir, in urging you in the strongest way possible to abort this rescue operation."

"That is not an option, now that we have already begun it," said the Admiral.

"Sir, if I may," said Chief of Intelligence. "Recently you have been expressing concern about the threat of Q boats."

"That is true enough." The old U-boat commander was constantly haunted by memories of what he called 'submarine traps'. Back in his day, heavily armed surface warships had masqueraded as merchant ships and had sunk at least fifteen of his comrades. These masqueraders would lure in curious

U-boats and then suddenly drop their fake costumes and blow the U-boat out of the water at close range. Dönitz constantly worried that the ghosts of sinkings past might come back to life.

His advisor said, "At your urging, Sir, I have been intensifying our assessment of precisely that threat."

"Do we have any current information in that regard?" asked Dönitz.

"As a matter of fact, Sir, we do have some modest intelligence." Dönitz chose not to comment on the obvious.

The advisor paused to make sure that he chose his next words carefully. "Because such programs are understandably cloaked in the highest secrecy, we, umm, have great difficulty obtaining information that, uhh, we would consider particularly reliable."

Dönitz said, "You seem to be stammering a bit there, Gottfried."

Ciske did not take the bait. "From what we can gather, our best estimate is that Britain may have fielded as many as nine raiders and the Americans half a dozen. That is one of the reasons we want to advise against any non-attack surface operations for any reason, Sir."

Dönitz pressed the case. "As much as I do share your concerns Mr. Ciske, I have to ask if we have any clear evidence of actual losses to these wonderful things."

"Not really, Sir. But we also know that lack of evidence is what these ships specialize in."

"Point well taken," said the admiral.

"If I might add, Sir," said Hoesch, his tactical chief, "the most threatening thing about these boats is precisely that we do not know how likely they are."

Dönitz nodded thoughtfully. "I think that is fair to say."

The strategics man pressed the point. "Well, Sir, our understanding is that Naval High Command in Berlin and the Führer himself have warned us that no rescue effort can be allowed to prevent our U-boats from submerging or jeopardizing the Cape mission. Should we be taking such unknown risks that are unnecessary?"

"I am well aware of our orders. That is why we have called in boats *506, 507* and the *Capellini* to release *Eisbar* boats to resume the mission, is it not?" asked Dönitz.

Hoesch said, "Yes, Sir. Of course, Sir. But should they themselves have to suddenly dive, any rescue effort at all will also risk the destruction of any other other boats we assign to the effort."

"You underestimate the efficiency of our crews, gentlemen," said the Admiral. "While we get faster with sharper pencils in this office, they keep besting their submerging speed."

Stohlman, the logistics man, was dangerously close to losing his mask of objectivity when he said, "Admiral, with all due respect, it is our sharper pencils that have given you those numbers."

The Admiral turned to face the subordinate straight on. "With all due respect, you say?"

"Begging your pardon, Sir," Hoesch said. "I think what Otto was trying to say was that we cannot help but take to heart your vigilance in reminding boat commanders about the increasing dangers of lethal air attack."

"Say more, please," said Dönitz.

"Well, Sir, you have been so clear about the numbers which you have told us are so unforgiving, no matter how good a boat is. A couple hours ago, Otto was reminding us about some of those numbers. Otto?"

"Please forgive the forcefulness of my concerns, Admiral," said Fregattenkapitän Otto Stohlman. He awaited an acceptance of his apology. Dönitz did not respond, but kept his locked eyes on him. The junior man resumed a little more tentatively. "I believe what Kapitän Hoesch may have been referring to was my recollection of your explanation last week of what would be required for a survivable emergency dive under air attack."

Dönitz still did not respond but continued with the eye-lock. Stohlman cleared his throat. "What I recall from your excellent instruction, Herr Admiral, was your concern that boat captains were becoming too complacent about the dangers of air attack whenever they did not see any approaching aircraft."

For the first time, Dönitz responded. "Yes. That is true enough."

Stohlman was thinking that perhaps he was beginning to dig himself out of his grave. "I was reminding all of us how you had explained that after a lookout spotted an aircraft at the maximum range of four miles, the boat would have only one minute before that plane was upon them."

Dönitz pressed, "Your point?"

"Well, if I understood you correctly, Sir, even an already fast-moving boat, with a minimum number of highly trained personnel topside would still only have modest odds, at best, of surviving an air attack. I simply ask what chance a stationary U-boat could have that was crowded topside with injured civilians?"

Dönitz was cornered by his own facts and he exploded. "What then are you expecting me to do? To throw back into the sea our own surviving allies and innocent women and children?"

"Yes!" said Wiedenhoef. "Unless you are willing to exchange the lives of our own men for theirs! Are we telling our men to kill the enemy and then die to save them?"

Dönitz stared into empty space. He was silent. So was everyone else. "It may not have to come to that. The rescue stands. Thank you, gentlemen. Dismissed."

Immediately, the superheated atmosphere was breached. "Herr Vizeadmiral, urgent message Berlin," announced the aide who snapped a paper at him.

Dönitz quickly read the brief message and said to himself, "Now what? Is Berlin eavesdropping here?"

He looked around as though to find a staff officer that he must have misplaced. "Peder!"

His Chief of Staff answered even before the second syllable of his name was spoken. "Sir!"

"Arrange *Pegasus* for immediate departure Berlin. I expect to return by supper."

Pegasus was the code name for the Bf 110 C-4 that was always at the ready for Dönitz to make quick hops to Berlin for consultations. The two-seat variant of the Messerschmitt fighter could top five hundred and sixty kilometers per hour. It carried armament and pilot capabilities for self-defense. A one-way trip could be made in under two hours.

By 1300 hours, Dönitz was standing before Grossadmiral Erich Johann Albert Raeder, Commander in Chief of the German Navy. One other superior was present: Adolf Hitler.

Hitler spoke. "Thank you, Admiral, for coming so quickly." As if there had been a choice in this life.

"By all means, mein Führer," replied Dönitz with a deep bow and light click of his heels.

Raeder began the dirty work by trying to lower the guard of his visitor. "Karl, the Führer and I would not have disturbed your pressing duties were it not for the urgency of this unfortunate Italian matter."

"Of course, Sir."

Hitler resumed. "Your commander Hartenstein is to be commended for risking life and limb to preserve the alliance with our Italian friends." This had what might have been the desired effect of almost throwing Dönitz off his game.

Hitler continued the set-up that he and Raeder had planned. "The young commander placed himself and his men in great danger to, shall we say, liberate those prisoners of war. Might even go down as the greatest prisoner of war escape in history. For such leadership, I'm not at all sure that it would be unseemly to consider this man for the Knight's Cross. Wouldn't you agree, Erich?"

Raeder, of course, was prepared. "By all means, mein Führer. I shall see to it immediately."

Hitler now got down to business. "On the other hand, Dönitz," he said with increasing volume and volatility, "I cannot, indeed I will not countenance jeopardizing vital mission, boats and crews for the sake of rescuing enemy combatants who will return to wage war against us! Is that absolutely clear, Vizeadmiral!" It was not a question.

Dönitz quickly responded, "Absolutely clear, mein Führer."

"Very good," continued Hitler whose face relaxed a bit. "You must fully appreciate the importance of our doing everything possible to discourage recruitment of allied sailors. That is why I want as many allied seamen killed as possible."

Hitler's high level subordinates had limitless ways of answering in the affirmative. "Of course, mein Führer."

"Therefore," said Hitler, "I will give the order that since foreign seamen cannot be taken prisoner, the U-boats are to surface after torpedoing and shoot up the lifeboats."

Now Dönitz started to say something that he had never expected to say in his wildest dreams. "But, mein Führer . . .."

Hitler cut him off in mid-sentence. "It is nonsense to offer provisions to survivors in their lifeboats, or to provide sailing instructions for their return home. I hereby order that ships and their crews are to be destroyed, even if the crews are in lifeboats."

Dönitz now went where few had trod and where even fewer had survived. "No, mein Führer. It goes against the honor of a seaman to shoot at shipwrecked survivors. I cannot issue such an order. My U-boat men are volunteers, waging a costly struggle in the belief they are fighting honorably for a good cause. Their combat morale would be undermined by this order. I must request that you withdraw it."

The seconds of silence were measured in three sets of heartbeats.

Dönitz ventured a little further. "If I may be so bold as to offer a less costly way to achieve your aim, mein Führer."

"Karl, I must warn you . . ." said Raeder.

Hitler held up a hand. "No, no Erich, let him continue," as if giving Dönitz enough rope to hang himself.

"Sir, as you know, our torpedo development has been proceeding with main focus on guidance and trigger technology. We could shift primary attention to vastly increasing explosive load to ensure greater personnel lethality."

Again, silence. Long silence.

Even Dönitz himself was surprised when the Führer acquiesced. "Do what you want, but no more offering assistance and sailing instructions."

"By all means, mein Führer," replied the man who tried not to let his exhalation be heard.

"I think that should be all, Dönitz," said Raeder.

Ironically, the man now being dismissed would be the very one to eventually replace both of the other two. By order of Hitler himself.

CHAPTER 32

IN THE WIND

15 September 1942
U-156
Stationary 130 miles northeast of Ascension Island
1130 hours

"**S**till nothing, Mr. Hacker?" asked Hartenstein of his senior radio man.

"Neither beast nor fowl, Sir."

It just felt too quiet.

"If you don't mind me asking, Captain," said the Chief Petty Officer. "How soon might we expect the three other boats?"

"Hard to say Oberbootsman. That is the double-edged sword of the silent service, is it not?"

"The silent service, Sir?"

"A term that our esteemed American counterparts are said to be using in the Pacific theatre. Your specialty, in fact, Hacker. Silence. You and sonar. The proof that God gives us only one mouth but two ears."

The long hours of monotony relaxed the skipper's bearing and even his tongue a bit so that he was a little more loquacious than usual. He reflected, "Hmm, strange. The silence that keeps us hidden is the same silence which keeps us in the dark. We dare not ask who is where."

This was more than Hacker had been able to hear all shift. The mind-numbing quiet was deafening. His hardest task was trying to distinguish between real sounds and those he imagined.

As if asking a second time would improve the odds, the skipper asked, "No signal traffic of any enemy movement in response to our in-the-clear?"

Hacker tried to be more specific. "As far as I can tell, Sir, the only transmissions seem to be routine merchant shipping on civilian wavelengths."

It occurred to the captain that there were a few more things needed to make the boat ready for any responding visitors. "Leutnant Franceschi, see to the making of a Red Cross flag that can be draped across the bow. I want the red cross to stand out from a bright white field. I want this so large that a plane high overhead can easily identify it. I want this in position by fourteen hundred hours. Do you understand? Any questions?"

Like many junior officers, Franceschi had already learned the hard way that he had better ask questions now if there was the slightest chance of having misunderstood an order. "Begging the Captain's pardon, Sir. Are we allowed to display a Red Cross?"

"No. The rules of war expressly forbid a warship from flying the Red Cross. Please carry on."

The First Watch Officer looked even more confused. "Aye …… Sir!"

Then Hartenstein climbed the conn tower, uncradled the phone, switched it to external speakers and broadcast to everyone inside and topside. "Attention please. This is Captain Hartenstein. Shortly after we began taking survivors aboard, I took the unusual action of broadcasting, in the open, a call for help from any vessels, including Allied ships. I explained that we had women, children and other civilians from Allied nations aboard. I promised to not attack if we were not attacked. I have received no response. In the meantime, U-boat Command in Paris has ordered three other U-boats to assist. They are on their way. Our plan is to re-distribute passengers among as many boats as possible. Later, our guests will be transferred to Axis surface ships which will then take people ashore. So, as to avoid any possible confusion, I have ordered members of the crew to fashion a large Red Cross on the bow of this boat. Please cooperate with any orders and requests from crew members. Thank you."

Hour upon hour, upon the increasingly heated metal deck, the wait for assisting U-boats dragged on. Two necessities converged to become the mother of one invention. As *U-156* waited to be relieved, so did every person on its deck. Boredom was the second problem. One group of men took to calling themselves The Whiz Kids. As each one answered the call of nature, a competition of distance and marksmanship answered both physical and entertainment needs. Since the wind constantly shifted, male passengers on all sides of the combat casino got to take a shot, so to speak.

"Alright, first up!" announced the self-appointed ringmaster. "Our three judge panel of experts will score for distance and arc. Mid-stream wind shift of so-called ammunition will result in forfeiture of score as well as the life of the contestant. Are we ready gentlemen?"

Cheers and jeers rose from the audience and from the line-up of contestants. "Silence, silence please! Our contestant needs concentration. Are you ready, sir?"

"Sure, sure," said the contestant who seemed hurried. For some reason.

He twisted and turned to arrange himself for the event. The master of ceremonies interrupted him with an attempted French imitation. "Oh no, no. Pardon moi, monsieur. You must first signal your intention with the declaration of intent: 'Oui, Oui.'"

"C'mon Froggie, you've got to be kidding," said the urgent contestant.

"Oh contraire. Ze rules are ze rules, no?"

"OK," he grumbled and said something too quiet for the satisfaction of the ringmaster who raised his own voice. "Please, please lau-DARE for ze glor-EE of Fahnss!"

"I said, 'Oui, Oui!'"

The director faced the crowd and raised his arms for all the multitude to answer back in unison, "Oui, Oui!"

The conductor then did a smart-about face and snapped a back-handed French salute to the contestant, "Feye-AIR when red-EE!"

The marksman made his necessary adjustments and then calculated for windage and elevation. He no sooner began his arc of triumph than the sea itself returned the gesture with a massive geyser of its own that jetted ten meters into the air. A behemoth breeched the depths with a deafening exhalation as *U 506* blew its ballasts and surfaced, parallel to *U-156*.

"We have a win-AIR!" shouted the barker.

No one applauded. No one moved. No one else made a sound. For that matter, no one breathed. Waves crashed against the side as the arriving U-boat bellowed forth the paralyzing blast of an oceanic foghorn.

Some of the contestants lost their reason to compete.

PART V
AMERICAN RESPONSE

CHAPTER 33

OBLIVIOUS

15 September 1942
B-24 Liberator "Better Late Than Never"
500 miles due west of and approaching Ascension Island
1400 hours

To a Liberator, the length of this trip was nothing to write home about. The B-24 was specifically designed for long range. It could fly non-stop, twenty-eight hundred miles, which bested the B-17's range by almost a thousand miles. To conserve fuel, it cruised well below its maximum speed which meant that the crew had been flying about four and a half hours.

"Hurry up and wait, hurry up and wait!" said someone over the intercom. "Thought we'd be past that in a bomber."

"Army's the Army, no matter where it is," said someone else.

"I get the point when you're stuck in the infantry and you've got to slog everywhere. But gee, they put you in the fastest thing they got, get you going two hundred and fifty miles an hour or better, and we're still sitting around waiting. Doing nothing. Just waiting."

"Speak for yourself," called back the pilot. "Yakky and I are doing plenty up here," he said, referring to his co-pilot. "If we were doing nothing, then you'd be doing plenty and you'd probably be water logged."

Jingles piped in, "Speaking for the rest of the family back here, we really do appreciate all you do for us, Pop. That must be why they pay you guys the big bucks. But it doesn't help things a whole lot that you painted us as a turtle, Sir."

"Yeah, was that your idea, L.T?" asked Hennessey.

"Sorry, gents," said the pilot. "The credit goes to the nose artist. When I told him that we'd name the plane *Better Late Than Never,* I suggested maybe a broken clock or something like that. He recommended something with a little more attitude. So, he's the one who came up with that cocky looking turtle dropping something on a dumb bunny."

"I don't get it, Sir," said Frankie on the waist gun.

"Gee, kid, we gotta explain everything to you?" said Spinoza on the nose gun. "See, we're always complaining about everything taking so long, right? So, the paint guy comes up with a turtle because turtles take so long to get anywhere. Follow me, kid? But the thing is, he still manages to nail the bunny. You know, like the old Tortoise and the Hare. Get it now?"

"What's the Tortoise and the Hare?" asked Frankie.

"Ah, forget it!" said the gunner.

"Besides," said the pilot, "we've only been up for what, how many hours, Dick?"

"Four," said the co-pilot of few words.

Dropsy, the bombardier, had to add his own mockery. "Are we there yet, Daddy?"

"Almost there. You can hold it," said Harden.

Miller, on the tail gun, said, "How much longer?"

This was the cue for the Navigator, 2nd Lt. Chuck Milberg. "Ah, according to my charts, I'd say another good two and a half hours.

CHAPTER 34

TWO BECOMING ONE

15 September 1942
U-156
Stationary 130 miles northeast of Ascension Island
1600 hours

The panic of yesterday had long since settled into changeless monotony. The losers had lost, the dead had died, and all that remained were the remains. Whomever you happened to dry out next to was now the person who knew you best. And, maybe, the person who would know you last. Long ago, people had said everything they had to say. Now, they talked about everything else.

Every single square inch of the deck was spoken for. Everyone had his place. Tony and Lyn had somehow managed to claim their spot on the wind-sheltered back side of the conning tower. It also provided them a modicum of privacy.

Lyn said, "Tony, do you ever think that things happen for a purpose?"

His vacant eyes stared right through her. "Not really. Things just happen."

"You mean like meeting each other in London?" she said. "Falling in love, losing one another and then bumping into each other again in the middle of the ocean, and falling in love all over again?"

"Pretty big coincidence, I'll give you that," he said.

Lyn tilted her head and she pursed a faint smile. "Too big, too many things to just be coincidence for me. I like to hope that there's a reason for things. I'm counting on this all leading somewhere."

He paused to give that last remark some considered thought. "Nice idea, if you can believe it."

"Tony, I've been doing some reading these last couple days."

"Reading?" said Tony. "With what?"

Lyn said, "Nothing I was able to bring along, I'm afraid."

Tony was almost beginning to get used to Lyn's mysteries. "But you've been reading?"

"Oh, something I've read and read so many times that I guess I kind of memorized parts of it," she said. "Some of the stories mean more to me than others, especially at certain times. For some reason, they've been coming back, stories about boats and near drownings and near sinkings and people getting saved. I've sort of been reading them in my memory. It's what makes me think that maybe all these crazy things have a purpose after all."

She stopped there, waiting for him to inquire. He didn't.

It took time for each of them to prepare for what the other might say next. "Tony, I once promised the rest of my life to someone. It turned out to be the rest of his life, not mine. I thought I could never do that again."

Tony pursed his lips in deep thought, nodding his head in resignation.

320

Lyn continued the one-sided conversation. "If I ever did that again, I would only promise the rest of my life to someone whom I knew would come through in the toughest times. That is how we have come to know each other. I've grown very fond of a man who has always come through for me in the worst times."

Tony looked up tentatively. "What are you saying?"

"Like I said, I think we are here for a reason, Tony. I very much would like to think that you and I have something together, way beyond this mess."

Tony almost looked like he was mulling over a business offer. "OK, maybe we just might make it. After all, how many couples take a cruise before the . . .?"

He shocked himself at almost having said such a word out loud.

For a long time, spoken words would have interfered with the conversation. In the gentle South Atlantic breezes, the two allowed themselves to doze for a brief moment on the deck of a Nazi U-boat.

It wasn't just because her back was tired that Lyn relaxed into Tony's arm-chair. And it wasn't just because of the cooling breeze that Tony wrapped his arms around the warmth that was Lyn. She drifted into the light dreams of a future where a little girl of her own asked, "Mummy? Did you and daddy always know each other?" Even wrapped together, Lyn and Tony did not know how close they really were. Tony also wafted through the same fantasies where he dreamed of a teenage son one day asking, "So Dad, where did you and mum meet?" Even in dreams, he chuckled his answer, "On the deck of a German U-boat."

Together on the rocking deck, they drifted in dreams together for twenty minutes, until the breeze shifted to revive them back to reality. Trying to feign some kind of a royal accent, Tony said, "So, me lady, with all our future hanging in the balance, as it were, would it not be fittin' for the two of us to get to know each other a wee bit?"

Playing the fair damsel, Lyn said, "And what honorable thing, pray tell, would ye be havin' in mind, in the midst of all the royal court round about us here?"

"Oh, nothin' unseemly, I assure thee. Only the sharin' of words and hearts, me lady."

"Then, good sir, have at it!" Dropping the game, Lyn nuzzled in close to his chest and spoke in a tone of intimacy. "So, what would you like to know, my dear?"

"I do like the sound of that," said the smitten soldier. "Only curious, and I'm not even sure you remember. Tell me if it's too personal, but twice I have noticed you speak in the voice of a little girl."

Lyn did not answer. She was too close for him to see. But he heard her sniffle. Somehow, he knew not to intrude, but to wait for her to choose whether and when to respond. She sniffled again. Eventually, the sniffling subsided. She let out a cleansing sigh and her breathing became more regular.

Just as Tony was sure that Lyn had drifted off to sleep, he heard her still, quiet voice. "Did you know that I was an orphan?"

"No, I didn't. In fact, I don't think you ever mentioned anything about having a family."

"Oh, I do have a family," said Lyn. "A very wonderful mum and dad. In fact, I worry most about them right now. I'm sure they're dying of anguish at the sinking of our ship. Especially mum. This is going to be hardest for her."

"I suppose that's what moms are for," said Tony.

"Oh, it's so much more than just that, Tony. This is going to bring back nightmares of how she and I first met. Mum and Daddy are my adoptive parents. I've always known that. But then I enlisted in the TANS and got assigned to the *Laconia.* That was when Mum and Daddy felt compelled to tell me the story of how I came to be an orphan."

Tony listened without comment.

"In the last war," Lyn said, "my birth-mother and I were on another ship. You're not going to believe the name of that one."

"I don't know," said Tony. "The *Queen Mary*?"

"The *Laconia,*" she said.

Tony looked a little confused. "Strange. I would never have thought the ship was that old."

"No, love, it was a different *Laconia*. It was torpedoed and sunk by a U-boat as well. My real mum's name was Mary Perth, and she drowned. I was maybe three years old. Another lady was swimming where I was floating. She saved me. Later she and her husband adopted me."

"This is incredible," said Tony.

"I only just learned about all this before boarding for this mission," she said. "I've been working so hard to come to terms with all of that. All during this trip, I've been dreaming a lot. Especially when I've been scared, I've had a lot of flashbacks, of things I never knew that I knew. Maybe that's what you've been hearing."

Tony's eyes were wide. "What an unbelievable coincidence!"

Lyn shrugged her shoulders. "It would be unbelievable if it were just a coincidence. But don't you see, love, how this all has to be more than coincidence?"

Tony gave it long thought. Then a faint smile and an almost imperceptible nod. "I don't know. Maybe. Sounds kind of churchy."

She didn't push the point.

DAVE GARWICK

CHAPTER 35

AS IN 'WAKE'

15 September 1942
"Better Late Than Never"
Eastbound over the South Atlantic nearing
"Wide Awake" station on Ascension Island
1630 hours

"**D**on't let us down now, Amelia," said navigator to pilot.

"So why would I put us down here in the middle of the South Atlantic?" said the pilot, as if he missed the point. "Besides, Freddie, this is your show. I'm just the driver. You tell me where to go."

"You mean that, boss?" said the navigator. "I get to tell you where to go?"

The Amelia and Freddie routine between pilot Harden and navigator Milberg was a reference to the ill-fated flight, five years earlier, of Amelia Earhart and her navigator Fred Noonan. That pair had simply vanished into thin air over the South Pacific as they were presumably closing in on one

Howland Island. The media had all kinds of tantalizing theories that ranged from the pair being taken prisoner by the Japanese to a Martian abduction.

For always being up in the air, it was the aviation community that was the one that was most down to earth. Nobody in the flying world was perplexed by the most likely scenarios. Either the pilot had not been able to overcome some mechanical failure or the navigator could not overcome some navigational confusion.

"You think that could happen to us, Sir?" asked the eighteen-year-old belly turret gunner.

The leader of the crew sensed the kid's anxiety. "Naw, Tiny, not too many Japs out this way."

"No," said the kid. "I mean, you know, like getting lost, looking for a stone somewhere in the middle of the ocean."

Even as young as he was, Harden was 'the old man' to the crew and he didn't like unnecessary complications. He shot his navigator a look like, "Now see what you've gone and done?"

The tunnel-visioned navigator finally looked up from his charts and glanced around to see what it was that he had done. Milberg took the cue. "Boss is right. Where Earhart was fixing to put down was about fifty times smaller than what we're looking for. That's why they call this one "The Rock." A pretty big one, Ascension."

The pilot looked over to his co-pilot. "Hey, Dick, what did you say they call the airfield?"

"Wide Awake," said the co-pilot, as assurance that he really was.

The bombardier took aim at the navigator. "Take that as a gentle reminder, Nav."

"Yeah, these boxcars don't have all that great a record with islands that have Wake in their name," said the tail gunner.

"*Now* what are you blathering about?" said Harden.

"No offense, Sir, but don't tell me you don't know about the first combat mission of the 24," referring to their type of bomber.

From the top turret, Hennessey said, "I've got a feeling you're going to tell us all."

"Well, gee, it was only a couple months ago." And then he remembered his manners and added, "Sarge."

Total silence told the gunner that he needed to explain a little more. "First time in action. More like first attempt at action. So, they send four of these babies out of Pearl to hit *Wake* Island. Only they never find the thing!"

"Well, not to worry," said the wiser-than-his-years leader. "Nimitz has had a whole three months to get it all figured out. Came up with a secret weapon."

"What's the secret weapon, Sir?" asked Frankie Sawyer, the young waist gunner.

"Us," said the co-pilot of few words.

The tail gunner just had to stoke the embers a bit more. "Yeah, just as long as you remember what they say, Sir. About pensions."

Harden said, "I'm afraid to ask."

Miller was only too happy to oblige. "Miss Ascension, your wife gets a pension."

"From what I hear, Otto, that's about all your wife will ever get from you anyway," said the engineer over the mic.

A new voice joined the intercom banter. "So, what do you do all by yourself back there anyway, Lately?" said nose gunner. Otto Miller had gotten the tail gunner moniker, "Johnny Come Lately", because he joked about always being the last one to land.

"Spend all my time praying that we don't all land at the same time," said Miller.

The pilot referred to the Navigator. "Well, if Mr. Milberg here can find the right address, I'll do my best to get us all down in the proper order."

CHAPTER 36

STRANGE CONFIDENCES

15 September 1942
U-156
Stationary, 130 miles northeast of Ascension Island
1700 hours

Hartenstein reached into the inside right pocket of his black leather command jacket and pulled out a silver cigarette case which was adorned with a striking emblem. The decoration was a black swastika on a round white field, all ringed in gold and placed over a subdued, golden, eight pointed starburst. He opened the shiny wafer case and held it out to Johnny Walker. "Cigarette?"

Walker warily kept his eyes locked on his host as he carefully reached to pick out one of the neatly tucked-in samples. His captor assured him, "Don't worry, my friend. These are perfectly safe. After you, I shall take one myself. In fact, it occurs to me that perhaps this is the origin of the custom of letting the other person choose first."

"I don't follow," said the Brit.

"So that you can be assured that your captor has not tricked you. How would I know which cigarette you would choose? Especially when I myself take from what you have left?"

Walker said, "You'll excuse me if I don't explain a way around that."

Hartenstein waved away the comment. "Ach! This nastiness of war need not also trample the small courtesies of civilized men."

Walker did not miss a beat. "That's probably why they offer a cigarette to a man who's about to be shot."

This gave Hartenstein a jolly good laugh. "You Brits can be so understatedly dramatic. You have been watching too many Hollywood fictions!"

Walker let slip a vague smile and nodded his head as he accepted the offer. "Thank you then for your kindness, Sir." The boat captain reached out with another Nazi emblazoned device to light Walker's smoke.

The first day's panic gave way to a boredom, absent of any horizon. The boat did not move, the seas were calm, and even the passing clouds gave no menace in their fluffy innocence. On Hartenstein's orders, crew members circulated in maintenance duties as a pretext for keeping an eye on their guests. The order of the day was, "wait."

Walker was beginning to relax. "If you don't mind me asking, Sir, I couldn't help but notice the insignia on your cigarette case."

Hartenstein said, "The German Cross. In gold, to be sure." He looked down in deep reflection. "And probably the last medal I'll ever receive after what I'm doing out here."

"Sir?"

"Our superiors all have ways of bestowing things on us, don't they?" said the skipper. "At one moment, they'll pin one thing on your chest. The next moment, they pin something else over your heart."

Walker motioned with his cigarette. "They gave you that for all the suckers like us you sent to the bottom with this boat?"

Hartenstein took a drag and squinted through the ascending smoke. "Well, not with this boat." He paused in reflection. "In fact, I had never sunk a single thing with any U-boat by the time they awarded this. Strangely enough, it was after this decoration that I sank my first seven ships. From this very bridge, no less."

"So, what then?" asked the Brit. "What was that medal for? Pushing papers?"

The host quietly chuckled. "Not really. This award in gold is for heroism in combat. Apparently, I had done sixty-five war patrols on torpedo boats before I got this vessel. Saw a bit of action in the Spanish Civil War. Then in the Bay of Biscay after hostilities were declared with you lovely people." The commander pursed his lips in a faint smile.

Walker nodded his head in a show of admiration. "Big deal then."

"Oh yes. Personally presented to me by Dönitz himself. The cigarette case is a personal gift that he gives each of his commanders. I confess that I am quite proud of that. Received it in March and haven't even had time to lose it," he said with that gleam in his eye.

"So how many?" asked Walker.

This time, the confusion was Hartenstein's. "I beg your pardon."

Walker said, "How many people like us have you sent to the bottom with this boat?"

"I truly have no idea," said Hartenstein. "It's like asking a soldier how many men he has killed. One does not ask that sort of question. Most of us have no idea. One of the great old Prussian generals we studied, his name was Clausewitz, talked about something he called 'the fog of war.' We U-boats spend a lot of time in the fog."

"Yeah, but all snipers keep track of their kills," said Walker. "You're just a naval sniper, aren't you?"

The U-boat commander looked up in reflection and nodded his head. "Yes, I do see your point. I think that is fair enough. And, yes, we do in fact keep track of our kills, not of men but of ships. We have no way of knowing how many people are on board a given vessel at a given point in time. We count tonnage, Mr. Walker."

The British officer said, "Makes it a little easier on the conscience, doesn't it, to count tons rather than souls?"

The German paused in reflection. "Hmm . . . I sometimes wonder the same thing myself."

"So then," said Walker, "how much tonnage have you sent to the bottom?"

"Just shy of ninety-three thousand tons, counting our biggest prize," said the captain.

"Who was that?"

"You."

Walker was taken aback. "Us? We were your biggest kill?"

"Oh, yes. By far. Three times bigger than the next largest," said Hartenstein. "Five times larger than our average target."

The British target said, "And how many of these so-called targets?"

Hartenstein didn't even have to think. "Seventeen to date. Not counting four others that we damaged but failed to sink."

Walker shifted to a less casual tone. "So then, you must have known that we were a passenger liner when you attacked."

The U-boat captain pulled a long drag. "Obviously. But passenger liners these days are often converted into troop ships.

You can appreciate why we would take, shall we say, a special interest in troop ships?"

Walker's indignity was building. "So, you gambled the lives of civilians, even women and children, on the off-chance that you might be sinking a troop ship?"

"Mr. Walker," said Hartenstein, "I can appreciate how wrong this all seems from your perspective. But you know as well as I, that both sides of combat not only gamble with innocent lives but sometimes deliberately sacrifice them. I am sure you are painfully aware of what bombers on both sides are doing to entire cities." Hartenstein could have had no idea how prescient he was.

Walker had nothing to say.

Hartenstein paused and locked eyes on his guest. "Besides, my friend, my actions here were not, how do you say it, as cavalier as all that. Were you and your good captain intending to use women and children as a shield behind which to hide?"

This was a new one on Walker. "I beg your pardon?"

"Oh, come now," Hartenstein said. "Are you going to stand here and deny that you knew that you took women and children on board a ship that had been refitted as an armed merchant cruiser?"

Walker was incredulous. "How could you possibly know that?"

"Mr. Walker, a U-boat is not a cowboy who shoots from the hip in a western movie," said the skipper. "We stalked you closely for many hours to determine whether or not your so-called passenger liner was a legitimate target. We counted no less than eight six-inch guns and two high-angle guns. You were running a zig zag evasion pattern."

Walker was silent once more. He exhaled a long breath of smoke.

Hartenstein pressed his point. "Are you aware of something called the duck test?"

"Afraid you've got me there again, old chap."

"Before I entered the Kriegsmarine, I began studies to become a lawyer. I think you folks call them, how do you say it, solicitors? Anyway, when they taught us about circumstantial evidence, they talked about the duck test. It simply says that if it quacks like a duck, walks like a duck, flies like a duck and swims like a duck, then you might safely assume that it might well be a duck. Quite frankly Mr. Walker, you failed the duck test."

Walker looked up quickly from his thoughts.

"You British have another fowl expression. I believe it is the idea of a dead duck."

Almost to himself, Walker slowly shook his head and muttered, "Bloody hell . . ."

"Quite literally so, Mr. Walker. But please don't think that I want to create a bloody hell or that I take this lightly. I actually would not have attacked if I had known there were women, children and other civilians aboard. But you left me little choice. You made it clear that you were a warship."

Walker said, "So, you fished us out to wash your hands?"

"No, not at all. It is our standard procedure after a successful attack to surface, only to capture the opposing commander and chief engineer, for intelligence purposes. We do not have the capacity to rescue enemy combatants, I'm afraid."

"But you did stay to rescue the rest of us," said Walker.

Hartenstein again took a long pull on his cigarette and then smudged out the butt on his shoe. "I would like you to think that I am a man driven only by kindness. God knows, I wish I could be. But you know as well as I, that I am a military commander under orders at war. This extended mission began in order to rescue Italian POW's, our own allies whom I had torpedoed.

Only then did we discover the rest of you. I simply could not throw you all back into the sea. I am not a saint. But neither am I a monster, Mr. Walker."

"Comm to Captain on bridge," came across the external speaker. Hartenstein unhooked the phone from its cradle on the side of the conning tower.

"Captain here," he said to the phone.

"Sir, message from *U-507*. She and *Capellini* will be surfacing within twenty minutes, Sir."

Hartenstein answered so quickly that he seemed to have rehearsed his lines. "Advise *507* to pull alongside and *Capellini* to remain submerged until *507* operations are complete and we signal *Capellini's* turn." There was no need to give enemy aircraft extra easy targets.

He then switched a selector knob to speaker. "Attention all crew and passengers. This is the captain. Make ready to receive two more U-boats which will be surfacing alongside within the hour. Two-thirds of passengers will be designated by crew to transfer to each of the boats. All boats will then rendezvous with surface vessels over the next two days to transfer passengers ashore. Please cooperate with all orders. Leutnants Peter, Francesci and Fischer please report to me at Conn topside. This is all."

Earlier in the day, approximately a fourth of the passengers had been transferred to the *506*. Having done all it could, *506* then immediately departed to get away from the potential target zone since coordinates had been relayed in the open. She was already vulnerable to air attack since hundreds of passengers on the deck forced her to run on the surface. *U-506* was now serving as the pathfinder for the other boats to follow on a north-northwest heading toward Dakar in Vichy-controlled French West Africa.

When all three junior officers reported, Hartenstein addressed them. "Gentlemen, I think you'll agree that the passenger transfer this afternoon was somewhat less than efficient. I want you to immediately organize our remaining guests into three boat groups. I want you to be firm but gentlemanly in how you deal with these people. They are at their wits end, and I do not want to create a mob reaction. Keep families together. Decide among yourselves how you want to do this. I want all groups ready within twenty minutes. Let's move, gentlemen."

By nightfall, the *507* and the Italian *Capellini* had their respective share of travelers and were trailing the *506*. By morning, *U-156* was once again alone.

CHAPTER 37

ASCENSION

The little island in the middle of nowhere was only about the size of cities that most people never know about. It lay just south of the equator, midway between Africa and South America, halfway between the equator and the Antarctic Circle. It rose two miles high as the tip of a volcano that was millions of years older than the human race. Not one soul even knew it existed until the Portuguese stumbled across it in 1501. They named it on and for the day which commemorated Jesus Christ's ascension into heaven. Now this island was the only place in twenty million square miles of the South Atlantic where mere mortals could also ascend into the sky.

The rocky spit had a way of rising up onto the stage of history every now and again. It was once a garrison which the British established to guard the exiled Napoleon on nearby St. Helena. It next appeared in the scientific journals of Darwin who visited it on the *HMS Beagle*. After a hundred years of relative obscurity, the island would not miss this world war the way it had missed the last one. In the last few months, Hitler's U-boats had become an increasing menace to merchant supply lines in the South Atlantic. After receiving permission from Britain, the United States began a ninety-day race to build a top-secret antisubmarine airbase on Ascension. The 38th Engineer Combat Regiment did the impossible from March to June, 1942. The first American reinforcement planes reached the base on the 20th of July. The main cadre arrived on August 14th. On September 15th, a certain B-24 Liberator arrived. The next morning, Ascension Island would mark its day of infamy in the annals of human history.

16 September 1942
United States 1st Composite Antisubmarine Squadron
Wideawake Airfield
0400 hours

"C'mon, Tesarek, get your back under this thing!" said Henzelman. "The two of us can't be hoisting this pig forever!"

The three ordnance men were hoisting up into the bomb rack another three-hundred-and-twenty-five-pound Mark XVII aerial depth charge. Henzelman had a bear-caliber body that had gotten him drafted onto the senior varsity football team when he was still in eighth grade. Clint Olsen was no slouch himself, with all 180 pounds of barrel chested muscle built close to the ground. Bob Tesarek had the height. All three of them were from the upper Midwest, so they had taken to calling themselves the Packers. Packing ordnance is what they did.

Compared to the garbage can depth charges dropped off surface ships, the air dropped Mark XVII was more cylindrical. It was therefore the "football." Henzelman and Olsen would use a t-bar grab-jaw to lift up the three-foot canister into the receiving rack of the Liberator's bomb bay. At six foot two, Tesarek's job was to crouch under the explosive load and bench-press it up into the rack while the other two would finagle it into the release catches. Back in high school, successful delivery of the football often used war imagery, such as "bombing" the other team or "obliterating" the opponents. Never did these wanna-be warriors imagine that that's exactly what they soon would be doing with a "football."

B-24 ordnance came in all sizes, shapes and weights. Liberators had only been dropping depth charges for less than a year. Antisubmarine warfare was not what this plane had been originally designed to do. From its very first depth charge attack, the Liberator had been plagued by unreliable releases of the weapons. Loading crews had to become masters of adaptation, but Tesarek's back was running out of time. "So how much longer is it going to take you guys to lock it in?"

"Shove it up just another inch or so," said Olsen. "... trying to get it to seat right. It's like it's a quarter-inch too long. Can't figure, the last one snugged in just fine."

Henzelmann offered practical wisdom. "Let me give her a little ball peen encouragement."

"Just try not to encourage the fuse, would'ja?" said Tesarek who was underneath.

As the crew chief, Henzelman was the quarterback who called out his cadence in the "hut-hut-hut" of three hammer taps until the canister seated itself into place. "OK, Tesarek, I think we're good." In a mocking, sing-songy voice he said, "You can come out now."

Tesarek eased back down. "This one just about killed me." As if to take him up on what he said, the three-hundred-pound depth charge dropped from its jerry-rigged latch. In football, the receiver usually sees the ball coming. Not in this game. Not this time.

Midnight air raid sirens just did not happen. At least not on American airfields. But it was a siren that was slicing through the early morning darkness. Every man rocketed out of deep sleep and was pulling on gear when the door burst open and half a dozen bare overhead lightbulbs burst on. The all-night Officer of the Day burst in. "Congratulations, gentlemen. Your plane just scored its first direct hit."

Until what just happened, Lieutenant Howard had been at the end of his all-nighter in the Orderly Room. He was not particularly concerned about how he woke up the flight crew that had been in dreamland throughout his shift. And, he did not like the fact that one of his men was the base's first casualty, which wouldn't have happened if not for these uninvited guests.

As if the groggy crew might have missed his tone, Howard turned up the attitude. "Time to rise and shine and bomb the bunny, turtle boys!"

This, of course, was a reference to the turtle nose art on their heavy bomber. It had already earned the crew more than a little good-natured kidding on the base.

"How about that? A bat-crap hotel with wake-up service!" griped the top-side gunner.

"Stow it, Hennessey, before you find out what other buildings around here are made of bat guano!" said the pilot. Even the base guardhouse was constructed of nature's local building material.

"Gentlemen," said the host-with-the-most finesse. "In case it escaped your attention, the name of this oceanside resort is called Wide. Awake. Airfield."

Lieutenant Harden apologized to the Officer of the Day. "Sorry about the manners of my crew, Lieutenant. But what's going on? Sirens, you busting in here in the middle of the night talking about a direct hit, something about bombing some rabbit."

"You guys going wheels up in forty-five is what's up," said a pleased-as-punch Lieutenant Howard.

"Come again?" asked Harden.

"You remember that Brit liner?" said Howard.

"Thought that got wrapped up yesterday," said the co-pilot in the longest string of speech anyone had ever heard from him. Two of the crew members got their heads together and shook hands. "You're on."

"Yeah," said the Ascension officer, "a lot of out and back but not much else." Referring to one of their light bombers, he said, "A Havoc drew fire from a pair of U-boats yesterday morning, so we sent out a couple B-25's. But they didn't see anything."

"So why now?" said the pilot.

"Got a priority message last night from the Brits at Freetown," said Howard. "They've got a couple ships on their way to look for floaters. Should be on point sometime this morning. Asked if we could do some fly-over this morning to help out. Richardson wants you boys up, first sun-up."

"Uh, one second," said Harden. "Was that you in my dreams, dear, or did you just say something about a bombing mission?"

"You don't want me in your dreams," said the all-nighter.

"So, what's that all about?" said one lieutenant to the other.

The Officer of the Day had a gift for stating the obvious. "Well, you are a bomber crew."

"Yeah, but I thought you were saying this is just a peek-a-boo mission," said the co-pilot.

Hennessey was silently counting words on his fingers. "That's fifteen, Jingles. Beat the last one by nine. You owe me."

Howard ignored the gamblers. "Not if we're lucky. That liner was bitten by a U-boat. That A-20 yesterday was shot at by two U-boats. Captain thinks you could have good fishing along the way. Hence, the depth charges you're getting fitted out with."

"Depth charges? We don't have the right racks and release gear for depth charges," said the bombardier. "We're tasked for land missions! We don't know a stinking thing about dropping depth charges!"

"That's why Richardson had crews jerry-rigging your bays all night, so you can cater depth charges on this run," said the base officer. "That's what the siren was about. Those depth charges are almost impossible to fit into the bomb racks. The crew had to gin up the release latches and one of them didn't hold. A three hundred pounder came loose and flattened one of my guys."

"Killed him?" asked Frankie.

The messenger was in a hurry. "Have no idea. Mess will be ready in fifteen. Captain needs to see you ASAP, Harden."

WITH EVERY MOUSE & MAN

Ten minutes later, 1st Lt. Jimmy Harden, pilot of the base's only long-ranger, was in the office of the base senior operations officer, Captain Robert C. Richardson III.

"First Lieutenant Harden reporting as ordered, Sir."

"At ease, Lieutenant," said the senior officer.

Harden changed from his rigid at-attention pose to the just as rigid at-ease position of legs spread at shoulder width, hands clasped behind his back and eyes facing forward, "Thank you, Sir."

Now that formalities were over and the necessary pecking order officially acknowledged, it was the prerogative of the senior man to relax things a bit. Richardson only outranked Harden by one bar anyway.

"Have a seat, Jim," said Richardson. "Smoke?"

Harden took the hospitality as permission to be honest. "Not before my first cup of Joe, if it's alright with you, Captain."

"Make it Rich when we're in here." Then he called out to the corporal in the front room, "Smitty, get a cup in here for the Lieutenant?"

"Right away, Sir!"

"You'll like it. Usually pretty fresh since that's about all that keeps the guys awake in here over the night shift. Except tonight. We've had more than enough to keep us all awake. I've let you and your boys sleep as long as possible for a reason."

The pilot hunched his shoulders forward to brace himself for the possibility of unwelcome news. "Kind of had a sense something was coming."

"Yeah, well, here's the thing, Jim. Freetown rang us up late last night and asked if they could trouble us. The Brit's can be nice and polite when they need something." Then he looked around for the thought he had dropped, ". . . if they could trouble us to send up some air cover. It's that *Laconia* thing. They've sent out two search vessels that should be arriving on station sometime this morning. U-boats in the area have been a little less than welcoming recently."

"But didn't our 25's handle things yesterday?" asked Harden.

"Glad you're already saying 'our.' That'll make this thing a little easier," said the captain.

"That bad, huh?"

"No, not really," said Richardson. "In fact, you might even have a little fun. How often does a Liberator get to go on a bombing mission without having to worry about enemy fighters or heavy flak?"

Especially for a combat pilot, it's not an easy thing to admit that you've never actually been in combat, especially when you're sitting in the middle of a war that everyone else is fighting. But Harden was about to place the lives of his entire crew on the line for something they had never trained to do.

Harden cleared his throat, "Uh . . . truth in advertising, Rich: this will be our first real life bombing mission. We've never done anything with depth charges. In fact, we've never yet hit a single thing in anger, as they say."

Richardson bit the inside of his lip while he took that in. "Anyway, the 25's don't have the range to spend much time hanging around the search area that these people are requesting. That's where you boys come in. Now, I don't have the authority to order you on missions. That's why I'm asking."

So now, Richardson was putting him in the position of risking the lives of his men for a mission that they did not have to do. In seconds, the young officer would have to balance duty to his men with duty to command, weighed on the scales of common sense and personal ego and then served up on a platter of honesty to the man before him and the men awaiting him.

After ten seconds of silence, Richardson took on a British accent, "So what do you say, old son? Can we . . . trouble you . . . to help out the old home office?"

The junior officer cocked his head in mock reflection. "Well, since you have gone to all the trouble to gas up our ride, check the oil and change the depth charges, how can I say no?"

There were two rapid knocks on the door of the closed office. "Yes?" said Richardson. The door opened and one of the clerks stuck in his head. "It's Tesarek, Sir. They need you right away."

CHAPTER 38

THE HELPING HAND STRIKES AGAIN

16 September 1942
U-156
Two hundred miles north northeast of sinking
0920 hours

In four short hours, the bomber crew was searching a couple hundred miles out to sea on its first real-life combat mission. They were about to make the acquaintance of a U-boat crew that was mopping up its twenty-second victory.

On *U-156*, Second Watch Officer Silvester Peters called down from the conning tower, "Bridge to Captain!"

Hartenstein was below deck, checking navigational charts. "Captain here."

"Peters, Sir. Lookout thinks he spotted a glint in the sky on the horizon due south."

One of the deck-top castaways noticed the lookouts pointing toward the horizon. He followed the direction of where they seemed to be pointing. He shielded his eyes with his hands as he gazed seaward. This attracted the attention of a couple others who did the same. Soon, the entire crowd was standing up and pointing as the noise of excitement quickly built into a cheering crowd of hopeful chatter.

A desperately hopeful voice cried out from somewhere in the closest lifeboat. "They see us!"

Another passenger sent up a prayer of sorts. "Thank God, they're sending help!"

A voice cracked with excitement from a teenager in the second lifeboat. "C'mon, baby!"

"It looks like your broadcast worked, Sir," said Mannesman to Hartenstein. "It sure took them long enough."

The skipper gave it some thought. "Could have taken some time to make it up through their chain of command. They're probably being a little cautious about what to do with a transmission in the clear from an enemy U-boat. Probably not a protocol for something like that."

"Better Late Than Never"

"L.T., you see something off to the right?" asked waist gunner Pfc Sawyer.

"Not sure I can make out anything. About how far? Anyone else see anything? How about you, Yakkey?"

"Nope."

"No, I think Frankie's right," said the tail gunner. "I think I see something."

Harden dipped the right wing to change course forty-five degrees. "Won't hurt to check it out. That's what we're here for. Make sure you can get us back on course if it turns out to be nothing, Chuck," he said to his navigator. "Check your guns, boys. Just in case."

Short bursts could be heard all around as the gunners made sure their weapons would not jam.

Just that quickly, a target clearly came into view. Harden began a safe orbit two miles away from what clearly was a German U-boat. "I think we hit pay dirt, gentlemen. Stay sharp."

Now he threw his voice hundreds of miles back to Ascension. "Turtle One to Home, over."

"Home to Turtle, go ahead, over."

"Turtle One to Home. We got a bunny. Latitude 3°48'15.15" Longitude 15°26'1.24". Appears to be towing four lifeboats. Moving north-northwest. Please advise. Over."

The radio was silent for a full minute. Harden repeated, "Turtle One, Home. Do you read? Over."

"Home, Turtle. Read you five by five. Stand by. Over."

U-156

The Executive Officer of the *U-156* kept his binoculars tracking the distant aircraft. "Our friend clearly sees us but she seems to be keeping a safe distance," Mannesman said to his commander.

Hartenstein also had his glasses up. "I cannot figure out what kind of plane we're dealing with. You've got younger eyes, Gert. How about you?"

"Not much help either, Sir. Unless the enemy has something new, her speed and size at that distance make me think we're probably dealing with a bomber, especially with the range required this far out."

"Makes sense," agreed the senior. He picked up the Conn phone. "Radio, this is the captain. Any intercepted traffic?"

"Aye, Sir. I'm guessing it's American, Sir." Fortunately, the man with the ears on was the senior radio operator, Erick Hacker, who was proficient in English. "If my English is correct, Sir, it sounds like a plane talking about bunnies and turtles. Must be code of some kind."

Every time the mystery plane turned away in its orbit, the commotion on deck died down a bit. Then the plane would return closer, which once more turned up the volume of hope.

Mannesman revealed his own hopefulness. "It is a good sign that our visitor has shown no aggressive moves, wouldn't you agree, Sir?"

"I hope so," said the cautiously optimistic commander. "Have Peters make sure that the Red Cross canvas is secured and prominent."

Then the captain called down to Radio. "Hacker, any radio traffic coming from aircraft to us?"

"No, Sir. No change at all."

"Try to raise them, Mr. Hacker. Identify ourselves and inform them that we are transporting Allied military and civilian survivors of *Laconia*. Be sure to say that we are operating under proposed cease fire. Ask their identity and intention. Keep repeating.

"I don't have a good feeling about this, Gert," said Hartenstein to his second. "Somebody out there does not seem to have decided what to do with us. One way or the other, they are not going to ignore us."

The Executive Officer asked a question that sounded more like a statement of fact. "Your orders, Sir."

"Immediately begin moving all deck visitors to the lifeboats in tow," said the commander.

Just then, the crowded deck erupted in cheers as the ever-enlarging bomber once again turned toward them in its orbit.

"Keep our guests positive," Hartenstein told his officers. "Tell them we are moving them into transfer boats to prepare for rescue assistance. Gert, we may have only minutes. Prepare crew for immediate crash dive."

Only four lifeboats remained. Each of the thirty-person capacity tubs had to carry upwards of fifty people. Chivalry once again died on the decks as everyone rushed and jostled to ensure a place on board. 'Women and children first' meant that they were the first to get overrun.

"C'mon Walker," yelled the Yank, "let's clear a path!" Tony grabbed Lyn's hand and pulled her into the surging mob.

"I need both hands. Whatever you do, hang on to my belt in back."

Walker was following behind, serving as icebreaker for a young mother with a toddler in her arms. The first man who stood in his way didn't get out the second word of protest before he was flattened by the Brit. Tony Corbetta was shouldering men aside while he led Lyn and she led two youngsters.

Tony shouted to Lyn, "I need you in that boat there to receive others."

This had happened before.

Lyn was not about to lose him now. "But . . ."

Tony knew what she was protesting and answered the question he wouldn't let her ask. "I'll follow after we get the others in."

Within thirty minutes, all guests had been transferred into the four lifeboats which were tethered one to the other, end to end.

Hartenstein picked up the deck phone. "Engines one quarter."

The four lifeboats trailed out from the stern like a rear-guard picket line.

"Better Late Than Never"

Jingles perked up with excitement. "L.T. we have a message coming from that U-boat! Can you believe it?"

"Not until I know what it is," said the pilot. "Would you be so kind as to let me in on it?"

The signal man all of a sudden remembered what he was there for. "Right. Sir. Here it is: '*U-156* TO UNIDENTIFIED

AIRCRAFT CIRCLING U-BOAT. PLEASE IDENTIFY YOURSELF. UNDER PROPOSED TEMPORARY CEASE FIRE, WE ARE TRANSPORTING TO SAFETY MILITARY AND CIVILIAN SURVIVORS OF *LACONIA* SINKING. ON BOARD WOMEN AND CHILDREN. WHAT IS YOUR INTENTION?'"

"Oh, what big teeth you have, grandma," said Harden.

Dingle was a little confused. "You want me to send that?"

Harden couldn't believe his ears. "Of course not. These things travel in wolf packs. That makes this one a wolf."

"Sir?"

"A wolf in grandma's clothing is my guess," explained the pilot.

He was an Allied pilot and that was an enemy boat. Period. Like every warrior in every war, he had heard all the stories of the enemy's cunning treachery. He was new to the war and even newer to antisubmarine warfare. There was no way that 1st Lt. Harden could have known that in the last four months alone, German U-boats had rescued over two dozen Allied survivors in well over a dozen separate incidents.

"Want to go a huntin'?" asked the bombardier, 2nd Lt. Howie Nichols.

"Maybe," said the pilot. "This would be a good time to check and recheck your arming switches, Dropsey. Especially those depth charges since we've never used those."

"What are we waitin' for, Sir?" asked Otto Miller on the tail gun.

"Waiting for orders from the big boys. We don't have any experience with this kind of stuff. Come to think of it, we don't have any experience, period," said Harden.

"But we do have a few tons of bombs and depth charges, right, Sir?" asked the nose gunner. "Why not just fly down the chute and sink the thing?"

This time, the answer came over the intercom from the topside gunner. "Well, for one thing, smart boy, this is the first time we've bombed something that can shoot back."

Spinoza, the nose gunner, returned the verbal fire. "With what? What can they do, throw torpedoes at us?"

The leader of this gang needed to settle down the men and get them to focus. "Men, if we get the green light on this, you've really got to keep your eyes peeled. Besides heavy machine guns, they also shoot a spit wad just for birds like us," said Harden. He was referring to the standard 3.7 cm SK C/30 anti-aircraft gun which was a favorite of the super U-boats. "That little piece of artillery can toss thirty projectiles a minute at us, and all they need is for just one of them to set off our payload."

United States 1st Composite Antisubmarine Squadron
Wideawake Airfield

The Executive Officer reminded Cpt. Richardson, "Sir, Turtle is waiting orders."

"Get back to them with a 'wait one.' I'll be back in a moment. First, notify Ronin's office that I'm on my way to see him immediately with a top priority." Richardson dashed out of his office to confer with Colonel James A. Ronin, the senior Army officer at Ascension.

The commanding officer did not let the intrusion interrupt whatever he was writing. "What's up, Rich?" asked the senior man who did not look up.

"Well, Sir, late last night, Freetown called to say that they had sent out a couple auxiliary ships to fish out whoever they could find from that *Laconia* sinking. They asked if we could lend some air cover. So, early this morning, I dispatched that B-24 transit crew to see if they could help out."

Ronin kept working on his project. "And?"

"Well, the thing is, Sir, those fly boys seem to have actually stumbled on a U-boat that's staying on the surface."

The boss looked up from his paperwork. "We sent out somebody else's plane to do *our* job?"

"Yes, Sir. They've got the range that none of our kites have to go out that far and spend any time at all on station. I didn't actually order them. You might say they volunteered. Sort of."

Ronin bobbed his head. "You might say, huh? Sorta volunteered? Please say you haven't rushed over here to tell me that they got into trouble." That's all he needed, to lose a Liberator and its crew that didn't even belong to him.

This time, Richardson could say something more than 'Yessir.' "No, Sir."

Ronin went back to his desk work. "So, they nailed it?"

Richardson hesitated just a moment, shifted his weight and cleared his throat. He wasn't sure that his next answer would be the correct one. His boss belonged to the he-who-hesitates-is-lost school of thought. "Not yet, Sir. They're waiting orders to attack."

Ronin looked up again. "Why do they need orders to take out a target of opportunity?"

"Well, that floating can seems to have four lifeboats in tow filled with men."

"Did Freetown say anything about some U-boat doing a rescue?" asked Ronin.

"Not to my knowledge, Sir."

"Sounds like bait to me, Rich. What are your thoughts?"

"That's exactly what I'm thinking. Reminds me of an old sniper's trick," said Richardson.

"Want to have the boys sneak in for a closer look?" asked the CO.

"No, Sir. I figure that's exactly what the Jerrys want them to do so they can blow them out of the sky. These sweethearts carry flyswatters. In fact, day before yesterday, a couple of those tubs tried to take a bite out of a Havoc. Didn't seem to be a whole lot of goodwill then."

Ronin thought for a moment. "Two U-boats then and another one now."

The junior officer said, "That's what bothers me, Sir. And those are only the ones we know about. Wondering if something's building. What if they've discovered us and they're fixing to blow up the field and the fuel dumps? They caused that mess a few months back on the Aruba refineries." Richardson would have flipped to know that the U-boat right now in his sights was the very one that had made that daring raid on Aruba.

The top guy relied on his next guy. "What do you propose, Rich?"

Richardson remembered what he once had been taught as a brand-new second lieutenant. This right here was what they liked to call a "bet your bars" kind of situation. If, against your better judgement, you followed the book and things went badly, you could be blamed for not using your head. On the other hand, if you departed from the book and things went poorly, you would certainly be blamed for not following procedure. A battlefield commander always had some authority to adapt orders to the situation at hand, but he had better be right. If you succeeded, you and your career continued. Otherwise . . .

The Captian threw the dice. "Take them out, Sir."

"I agree," said the Colonel. "You have my support."

"Better Late Than Never"

The crew aboard the heavy bomber was having a hard time staying awake. For the last three hours, they had been vigilant as hunting dogs on the trail of a scent. But since they spotted the U-boat, they had been standing off at a distance awaiting orders. Around and around and around they flew, when this would end, no one knew. In all their fantasies of heroic combat, abject boredom had not been part of the picture.

All the months of training and waiting and training and waiting now came down to this. It wasn't what they thought they had been trained for. But it really was what they had been trained for: hurry up and wait. And it was exactly what the officers had been taught to expect, that no plan ever survives the first ten seconds of action.

The pilot, Jimmy Harden, had been the one to name the plane and he was beginning to wonder if he had jinxed them by naming it *Better Late Than Never*.

Just then, the radioman said, "L.T., incoming from Home: 'Sink sub.'"

"Acknowledge 'Wilco,' Jingles." 'Wilco' was short for 'will comply.' "OK gentlemen," said Harden, "welcome to the war. Guns hot. Arm your switches, Dropsey. Confirm when bomb bays are open."

"Confirmed. Bomb bays are now open."

Then to his co-pilot, Harden said, "I don't know what they're going to toss at us, Dick, but let's really try to hold this thing steady. I'm not looking forward to knocking on their door more times than we have to."

"Gotcha," was all Schultz said.

Harden increased speed to more quickly complete a wide arc, keeping the plane as distant a target as possible. He was two miles out when he throttled up and leveled off at two hundred feet to line up for a stern to bow pass over the U-boat.

"Nose and Ball, keep your eyes open," Harden said to his nose gunner and to his ball turret gunner. They were the two who would have the best look-see at the U-boat on approach.

"Right, Sir," replied Cpl. Sal Spinoza in the nose.

Tiny Tim echoed the acknowledgment from the belly turret, "Roger that, Skipper."

As a typical B-24 crew, these gunners had been trained for high altitude bombing missions over land. On the aerial food chain, their natural enemy was the fighter. Tiny Tim in the ball turret was known for two things, both of which earned him the nickname from Charles Dickens' classic. Like all ball turret gunners who had to be squeezed into plexiglass bubbles under the B24's belly, his stature was, well, tiny. And, like his namesake, he was always the kid who would ask the question that others were thinking, but no one would ask. "Uh, beggin' Lieutenant's pardon, Sir. Are we expecting to see fighters out here? What are we looking for?"

"That boat's got some pretty heavy artillery down there," said Harden. "You see even the tiniest movement toward any of those things and I want you to dust the deck. Got it?"

"Roger that, Sir," answered both gunners.

U-156

On the waters below, every soul on and off the U-boat had been holding his breath to see what the plane was going to do. Every single mind had been asking the same question of why it had been just floating in the air and not doing anything. Surely it had spotted them, or why would it be hanging around at all?

Since Captain Hartenstein had deferred to his better-sighted Executive Officer, Mannesman had been glued to his binoculars every second since the aircraft had been in sight. "Sir! She has made a turn and is lining up for an approach on our stern."

All too soon, it could be seen that this was indeed a bird of prey that had made up its mind as it charged through the skies. Like an American bald eagle, it was at once a glorious sign of freedom to some and a terrifying predator to others.

Four lifeboats of bedraggled victims suddenly became a cheering section of spectators who rose to their feet to wave in the B-24. None of them knew that the approaching plane was called a Liberator. Someone said, "Have you ever seen anything so beautiful?" The plane adjusted its glide path. "Look! He's waggling his wings!" Everyone was waving with both hands. Some almost fell out of their boats in their excitement.

Hartenstein was not so sure. Was this plane the answer to his broadcast prayers for assistance? Still, he felt like a rabbit staring up into the beak of an eagle coming straight for him. Since he had no way of reading the minds of flying men, he had to prepare for the worst scenario. He immediately picked up the phone, switched it to loudspeaker and commanded, "Crew, cut loose all lifeboats. Attention lifeboats, move away as quickly as possible."

He needed to rapidly separate from the lifeboats to protect them from becoming collateral damage in the event of crossfire. He also needed top speed so that if the bird opened its explosive talons, the U-boat could make its fastest dive for cover in the rabbit hole of the deep. He switched to internal communications, "Engines all ahead full! Engines all ahead full!"

The job of an Executive Officer is to read his captain's mind. Hartenstein's defensive orders made his danger assessment all too clear. "Sir! Should we order guns manned?"

Hartenstein was still playing both horns of the dilemma. "Not yet. We cannot be sure of their intentions and I do not want to force an unnecessary attack."

On the U-boat, the question was what the men in the plane would do. On that bomber at that very moment, the question was what the men in the U-boat would do. The flyboys had never yet been in combat, much less antisubmarine operations. "Nosey" looked down at the waves racing beneath them on the approach. It all of a sudden dawned on him that he would be the very first one on either side to take a swing. He had never shot anyone in his entire life. As a kid, he had been in a couple scuffles. But each little gladiator had spent most of his time hopping around, waiting to see if the other guy really was going to do this. He muttered to himself, "If I open fire, then they'll probably shoot back and I'm just hanging out in the wind. But if I don't fire, then maybe they won't either." Already he was thinking more like a combat-experienced soldier whose main concern was just getting out of this thing alive.

Underneath, in the ball turret, Tiny was already thinking that he would open fire only if and when Nosey fired first. After all, Sal was the one up front and would see things first.

Every inch inside the entire bomber, every molecule of air, and every cell of every crewman vibrated in thunderous synchrony with the forty-eight hundred horsepower of its four turbo supercharged, radial Pratt and Whitney engines. Two hundred feet below, the same thing was happening on and near the *U-156* as rolling thunder approached. The rumble grew louder and louder and soon was felt more than it was heard. The deck itself shivered from the approaching engines above and from the U-boat's desperate engines below.

The raptor quickly doubled in size, doubled again and yet once more. Just as it passed over the first lifeboat in line, the bomber dropped its first "stick" of three depth charges. The first canister fell ten feet short of the stern and exploded three seconds below the surface. The shock wave and ripple surge lifted the stern screws out of the water before the U-boat crashed back down, throwing all deck personnel off their feet.

The other two depth charges fell wide. But the waves of those eruptions summated with those of the first charge and with the splash of the U-boat. A ten-foot-high rolling pin of water capsized two of the lifeboats and spilled out most of the victims from the other two.

"Crash dive! Crash dive!" ordered the U-boat commander. Within mere seconds, all deck personnel had scrambled down hatches which were then locked tight. The only people on the sea now were those caught between the vanishing U-boat that had rescued them and the approaching bomber that should have rescued them.

After the raptor had done its work from above, the sharks and barracudas began their work from below. With all eyes cast skyward, none of the swimmers even noticed when two among them were silently jerked out of sight. Then someone screamed. Another called the alarm, "Sharks! Sharks!" A chorus of screams distracted all eyes from the approaching hell on high.

"Better Late Than Never"
Preparing for pass #2

Normally when he wasn't trying to dust off enemy fighters, the main job of the top turret gunner was to be the plane's engineer and keep mechanical things working. But there were no enemy fighters. So, the crew's top sergeant also saw his role as kicking a little butt from time to time.

One well-crafted piece of sarcasm could accomplish so much in a situation like this. The same remark could establish dominance and mollify the private insecurity of a man who was too old to be one of the guys but too outranked to be one of the officers. That same remark could also coach and discipline the younger troops. It was expected that a senior sergeant should be thought of as a jerk, he really wasn't one. He used humor to cushion the heavy hand. Not that Hennessy was conscious of all these motives. That was college-boy stuff. For him, the mouth just came naturally. "Engineer to gunners. What happened? All your guns jam up at the same time?"

The truth is, the senior man had always wondered if "his boys" would freeze up their first time under the gun. It was all too common in combat. So he said, "Need the engineer here to show you how to work those new-fangled shooty things?"

"Didn't hear anything coming from your gun either," said the nose gunner.

"Yeah, well, lookin' up the sky here makes it kind of hard for me to hit anything on the water," the Sarge said.

"No one on that deck was reaching for anything," said ball gunner, Tiny Tim.

"This ain't no Gunfight at the OK Corral, boys," said Hennessey. "You don't have to wait until they draw first."

2nd Lt. Milberg, the navigator said, "Yeah, what the devil was that all about? Not even making an attempt to take a pot shot? They sure had time to set up for it."

"I was thinking the same thing," said Harden. "But looks like we have to make another run at 'em."

The bombardier was a little chagrined. "Sorry about that, boss. This low-level stuff goes pretty fast."

"Don't worry about it, Dropsey," said the pilot. "Practice makes perfect. Hang on ladies. Round two." He banked the plane to port for another pass.

The intercom was just like a party line back home where every farm took turns using the same phone line. In the plane, everyone was constantly hooked into one seamless conversation with everybody else.

Ball Gunner joined in. "Saw something on that last pass, Sir."

"What'd you see, Tiny?" asked Harden.

"Well, Sir, I think I saw something like a big Red Cross on the front of that sub."

"Well, sure didn't look like any hospital ship to me," said Harden. "War ships are not allowed to use Red Crosses. That's just the wolf dressing up as Granny, right Tiny?"

"Guess so, Sir."

In the glass nose roost, Spinoza was the first to spot the red frothy killing field rapidly approaching below. "L.T.! They're being torn to shreds by sharks! I'm going to dust 'em off."

"Hold your fire!" said Harden. "You'll kill everybody!"

Two light-weight children had been knocked into the water by the first blast. Lyn was not going to lose another child. She immediately threw caution to the water and jumped in to rescue them. Just as quickly as she had entered the water, she grabbed each of them and pushed them back into the lifeboat. She turned to check for others when she spotted Tony freestyling toward her. "Lyn, get out! Sharks! Get out now!" But the gunwales on the rocking hull were so high that the exhausted and water-logged woman could do no more than hang on.

The slower that Lyn moved, the faster that Tony did. "C'mon, babe. Kick!" As she did, Tony hoisted her up and in.

When she turned around, she saw him still in the water. But he was not alone. A fin was making a bee line straight for him. She leaned over the gunwale and screamed, "Give me your hands!"

The predator was ten feet away by the time Tony got his arms over the side. But the lower half of his body was more than enough for bloody jaws to grab. She knew it was over.

While a real hunter shark was rocketing up from the deep, the hunted German shark was desperately trying to claw its way back down into the deep.

The conning tower of the U-boat was about half submerged when two depth charges dropped from the sky and kerplunked close to the hull. Before the raindrops settled, two massive geysers erupted beneath the U-boat, right under the conning tower. The U-boat dove out of sight, the bomber winged off in flight, the living huddled and the dead floated. Hundreds who had survived attack from below only four days earlier, had not survived help from above.

The lightning, thunder and rain of the attack were replaced by the gentle swells of silence. As the waves rocked Lyn back and forth into a semi daze, she drifted back to her Catholic girlfriends who mocked the nuns over an ancient rhyme: *As soon as a coin in the kettle rings, then out of Purgatory a soul shall spring.* Lyn wondered if this was Purgatory, since death had neither consumed her from below nor claimed her from above. But she also knew that she would not be stuck in the middle for long. The only thing she didn't know was what coin would spring her.

CHAPTER 39

TWO BECOMING ONE. AGAIN.

The blast concussion not only damaged the U-boat's controls, but it crushed anything that was in the water. Even the sharks took a mighty wallop that shocked them into flight. Several swimmers had dived under the water to escape shrapnel. Anyone whose head was submerged was instantly killed by the crushing concussion. These were the ones who floated to the surface with burst eyeballs hanging by occular muscles and optic nerves.

Everybody else in the water felt like he had been kicked by a horse in whatever part of his body had been below the waterline. Eventually, with Lyn's tugging, Tony flopped into the lifeboat. When he caught his breath, he helped Lyn drag others aboard. Before the sharks returned, a couple dozen other swimmers filled the two remaining lifeboats. Suddenly, all was quiet. No U-boat, no bomber, no sharks, no screaming. Just coughing.

Everybody was coughing. Everyone was winded. Everyone had swallowed seawater. A few had blood trickling from their mouths and noses.

"Hemoptysis," said the nurse.

"Hmm?" asked her almost-fiancé, against whom she was reclining.

"Bleeding from the lungs," she said. "These poor sods can't catch their breath. I think the explosions damaged their lungs. Concussion."

"Why just them? Most of us were in the water," said Tony. "Why not Eddie? Helen over there? Bobby's doing OK. So am I."

"I don't know, love. I think the four of you were clinging to the boat when the blasts went off, right?"

"Yeah, but we were still in the water like the others," he said.

The nurse said, "Where did you feel the kick?"

"Right in the back. Hurts like everything."

"But not your chest, right? Your chest was out of the water," she said. "The four of you were half out of the water, but I think the rest of them took the concussion to the lungs. You're feeling OK, aren't you, love?"

Tony groaned. "Except where it hit me, yeah."

She placed her head on his chest and held his hand. Tony had not yet learned to pay attention to where the nurse placed her ear or where she placed her fingers when she held his hand. She knew him better than he knew himself.

By nightfall, every one of the bleeders had died and had been gently laid to rest overboard. Tony and Lyn could not help but notice that the same ritual was happening on the other boat. Sometimes, the deceased would gently float for a minute or two before quietly and suddenly disappearing.

There were two groups of survivors in this boat. There was Lyn and the two children. Then there was Tony and the other three who had come to call themselves "the clingers." They were the ones who had been hanging onto the side of the boat when the depth charges went off. In another way, Lyn was in a class by herself. She was the only one who had the power to simply look at a person and see inside the body.

Throughout the waning day, the nurse noted that each of the clingers seemed to be growing a bit "shocky." They talked less, their eyes seemed a little vacant and they seemed increasingly pale. By twilight, each of the four began complaining about increasing abdominal pain.

"Dang it, nurse," teased her prime patient. "That horse must have kicked me a whole lot harder than I thought. Feels like I've got a knife in my gut. No, it's down lower." Always trying to make a joke, he said, "That make me a low-down patient?"

She knew all too well what it did make him. And there was no way that she was going to tell him or anyone else. That made her feel all that much more alone. That is, until she looked at the two littlest castaways, an eight-year-old little girl and a five-year-old-little boy. They weren't even brother and sister. Until now. They held on to each other as the most important person left in each of their little worlds. Long dormant terrors awakened within Lyn as she realized that she knew exactly what they were going through. At least as much as one person could know about another. A memory appeared from a children's hospital of long ago. That is when and where another little girl had decided to become just like Nurse Cummings.

Lyn leaned close to Tony. "Will you excuse me, love? I need to hire a couple little assistants to help me."

Tony squeezed shut his eyes, pursed his lips in pain and held his breath for a few seconds. Then he relaxed. "Sure, go ahead. I'm fine."

She bent down to walk over to the youngsters and then knelt before them. "Children? I need your help. You know what a nurse is, right?"

The little girl said, "Yes, ma'am. She gives shots."

"Well, not always. I'm a nurse and I do lots of things besides give shots."

"Like what, ma'am?" asked the polite, little boy.

"Well, when people are sick," said Lyn, "I try to make them feel as good as I can. The four grown-ups here are sick and I could use your help washing their faces and getting things I need. Do you think you two could be my nurse's assistants?"

"I could sing them some songs," the little guy said.

"Ok then, be sure to stay right beside me the whole time. OK?"

The nurse knew that her little caregivers needed care themselves. It had been only four hours since the attack, but the soaking cold alone had burned up tremendous energy inside everyone. Especially for a child, the tummy is close to the heart. Lyn noticed the small on-board box of survival staples.

"Nurse's helpers need to keep up their strength," she said with an exaggerated show of resolute courage as she unwrapped one biscuit for each child. No one else in the boat would be needing rations, except Lyn herself. However, she would not practice what she preached about keeping strong, because she needed to protect the reserves for the children.

Soon it was pitch black and she could no longer keep an eye on her patients. "Sally and Tommy, I need you to stay with Tony here while I check on the others." She moved from one clinger to another checking pulse, respiration and alertness.

Everyone's abdominal pain was increasing. Helen was the first to stop struggling. Lyn knew there was no one who could help lift. She used her patient transfer skills that were honed to comfort those who couldn't move on their own. Lyn managed to roll the woman over the side, hanging on to her to break the fall and mute the splash.

Tony himself was struggling with excruciating paroxysms of agony that ebbed and flowed. For the sake of little ears, he tried to restrain his moans and groans. As each wave of gripping pain began, he held his breath and pushed as hard as he could to hang on. The intensity would build and build to a crescendo that was always just out of reach. Each breath further shoved a hot blade of agony across his abdomen, up his right arm and across his upper back. Then it would subside.

During the next five minutes of blissful peace, he noticed increasingly fewer groans throughout the dark boat. The little nurses were wiping his brow with soaked rags. He was overwhelmed by their brave compassions.

He was almost out of breath but managed to say, "I hope I don't scare you too much. The pain is going to come again. It hurts, but I'm really OK." He huffed and caught his breath. "I love your songs, and I love you cooling my head. Don't worry. Looks bad. But I'll be fine. Okay?"

Tony started to breathe harder and faster. "OK, here it comes again." He held his breath, pushed against the pain and strained out a strangled gritting sound until he could hold his breath no longer. Then he took short panting breaths as the agony reached a peak and then slowly eased off.

When the torture subsided, Lyn was by his side. There were no more sounds in the boat. "They're gone, aren't they?" he asked Lyn. She squeezed his hand. "You're always taking my pulse, aren't you?"

"Can't put anything past you, Yank. You're a clever one, you are."

"I'm not going to make it, am I?"

"I think you four sustained abdominal bleeding."

"Sustained something," he agreed. "Oh crap, here it comes again."

"Bite on this," said Lyn as she gave him a rag to bite on. "Try to puff out your breath instead of holding it. Puff out your cheeks! Puff out your cheeks!"

When this round subsided, Tony realized that they'd better say what they wanted to say. Over all the days that they had been getting to know one another, they had danced around each other's hearts with romantic banter that was always just shy of declaration. He knew that in this ark, they were the last pair that he would ever be part of on earth. He needed to be sure that they were indeed a pair before they became extinct. "Lyn, Lyn, I love you." He took two rapid puffs. "So much. So much." Three more puffs. "I'm so sorry about this. I love you." Two more puffs. "You've got to remember. I love you."

She could not get out any of her own words. Her throat choked off each time she tried to speak. His voice got weaker so that she could only read his lips by touching them with hers. Until his lips moved no more, she breathed his last.

PART VI
AFTERMATH

CHAPTER 40

WE TOLD YOU SO

16 September 1942
Headquarters, Commander of Submarines
Avenue Maréchal Maunoury
Paris
2304 hours

Dönitz and his command staff were all awake at this late hour. His aide, Korvettenkapitän Joachim Kittel, stepped briskly out of the communications center, speed-walking straight for Dönitz. What he had in his hands was a message that he deemed somehow so upsetting that it was for Dönitz's eyes only. But he also wanted his colleagues on alert that something was probably about to happen, so he passed through three senior staff officers as he signaled trouble with barely raised eyebrows.

Moving at full speed until he was directly in front of the Admiral, Kittel came to attention, clicked his heels together, and bent at the waist as he snapped him a radio message. "Vizeadmiral, Sir. Message from *Eisbar* leader."

"Read it aloud, please," said Dönitz.

The Lieutenant Commander cleared his throat, "Begging your pardon, Sir. You might wish to look at this first. Sir."

Dönitz took a deep breath and slowly reached for the memo. Though the message was only a small paragraph, he read it for almost a full minute. He betrayed no emotion but handed it back to his aide.

Dönitz called out to his Chief of Staff, "Altenbush, assemble all staff officers here in precisely one hour!" The Admiral had immediate work to do with his tactical advisor. "I want Hoesch in my office in ten minutes." He snatched the message from Kittel and quickly exited to his office.

Precisely one hour later, the senior staff snapped to attention as the Commander of U-boat Operations marched back to the same spot with Kapitän zür See Gunther Hoesch in close trail.

The commandant immediately got to the point. "This received from *Eisbar* leader one hour ago: WHILE TOWING FOUR LIFEBOATS IN CLEAR WEATHER AND DISPLAYING LARGE RED CROSS FLAG FROM THE BRIDGE, WAS BOMBED BY AMERICAN BOMBER. AIRCRAFT DROPPED FIVE BOMBS. HAVE TRANSFERRED SURVIVORS TO LIFEBOATS AND AM ABANDONING RESCUE WORK. PROCEEDING WESTWARDS. REPAIRS IN HAND."

Dönitz drew the bottom line. "Gentlemen, to the point. We will not be put in this unfortunate dilemma again. We must ensure that, henceforth, boat commanders never again have the discretion to place their boats in jeopardy by conducting rescue operations. Regardless of circumstances. Gunther, please read the War Order we have just drafted."

The tactical advisor came to attention and recited the order.

"Number One: All efforts to save survivors of sunken ships, such as the fishing out of swimming men and putting them on lifeboats, the righting of overturned lifeboats, or the handing over of food and water must stop. Rescue contradicts the most basic demands of the war: the destruction of hostile ships and their crews.

Number Two: The orders concerning the bringing in of captains and chief engineers stay in effect.

Number Three: Survivors are to be saved only if their statements are important for the boat."

"Any suggestions?" said Dönitz.

The strategics advisor, the slickly quaffed Rudolph Motschenbacher, said, "Sir, I believe I speak for the entire staff when I say that you have drafted a necessary and superlative directive."

Dönitz again was less than impressed with the predictable adulation from the man whose skills had most to do with strategy of self-promotion. "Thank you, Rudi." Keeping his eyes on Motschenbacher, he said, "Any substantive comments?"

"If it please the Admiral," said Otto Stohlman. "Your courageous risks were thrown back in your face by an unworthy and opportunistic enemy. I would humbly suggest that the War Order be forcefully punctuated with a statement about the dishonorable treachery of the enemy."

"Do you have a particular statement in mind?" asked the commandant.

"Yes, Sir. Something like this: 'Stay firm. Remember that the enemy has no regard for women and children when bombing German cities!'"

"Excellent," Dönitz said. "Herr Altenbusch, append that statement as Number Four and transmit immediately to all boats. Dismissed."

So became The Laconia Order. Three years later, that directive would have Dönitz fighting for his very life at the Nuremburg War Crimes Trial on charges of ordering murder on the high seas.

CHAPTER 41

APPETITE

14 October 1942
U-156
Surfaced
198 miles northwest of Ascension Island

Twenty-eight days later, a lifeboat with one solitary soul was intercepted by the Vichy French cruiser *Le Gloire*.

The currents had kept Lyn's boat on a straighter course than that of *U-156*. The hunter had circled back and forth looking for other prey in the same area. While Lyn had drifted east toward Africa, that twenty-eighth day after the bombing found the U-boat two hundred miles further west. It had been three weeks since either of them had taken a bite of anything. Just a week after sinking the *Laconia,* the U-boat had claimed its last ship and its one last seaman.

Standing beside his captain in the conning tower, Mannesman took off his cap and let the wind blow his hair wild in the cloudless sunshine. "Now this is the kind of day that I enlisted for in the Kriegsmarine!"

Hartenstein stretched out his arms and took in a lungful of ocean air. "It's a U-boat day for sure. Haven't seen prey or predator for some time. Excellent visibility both up and down. I'd like you to rotate the crew topside so our boys can clear their lungs."

The Executive Officer said, "Yes, Sir. I'll have Peters keep it to a half dozen at a time so we can crash dive if necessary."

"Yes. About crash dives." Hartenstein didn't have to look at the records to have the last dive trial times all graphed in his mind. "I don't like the numbers, Gert."

The second-in-command pursed his lips and nodded in silent agreement.

Hartenstein said, "We came too close to being nailed by that bomber. It was only blind luck that they couldn't bomb as well as they could fly."

The Executive Officer now had another opportunity to weigh integrity against personal gain. "Not to quibble, Sir, but we could have dived a whole lot faster."

Hartenstein snapped his head up to lock eyes with the subordinate. He knew that Mannesman was being courteous in not stating the obvious. It was the captain's delayed order rather than the speed of the crew that almost sank the boat. When he finished that discussion in his mind, the captain broke eye contact. "You are correct, Gert."

"Please excuse my bluntness, Sir."

The boss paused and let out a breath. "I respect you for your courage in stating the truth. I will not repeat that diving error again." Almost to himself he reflected, "It did not help those people either."

The second-in-command may have waited just a bit too long to respond. "Nevertheless, Sir, I believe you are entirely correct about the dive times. At the beginning of this patrol, we were hitting the thirty-five second goal consistently. Now we cannot seem to break the mark of forty seconds."

"When did our times start to go down, Gert?"

"That is what bothers me, Sir. It was after the bomber. One would think that our dive times would have improved after that."

This puzzled the captain. "Exactly. Why would these numbers be going the wrong direction?"

"I'm not sure, Sir. But I've been thinking that the crew seems different. Slower, somehow. Not as spirited. No bragging. No joking. Even their card games seem boring."

Hartenstein reflected, "We've been out this long before. So, it's not the length of the patrol."

"If you'll pardon me for mentioning this, Sir. But I've been noticing the same things about you. Even the number of dive drills has gone down, Sir."

Hartenstein said nothing.

"Truth is, Sir, I'm thinking the same thing about myself."

"How do you mean, Mannesman?"

"Well, this is crazy, Sir. But I find myself thinking about those people we had to put off. Kind of got to know a couple of them. You know how the men gave up their bunks and then took up collections for those people?"

"Hmm."

"I think it was easier before," said Mannesman, "when all we thought about were targets and tonnage. It's not just numbers anymore."

U-156 would prowl another month on this patrol. It would hunt yet two more months on another tour. But it would never again claim another victim. This shark had rarely gone more than two or three days without feeding. But it would now trawl the depths as one that had lost its appetite. It would never again take another bite.

CHAPTER 42

CASABLANCA

12 November 1942
Vichy Prisoner of War Camp just outside Casablanca
Mediouna, Morocco
Dawn

For the last four days, silent dogfights could be seen high overhead. Detonations miles distant toward the coast were not only from bombers. Some of the nurses had served on ships and they recognized the two-part rhythms of naval bombardment. A roar of distant thunder followed by a four second pause would be punctuated by another rumble of impacting rounds, all at once, time after time, after time, after time. Each round of thunder transformed the months of monotonous existence into a moment of great expectations. The women did not know it, but Casablanca was on fire. These were the opening rounds of Operation Torch to liberate French West Africa.

For about a week now, the guards had been acting differently among the Allied women prisoners of the Vichy POW camp in Mediouna, Morocco. To a casual observer, the women might seem to have had a lot in common, since most of them were from the several nations of the United Kingdom. All of them spoke English. But they ranged in age from eighteen to sixty-three years of age. Many had never been married and some had husbands, though none of them knew where. Several were widows, and one had been twice, sort of. Some of the married had children and others did not.

The women came over many different kinds of paths to be in this particular camp. Some of them had been civilians in colonial posts, some were military, and one was both, sort of.

All were homesick, all had injuries and some had wounds that were visible. Some of the visible traumas were protected with ragged, makeshift bandages. Other women had recoiled into protective shells of isolated despair.

The women who had found ways to take things in stride were the ones who reached out to one another. Or maybe it was the other way around. For the last three nights, these women had no interest in sleeping. They stayed awake to listen to the music of battle. Each night turned Barracks 14J into a girls' pajama party of all-night chattering. When the guard control station snapped off all the lights in all the barracks, the muffled silly giggling would commence. Giddy dreamers would plan what they would do, what they would wear, what they would eat, where they would go and most importantly whom they would hold when their dreary days would be rescued by shining knights.

Some of the older girls had given the nickname of "Beautiful Dreamer" to the eighteen-year-old with long, yellow hair. She said, "The first thing I'm going to do when I get back is to go straight to a cinema."

Brunette-haired Millie had become the older, encouraging sister who played along with her. "So, what are you going to see?"

Beautiful Dreamer did not hesitate. "Oh, Bogie for sure!"

Tillie was the more substantial farm girl from North Wales who had learned to entertain herself because she had grown up far from neighborhood playmates. "Just imagine," she said without pausing for a breath, "What if one of those dashing pilots up there had to parachute out of his smoking Spitfire and he was on the run and he burst into our barracks to hide out and he turned out to be Sam Spade played by Bogie?"

Kelly was the older red-head with all the common sense of gravity. She marveled and just shook her head in smiling admiration of these young, free spirits. "Well, doesn't hurt to dream, Cinderella."

None of them had any way of knowing that right about now, Humphrey Bogart and Ingrid Bergman were about to open the world premiere of the blockbuster movie *Casablanca*. The Allies were timing that to coordinate with the liberation of Morocco. What the women were hearing at this very moment was the real-life soundtrack to the movie.

These days, the women were more frequently being confined to their stuffy barracks. It did not escape their attention that each time they were confined, they would feel the rumble of trucks. When allowed outside, they would be ordered to keep their eyes down. The guards whom they had come to know were increasingly being replaced with unfamiliar faces. These new minders did not seem aware of some of the kindnesses that had evolved over time. There were no favors and even less forgiveness. Things were much more by the books.

"So, what's up with you, mystery lady?" Lily asked one of the quieter ones. "You haven't said a word. What about your plans?"

"Oh, I don't know. Main thing is my mum and dad. I'm sure they think I'm dead." Then she chuckled a little, "When I show up, they may be the ones who drop dead!"

"How about your man?" asked Kelly.

"He's," Lyn paused and lowered her head a bit, "he's moved on."

"A real jerk, huh?"

A faint smile and a distant serenity came over the quiet one. "Not in the least. He was the finest person I think I've ever known. We were hoping to marry."

"But . . . he moved on?" Lily asked.

Lyn's only answer was the tiny rivulet of one tear down her left cheek.

"I'm so sorry," Lily said. "I shouldn't have pried."

Lyn pursed an appreciative smile, looked down to arrange something or other and quietly hummed to comfort herself.

"It's a beautiful melody, really it is," said her friend. "What is it?"

"Just a song that my mother left me with. When my adoptive mother took me in, they say I was still humming it. I've been humming it as long as I can remember," Lyn said.

"Does it have words?" asked her curious friend.

Lyn searched her memory. "As a matter of fact, I learned some of the words a little later, but I didn't understand what they meant. The preacher once told a story about how it was written." She looked down and faintly smiled. "In these last couple months, that story and those words have come to mean a lot. That's probably why you catch me humming it all the time."

"So then?" asked the audience of one.

"So then, what?"

"Well, are you going to tell me the story or what?"

"Oh, you probably won't believe it."

Lily said, "Try me."

Lyn noticed that nobody else was talking in the barracks. Everyone seemed to have dropped asleep right in the middle of their own conversations. Lyn lowered her voice to a whisper. She and Lily scooted closer to hear each other.

"Well, I don't remember the names and dates and all. I think it was sometime in the late 1800's or so," began the storyteller. "Anyway, this American business chap sends his family ahead of him to Europe for some reason. His wife and four girls on a ship for France I think. Somewhere near Ireland their ship collides with another and sinks and only the wife survives. The four girls all die."

Lily said, "This is supposed to have really happened?"

"That's what they say. Of course, the poor sod is devastated and boards the next ship to France to meet up with his wife. In route, his ship supposedly passes right over where the first one went down. The captain stops the liner so the mourners on board can pay their respects. This American chap is standing on the deck and looks down at those waters. Can you believe it?"

"This is totally unbelievable!" said star-struck Lily.

The storyteller herself was once again becoming a little overwhelmed. "Well, the story gets even better." She sniffed. "Then and there, he composes the verses to that song."

Lily's eyes were filling with tears. "I can't even imagine what that would be like. But you just survived a sinking yourself, didn't you?"

"In fact, I've survived two sinkings. Both were torpedoes. The first one took my mum. This last one took my fiancée. That's why the words mean so much to me."

"What are the words?"

"They go like this:

When peace like a river attendeth my way,
When sorrows like sea billows roll,

Whatever my lot, Thou hast taught me to say
It is well, it is well with my soul.

Though Satan should buffet, though trials should come,
Let this blest assurance control,
That Christ has regarded my helpless estate,
And hath shed His own blood for my soul."

Lyn faded off and then suddenly snapped back to the moment. "And it goes on like that. You probably aren't wanting a sermon though."

Lily was not done. "No, go on. Please."

"Let's see:

But Lord, 'tis for Thee, for Thy coming we wait,
The sky not the grave is our goal.
Oh trumpet of the angel! Oh, voice of the Lord!
Blessed hope, blessed rest for my soul.

And Lord haste the day when my faith shall be sight,
The clouds be rolled back as a scroll;
The trumpet shall sound and the Lord shall descend.
It is well, it is well with my soul."

A long silence followed.

Lily asked, "You believe all that?"

"I do," said Lyn.

Lily said, "But you don't seem all that excited about getting out of here."

"I guess I kind of try to make my peace wherever I am at the moment," said Lyn. "Not always good at that, but do what I can. I'm not very good imagining what's next in this world. Maybe I'm glad for that. There's always something. Everything seems to be so fleeting anyway."

"Kind of hopeless then, isn't it?" Lily said.

Lyn perked up. "Oh no, not at all. Just that I keep hoping for something other than the next bloody round."

"Like what?"

"You know, I've survived two sinkings, the Blitz, and now this," said Lyn. "And I'm still going to wind up dead like everyone else. That song is about the only hope I've got, that all of this is not all there is."

Three nights of sleeplessness had rendered everyone nearly comatose by now. Lyn and Lily succumbed like everyone else. The next thing they knew was a loud whisper.

"Hey, any of you awake?" No one answered.

"C'mon! Wake up!"

"Would you shut up?" came a groggy voice from across the dark room.

"Yeah, knock it off, why dont'cha? It's the middle of the night."

The wake-up caller persisted. "No, it ain't! I wake up the same time every morning when I hear the guards and the dogs coming to roust us. I don't hear anything. Not a bleedin' sound."

"Hey, she's right." Others were starting to come to.

"Hey, keep it down or House Mom's going to come busting in on us!"

"I don't think so, Milly. I don't think there's anybody outside."

Then, in the darkness, it dawned on them. "Hey, everything's totally quiet. No bombing. No planes. No trucks. That's how we must have fallen asleep."

"Who wants to look outside?"

"Yeah, right. And wind up in the hole for a week."

"Wait. Listen. You hear that?" Lots and lots of women's voices and hurried shuffling seemed to be coming from outside.

Lily was nearest to an aggressive banging on the door which almost shocked her off the wooden palette that served as her sleeping platform. An excited voice that was too loud for that time of the morning insisted, "Open up. There's no one out here. Everyone's gone!"

"Go on, Lily. Open it. Just a little."

Ever so carefully, she cracked the door. The woman on the other side pushed it further open. The flurry of a thousand feet could be heard and murmurs quickly summated to the cheers of a mob. Barracks 14J emptied to join the growing party in the assembly area. The earliest, pre-dawn lighting of the sky was enough to reveal no one in a uniform, no one in any of the guard towers. Just fifteen hundred cheering souls.

Except for one who watched from the doorway. She appeared to be talking to someone whom no one else could see.

CHAPTER 43

HERO

16 November 1942
U-boat pens
Lorient, Vichy France

T he pilot boat slowly guided *U-156* toward the receiving pen. All forty-three non-essential crew stood at attention on the deck. In the conning tower, the commander and his executive officer presided over the crew.

"Even unshaven, the men look good," said Mannesman.

Hartenstein let out a breath of resignation, "Well, I'm glad something does."

"Beg your pardon, Sir?"

The captain nodded toward the suspension wire which was dangling only three victory pennants. "Our longest patrol with the least tonnage. Last time we came in with eleven pennants, Gert."

"True. But we bagged our largest so far."

"Along with fourteen hundred of our own allies," said the skipper.

For the second time in his career, that he knew about, Korvettenkapitän Werner Hartenstein obediently made his way toward what he thought might well be the open jaws of the Gestapo. He had never heard of a U-boat commander being executed. Yet. At the same time, he would put nothing above the Gestapo. There was always a first time for everything.

Mannesman raised his binoculars to inspect the small receiving party on the pier. "Well, Sir, don't see any men in black leather trench coats."

Hartenstein gave a perfunctory chuckle.

"I do see a couple others, Sir. You might want to take a look."

He handed over the binoculars. Hartenstein saw none other than Grossadmiral Karl Dönitz. Beside the grand man was someone else with a photo tripod. Behind them was the customary welcome band. "I wonder what tune he has ordered them to play."

Twenty minutes later, the senior officer of the boat hopped off the deck of one world onto the pier of another. Hartenstein quickly stepped up to the senior officer of Germany's U-boat service. That was the customary signal for the band to halt wherever it was in the music. The junior man snapped a crisp salute, "Korvettenkapitän Werner Hartenstein reporting. *U-156* conclusion of war patrol. Sir!"

The Grossadmiral seemed almost fatherly. "Welcome home, Werner. It has been a long and, well, shall we say, adventurous voyage?"

"Yes, Sir!" responded Hartenstein to his commander. To himself he wondered if this is when the hammer would fall.

Dönitz slowly inspected Hartenstein, top to bottom. "If my memory serves, I believe that the last time we met was when I presented you with the German Cross. In gold, no less. That would have been only in February, according to my records."

"Yes, Sir!" He dared not correct Dönitz that the medal had been awarded in February, but not presented by the Grossadmiral until March, when they returned from their second war patrol.

With a subdued smile the Admiral said, "You seem to be getting into a habit of making this old man fly down here every time you return."

This is it, thought Hartenstein, who cleared his throat. "Yes, Sir."

Dönitz did not have to tell the commander to remain at attention. Instead he turned to the photographer with the tripod. "Are you ready?"

The tripod itself seemed to snap to attention as the Grossadmiral reached out to receive a box from an aide.

"Korvettenkapitän Werner Hartenstein, the Führer himself has ordered me to present to you the Knight's Cross of the Iron Cross for valor in saving the lives of over three hundred and fifty Italian allies at great risk to self, crew and boat." The band immediately struck up "Deutschland Über Alles" as Dönitz pinned the medal on Hartenstein, only the sixty-second U-boat officer so honored. The Grossadmiral took one step back and saluted Hartenstein who returned the salute.

Then Dönitz gestured the band to pause and he raised his voice to the crew which was still at attention on the U-boat. "This award to your commander is also an award to each of you. Your faithful courage made this possible. I salute you." And he did. From the conning tower, Mannesman ordered the men to return the salute. Then they spontaneously erupted in cheers.

Dönitz leaned closer to a stunned and speechless Hartenstein. "After the customary debriefings, I do not want to see you and your men until January 10th. You will then prepare to leave for your next patrol on January 16th. Until then you all take a well-deserved Christmas and New Year's rest. That is an order. Carry on."

"Yes, Sir."

CHAPTER 44

PARADOX

3 January 1943
Luther Church, Pastor's Study
Plauen, Germany

At precisely 1322 hours on the third day of 1943, Kapitänleutnant Werner Hartenstein suffered his first injury of the Second World War. After years of sure-footed dancing on rolling decks, the sea captain was felled by the ice-glazed ruts of his boyhood neighborhood.

"All I've got to do is break a leg a week before reporting back," he said to himself.

He lay flat on his back while half a dozen others rushed to assist him. An elderly lady stooped over the fallen hero. "Kapitan Hartenstein! Are you all right?"

"Nothing injured but my pride, Frau Schneller. I seem to have forgotten how to walk on land."

His boyhood boss, the shoemaker, mockingly waggled his finger at him, "So, I see you're still running on slippery streets, young man."

"Oh, I wish I had a good excuse like that Herr Demler," said Hartenstein as he carefully positioned himself on all fours on his way to the vertical. "Thank you, everyone. I think I'll be fine."

In the first days of the new year, even the bracing winter air felt clean and new. From three blocks away, the sea captain spotted the lighthouse of the church's familiar five-story tower with its tarnished bronze bell cap. Not that he needed any assistance finding the church that he and his family had walked to for decades.

He approached a complex of variously sized and shaped dark brown stone buildings that collectively were Luther Church. Luther Hall was the annex where non-worship activities, meetings and the Pastor's office were located. He couldn't help wondering how many New Years the old church had seen. In fact, Plauen's second oldest church had just celebrated its two hundred and twenty-first anniversary which was relatively young in the town's more than eight hundred years. Other churches had succumbed to plagues, town-leveling fires, and wars upon wars. During the Battle of Leipzig, the church served as a hospital. Today it would be called upon as a hospital of a different sort.

When Hartenstein opened the door to the main entrance, Pastor Achterhof came out of his study to greet the visitor in the parlor. The U-boat commander extended his hand, "Thank you for taking time out of your busy schedule to meet with me, Herr Pastor."

"Well, I don't think I'm going anywhere soon, unlike you, Wernie. Besides, I am the one who is humbled to somehow rate a private audience with Plauen's celebrity war hero!" he said with a wink. Hartenstein blushed to be treated like this by the man who had been his pastor since he was a small boy.

Pastor Achterhof's study was redolent of cherrywood pipe tobacco and leather-bound biblical commentaries.

"So, what's on your mind, young Werner?"

"I don't feel all that young anymore, Pastor."

"I'm sure you don't. But you and I do go back a long ways to when you really were young. Do you finally have your eyes on some lucky young lady? Lotte perhaps? And you're wanting to make arrangements, I presume?"

Werner tried to suppress a laugh. "Oh no, I wish it were that. But I think I want to wait until I'm sure I can be around for a wedding."

The pastor slowed things down a bit. "Is it about the war itself?"

"It is." Hartenstein lowered his head into his hands and rubbed his face like he was trying to scrub something off.

"You know, Werner, we're all very proud of you. Knight's Cross, is it?"

Werner looked to the floor and pursed his lips in concentration.

"What do you need to say, son?"

"That's part of the problem, Pastor. I can't. Not allowed to. Everything I do is classified."

"This have to do with something else hanging around your neck?"

The captain looked up. As always, Achterhof had a sense about things. "All I can say is that I don't feel good about how I got that medal."

"Most real heroes don't, young friend. In the last war, more men threw away their medals than most will ever know."

"I do my best to do the right thing. Sometimes I'm forced to see my work up close. It stinks, Pastor."

"So does an outhouse, Werner. Sometimes, what is necessary is revolting to look at, and even worse to smell."

"But I have to wear it. Right under my nose."

"In church we pray for you by name every Sunday. You and everyone else who is away. We pray for your safety."

"Thank you, Pastor. But in my particular line of work, I've learned that everyone dies."

"You had to go to war to learn that?" said the pastor. "You know, war actually does not increase the death rate."

Hartenstein nodded thoughtfully as he digested that thought for a couple seconds. "So, I've been thinking a lot about what comes after all this."

Achterhof didn't want to force the issue. "You mean after the war is over?"

"No, I mean . . . after." Werner paused, as if looking for a word. "After, you know, after *everything* is over."

"You always did have a philosophical streak in you, even as a young boy, Wernie. Always with the questions. Very good questions, in fact."

With no little exasperation, Hartenstein replied that this was not a hypothetical exercise. Since his last visit home, he had had to see his handiwork up close on the faces and bodies of hundreds upon hundreds of his victims.

The commander took a deep breath and let it out slowly. "Pastor, I have, uh . . ." and then he cleared his throat. Then he tried again, emphasizing the third word, "I have .... *had* ..... to kill dozens of men. And women. And God help me, even children." Another deep breath and exhalation, "And perhaps many more yet to come."

"Of course, Werner. In your position, I would assume so. But this is nothing new to you, is it?"

"That's the problem. It seems to get harder, Pastor."

"Maybe that is a good thing, Werner. Many people have to inflict pain: parents, doctors, dentists, nurses. I hope none of them enjoys it."

Werner said, "But those people are trying to accomplish something good."

"Are you not trying to do a good thing? To defend your home?" asked the pastor.

The penitent paused to consider that. "You made us memorize the commandments."

"Ah, you do remember!"

"That's my problem, sir. Especially the one that forbids killing."

"More precisely," said the Pastor, "the Hebrew word there is better translated 'murder.' What it was that God forbid was someone taking life into his own hands, all by himself."

"Nice technicality," said the commander.

"Are you sure that you wouldn't rather talk about the ways of young lovers, Werner? It would be easier."

Hartenstein just gave a faint smile of acknowledgment. "How do you come to terms with that commandment?"

Not even aged sages can experience most things. "Wernie, I'll be honest with you. I have never had to come to terms with that commandment in the same way that you do. I never had to go to war."

The one who did have to go to war did not know what to say. He dared not give voice to thoughts of unfairness that were going through his mind.

The pastor continued. "I'm sure you recall who it was that God gave the Ten Commandments to."

"Abraham, I think," said the former confirmation student.

"Werner!"

Quickly, Werner tried again. "Or Moses?"

The pastor slowly shook his head as he lowered it into his hands. He let out a sigh and looked back at his former student. "But did you know that, later, God did order Moses to kill? Even entire villages?"

"Now, I'm even more confused," said the student.

Achterhof nodded. "Of course you are."

"I'm needing help, Pastor, not riddles. God says He does not want us to kill, but sometimes He does want us to kill?"

"He forbids us to murder, but sometimes we are to kill, Werner. At least, when He is the one who orders us to do it. Has God ordered you to kill?"

"I don't know," said the U-boat commander. "I have never heard God speak out loud to me the way He does in the Bible."

"Me either," confessed the tired old servant.

The captain said, "I do what I have to do." He paused for a full twenty seconds. "But I hate it."

"I am glad to hear that, Werner."

Hartenstein looked downward and for a full three minutes of total silence his eyes roamed for an answer. "What if I have to face God for all of this?"

"I don't know," said the pastor. "Maybe ask His Son to stand in for you?"

CHAPTER 45

WITH EVERY MOUSE AND MAN

2 Mar 1943
U-156 surfaced
17 Miles North of Trinidad's Grande Boca
11° 2'26.86"N 61°47'29.30"W
1700 hours

At top speed and maximum down-angle, the boat put a fair amount of water between it and the four depth charges that had just hit in less than two minutes. Nevertheless, the boat shook violently and two crew sustained minor head injuries. Then, as suddenly as it started, it was over.

"Lucky shot," muttered Hartenstein after ten minutes of silence discipline.

In the conning tower, Hartenstein had just directed his second-in-command to begin rotating the crew topside for fresh air. The sky had been clear for maximum visibility. The B-18 bomber had no opportunity for sneak attack. It came in from the east and was well illuminated by the descending sun.

Lookout spotted it almost at the maximum range of about thirteen kilometers which gave the boat a fair chance of evasion.

"We are pretty close to land-based aerial operations, Sir," advised the Watch Officer.

Things seemed to be coming full circle. They had been here before. This is where it had all begun thirteen long months ago on their very first war patrol. They had made world headlines in what came to be known as the audacious Attack on Aruba. U-156 had been the dagger of Germany's furthest penetration into western waters. Long before the Allies had developed ways to counter U-boats, Hartenstein had been able to cruise unmolested and lob shells with impunity, to his heart's content. They sank 33,000 tons of shipping, blew up an oil refinery and killed dozens of merchant seamen. This time, it would be different because there were no longer any free lunches. Squadrons of hunter-killer aircraft made sure that no U-boat could surface to take a bite without having to pay for it.

"I want that convoy," said the commander who was looking for outbound Convoy TB-4. He did not know that when that bomber had disappeared after just one pass, it scrambled an entire swarm of other hunters.

At 2030 hours he raised the periscope and saw no evidence of surface activity in the darkness. "Surface!" he ordered. "Let's get some fresh air and charge up those batteries."

"Surfaced, Sir," came the notice that it was safe for him to break the watertight seal and clamber up the conning tower. He was followed by the routine entourage of surface crew who were hustling to man their respective deck positions. With all the noise and commotion of surfacing and clanging open the hatch, he did not hear the noise of another Bolo antisubmarine medium bomber. In less than five minutes and four hundred meters to stern, a spotlight projected out of the sky. It was clear that some night hunter knew they were there.

"Fire!" yelled the commander to his gun crew. He grabbed his mic and ordered, "Helm, prepare for crash dive on my command. Engines full ahead!"

Immediately, 3.7 cm red tracer rounds launched every other second from the boat's SK C/30U. The airborne spotlight winked out and the bomber broke off. "Dive! Dive!" ordered the skipper. The deck crew scrambled down the hatch and the boat descended into inky safety.

For thunder that never came, the crew waited in silence a full twenty minutes before their captain gave the all clear. "Congratulations gentlemen," announced Mannesman. "We achieved our dive time of thirty-five seconds." No chuckles and no cheers.

At 2300 hours, Hartenstein raised the periscope and saw no lights on the surface. He thought out loud, "All right then. Quiet long enough. Prepare to surface."

Mannesman double checked the skipper's intentions, if not his wisdom. "Sir?"

"That convoy is close and I don't want her to slip by while we hide. Blow tanks and surface."

He scittered up the hatch to not lose a second when it was clear to break seal. "We are surfaced, Sir."

With the deck crew right on his heels, he opened the hatch and was rudely greeted by the same patiently stalking bomber which now growled in on another attack. Four depth charges straddled the boat and exploded eight meters below. Immediately, the conning tower party dropped back down as the skipper ordered yet another crash dive. The boat was now damaged. Unbeknownst to Hartenstein, a fuel line was rupturing a trailing slick of oil that could easily reveal the boat.

"Not the good old days anymore, is it, Sir?" quipped his Executive Officer.

"You have a way of stating the obvious, Henry," replied the boss. "Things around here have obviously tightened up."

"Perhaps it is a different convoy that is reserved for us?"

"Perhaps. To paraphrase an old line, ''Tis better to have surfaced and lost, than to never have surfaced at all,' eh Gert?"

"Sir?" asked Mannesman.

"Nothing. Just a bad joke on a good poet."

Then to his Third Watch Officer, "Leutnant Fischer, get us out of here, due east but south and parallel to the shipping lanes. I want to be able to turn and intersect at will."

The next day, 3 March, at 1300 hours, while running deep and safe, three more depth charges exploded harmlessly, high overhead.

"Do you think our friends are playing with some kind of new toy that can see us?" asked the second-in-command.

Hartenstein called out to his senior radioman, "Hacker, have you boys picked up anything out of the ordinary?"

"Not at all, Sir. We've been trying to pick out anything unusual, but we've had no luck at all, Sir."

The skipper grabbed the intercom phone and called for his chief engineer. "Hansie, anything unusual on your end?"

"Could be nothing, but we've been keeping a watch on what could be a small drop in oil pressure, aft in one of the diesels," said the chief mechanic.

"How long?"

"Only since a couple of those kettlebangers bounced us around."

Hartenstein asked, "Think it's enough to trail an oil slick?"

"Hard to tell," said the engineer. "Wouldn't be too surprised though."

Hartenstein turned back to Mannesman, "There's our Judas. All we can do is stay deep, long enough for them to lose the scent."

For the next eighteen hours that's exactly what they did. At 0500 hours the next day the radioman heard a near distant convoy. Watch Officer Fischer awoke Hartenstein who sprang to command. To the radioman he asked, "What do we have, Mr. Jung?"

"Sir! Convoy approximately thirty-two hundred meters out and moving away. But a single set of screws is closing rapidly, Sir."

"Someone must have heard us. Take her down to one-eighty. I want total sound discipline. Brace for depth charges."

As though his order had just given permission to the enemy, the explosions began, each preceded by the click sound of a trigger mechanism: Click: Wham! Click: Ka-bloom! Click: Blam!

The lights flickered throughout the boat. Silence.

Then again, only much closer. Click: Ka-rumpf! Click: Ka-rumpf! Click: Ka-rumpf!

Pipefittings sprang high pressure jets of water. Two torpedo men were knocked off their feet into unconsciousness. Silence.

Then another trinity of terror. Click: Ka-blam! Click: Whump! Click: Whump!

Silence. More silence.

"Screws fading, Sir," whispered the young man who replaced his headphones which he had earlier removed to protect his hearing. Hartenstein nodded but said nothing for another ten minutes of sacred silence. Then he broke silence discipline, "Damage reports."

He picked up the phone to contact engineering. "You boys OK?" he asked.

"A much larger drop in oil pressure on the other diesel, Werner." The Chief engineer held the same rank as the commander and so under certain circumstances, such as over the phone, he could address the skipper by first name. "I have no doubt now that we're bleeding for the whole world to see upstairs."

"What do you recommend, Hans?"

U-156 was badly injured. A long way down, a long way from home. And well known to some very, very intent hunters.

"We could proceed on one diesel at a time while we try to fix any oil leaks," replied the mechanical expert.

"I agree. Let's do it now, Hansie." For the next thirty-nine hours, *U-156* proceeded, mercifully unmolested. All oil leaks were repaired and the hunted hunter proceeded due northeast. Well into the darkness of 2000 hours on 5 March, the captain voiced a concern that was beginning to creep into the minds of a few others, as well. "If we don't send a message back home, they will soon be notifying our families that we are lost at sea."

"Hopefully, our oil slick and our disappearance have convinced our friends upstairs of the same thing," said Mannesman.

"Alright then," said the skipper, "let's surface. Blow tanks and bring us to ten meters."

"Ten meters, Sir."

"Periscope up." Hartenstein scanned in all directions and pronounced, "Surface!"

He couldn't help remembering the last time he had opened the hatch. It was quieter now. He wanted to linger in the clear and pleasant night air. But he knew that the stillness could be the stalking space of a predator. Immediately, he picked up the telephone handset and dictated the following message for the radioman to send to Berlin: GRID ED 4681 210 DEGREES 22 EELS, TRADE WIND 3, EXTREMELY HEAVY AIR ATTACK AND ENEMY COUNTERMEASURES. REQUEST ORDERS *U-156*.

Berlin must have been waiting for his signal. The reply came in ten minutes.

BETTER HUNTING.

In other words, "Two months at sea and no torpedoes fired? You'd better do better." It was amazing how much information could be conveyed in just two words.

There were two of something else. In addition to *U-156* and Headquarters, there were two other silent listeners in this conversation. One was a radio operator at Edinburgh Field, three hundred and twenty miles west in Trinidad. The other eavesdropper was at Seawell airfield, two hundred and ninety miles northwest in Barbados. Between the two of them, the precise location of the *U-156* was triangulated. At first light the next morning, an air armada of submarine hunter killers was dispatched.

6 Mar 1943
U-156
1530 hours

With all the aerial surprises, the boat did its wandering well below the surface. Listening would have to be its looking unless possible noises warranted a periscope view.

Hartenstein spoke to his most junior officer who was the Second Watch Officer.

"Mr. Peters, we've put enough water between us and the airfields of those blessed birds. Prepare a course change to put us on a due north projection. Hopefully, we can intercept some convoy activity. I'm going to close my eyes for a few hours. You have the conn. Let me know if you hear anything."

Dear Mutti and Papa,

It has been two months since I last ate with you. I always miss you when I am so far away on these voyages. I miss our quiet times when we sit together in the evening, reading by the fire. How you always fetch us cocoa when the evening gets colder. How we each read little snippets to each other. It's like we each get to read three books at once. Our cook is Smutje and he does a very fine job with what he has. But, of course, his cooking is not yours, Mutti. As I'm sure you can imagine, we don't have daytime or nighttime down here. Nighttime is whenever I can grab a couple hours to myself. I am fortunate because a captain has the most space and privacy. I find that I make nighttime in three ways. I always talk with one of you like I'm doing now. Then I read. Right now, I'm rereading Twenty Thousand Leagues Under the Sea. Finally, I read my Bible and say my prayers like we promised Pastor Achterhof in Confirmation. Tomorrow night, I think I will talk with little Rudi. But for now, I must try to sleep after my devotions. A captain never knows how long he'll be uninterrupted. Papa, with all my travels, do you think there is any chance I might be able to join you in the export business?

Love, Werner.

7 *Mar 1943*
U-156
320 kilometers northeast of Martinique
1100 hours

Almost forty hours had passed since all the aerial drama. No sounds or sightings of any kind had been detected. The watch party was on highest alert for air visitors as the boat recharged its batteries.

"Hey Willie," said one of the lookouts to the other. "If they called off the war, think they'd let us know?"

"Probably not. That would make too much sense," said his partner who scanned the skies in the opposite direction.

Cynical humor was the lingua franca of the bored. "We ought to call that team there 'The Apostles,'" said Willie.

Gunther said, "I have no idea what you're talking about."

Willie couldn't pass up a friendly shot. "That's because you never went to church, you heathen."

"Yeah. Well, you're in the same boat as me," said his friend.

"Got that right," said Willie. "No, looking at those guys down there reminded me how I always thought that the apostles had to have been the worst fisherman in the whole world. They never seemed to catch a thing."

He was referring to Fish 3, the third group of guys who were trying their luck at catching something for dinner. The cook had offered up some meat scraps for bait. He promised that whatever the topside parties could catch, he would prepare for the next meal. That got the men to organize a little contest. Each rotation going topside for a little breather would be designated as a fishing team. Fish 1 so far took the lead with beginners' luck, bringing in six good sized something. Nobody was sure what they were. The current team still hadn't gotten a bite.

"I can see the men perking up," Mannesman said to Hartenstein. "They're already talking about how many kills they've scored."

"Speaking of which, I'd like you to set up a back and forth pattern across the axis of the projected convoy lanes, switching back every three to four hours on an irregular schedule," said the captain who retired to his private space.

Dear Rudi,

How is my special pal? Do you know that I am writing this over one hundred meters under the ocean? And the paper is not even getting wet! Outside my U-boat there are whales and sharks and jellyfish swimming alongside us. But guess what? I can't even see them because we don't have any windows in this kind of a boat. I'll bet you're wondering how we can see where we're going if we don't have windows. Well, there is a young man who works for me whose name is Alfred. He reminds me of you. I think you're going to look just like him when you get bigger. Alfred and two of his friends are kind of our windows. They listen really carefully with special earphones to hear all the sounds outside. That's how we know what's out there. By the way, do you know what book I'm reading?

I'm reading Twenty Thousand Leagues Under the Sea because I know that this is what you are reading too. I'm on page fifty-three tonight. Take good care of your mom and dad for me, OK?

Love, Uncle Werner

8 Mar 1943
1300 hours

"Something's changed, Sir," Mannesman said to his boss.

Hartenstein knew exactly what he was saying. But even to his trusted assistant, the commander could not voice the fact that they hadn't so much as seen a target in almost six months. "Harder to catch and easier to get caught. Means we've got to be better, eh Gert?"

"Kind of takes all the fun out of it," Mannesman said.

"The *Laconia* did that for me," said Hartenstein. "As long as we're trying to do our duty, I'll be happy to not go through that again."

"Yes, Sir. Very true, Sir," agreed the Executive Officer. "Do you think it might help the men maintain their edge if we ran a few more crash dive drills?"

"I think you may have a good point, Gert. Once the batteries are charged and we get the rest of the crew rotated top-side for air, let's run them through it, said the captain. I'm going to bunk down for a bit. Let me know when things are wrapped up."

Dear Hildi,

How's "Cookie?" I can still taste the wonderful cookies you made for me when I left for sea again. You made them crunchy, just the way I like them. Do you know how I can still taste them? Well, I never know how long I'll be gone. So just to be sure, I cut each cookie into four parts. To be a U-boat captain, I had to learn how to do math. So, I figured that since you gave me six dozen cookies, if I cut each of them into four smaller cookies, then I would have . . . oh, no, you have to figure that one out for yourself. Let's just say that right now I'm eating my fifty-first cookie and . . . Whoops! I just dropped a crumb on the letter and it left a little grease stain, just to prove how much I love it. By the way, on this trip I've traveled about twelve hundred leagues under the sea. And if you will look in the evening sky, you will see that I have hung up the moon and dusted off all the stars, just for you.

Love, Uncle . . .

The battle claxon erupted and Hartenstein was jolted back into the present as he smacked his head against the wall. He instinctively stuffed the unfinished letter into his water-repellant pouch. Surface-basking in the tropical waters, *U-156* had been caught totally by surprise. Twenty miles earlier, radar on an American PBY "flying boat" had detected the sitting duck. Cloud cover prevented the conning tower watch from spotting the approach. One mile aft, the very heavily armed sub hunter cut its engines and quietly floated down through the clouds. Four MK-44 depth charges dropped from only a couple dozen meters overhead.

The four charges exploded in unison only five meters from the boat. The shock detonated one of the U-boat's torpedoes. The boat snapped neatly in half, spilling out materiel as well as the dead among eleven struggling crew. The attacking plane came around for another drop. This time it released a life raft and a medical bag tied to life jackets. By the time it zoomed over a third time, six of the survivors were gone and five had made it into the inflatable raft.

Before the *USS Barney* arrived on the scene to rescue survivors, so had the shark feeding frenzy. No trace of anything remained. All were gone. With every mouse and man, as the victims themselves used to say. The destroyer found only two things: a floating bag and within it an unfinished letter to some niece named Hildi.

Kapitänleutnant Gustav Julius Werner Hartenstein was now finally dismissed from ever again having to wound his conscience.

DAVE GARWICK

CHAPTER 46

SINS OF THE FATHERS VISITED

12 April 1945
Plauen, Germany

O ver the months and seas, bombers had tried four times to kill Werner Hartenstein before finally accomplishing the goal on the fifth attempt. As though to burn out even his roots, bombers came again, this time to his hometown of Plauen. The birds of prey had just perfected their technique the week before in the firebombing of Dresden. Now, hundreds of British Lancasters and American B-17's dropped over fifty-seven hundred tons of explosives on the small medieval city that had no military significance whatsoever. Seventy-five percent of the city was destroyed, effectively ending its main wartime industrial production of lace and doilies.

Eleven-year-old Hildi Mauser shivered on the pile of rubble outside the shell of their fragmented house. Her little brother kept himself warm by climbing over debris and moving aside smaller chunks of building wreckage to look for treasures.

Mother called to children, "Hildi, I need your help to make a cooking pit so we can make supper later on. Rudi, help your father dig out that shelter hole for us."

"But mom, why can't we make supper in the kitchen?" asked Hildi.

"For the same reason that we can't sleep inside or use the basement. The house is shaky and it might fall down on us."

Three nights ago, two five hundred pound bombs had fallen on either end of their street. Five homes had been blasted to smithereens and no trace of the families had ever been found. Some held on to the distant hope that at least some of these people had taken shelter in the public storage caves further away.

In the last war, Father had learned about shell fragments the hard way. He still carried shrapnel in one leg from an artillery barrage. That ever-present pain left him with a pronounced limp. But it also rendered him an otherwise healthy younger man who was nevertheless designated as non-able bodied for military call up.

"Rudi, I need your help to move some of the chunks so I can dig the hole."

"What for, Daddy? The bombers have not come back."

"Well, they might. And if they do, we need some place to take cover. Besides, we need some place to sleep and get out of the rain."

Isolated fires were burning all throughout town. A mist of combusted human and non-human particles turned the air into a gossamer haze that carried the familiar pungence of burning buildings. But there was also a note of something that no one had ever experienced, but which everyone recognized. The human animal instinctively knows, but can neither quite describe nor ever forget, the smell of its own kind in death. Every nose breathed in, and thereby ingested, the remains of two thousand, four hundred and forty-three men, women and children who had been crushed, disintegrated, suffocated, carbonized, melted, roasted or simply vaporized throughout fourteen air raids.

Rudi looked at the big job in front of him. "But Hansie said his mom and dad said it's OK to go back into their house. So, why can't we?"

There was indeed a part of Walter that did feel a little silly, being the only one on the block who was making his family go through all of this. He wondered if this is how Noah must have felt while he was building the ark.

Hildi said, "Yeah, Daddy. How is a hole going to save us, anyway?"

As tired as he was, Walter had to admit that the kids were owed some explanations if they were going to have to stand out like this.

"Well, first off, Hansie's house might not be as shaky as ours. And in the last war, hiding in the ground saved my life, more than once, when bombs started dropping."

Not far away, a massive explosion meant that time had run out on an unexploded bomb. As well as on the seven children who had been playing nearby.

Charlotte chose this as a terribly teachable moment. "You see, children? Even though the bombers are not here, it is still very, very dangerous."

The children just stared at her. Without another word, each set about helping their parents with their respective excavations. An hour later, Rudi's friend, Hansie Schiller, came over to the work party.

"Wanna play, Rudi?" said a carefree spirit.

Rudi, however, had just moved one more explosion further away from the age of innocence. "Naw, we have to dig our hole for tonight."

"What for?" said Hansie.

"So we don't get blown up or have our house fall down on top of us," said the young veteran.

"So, can I help?"

Rudi looked to his dad who said, "Well, only if your parents say it's OK. Maybe they need your help at your place."

"Naw," said Hansie. "They told us to go outside and play, so we wouldn't be in the way."

"Well, ask them anyway, and then come back if it's OK. Tell them you can stay for supper if you want to," said Walter.

"Can Rudi come with me?" said the hopeful helper.

Walter did not want Rudi going inside any buildings. He also didn't want to get into that particular discussion in front of the little neighbor. "Not this time, Hansie. I need his help right now."

Hansie skipped off to his place which was only three houses away. He was back inside of five minutes and completely out of breath. "Mom said it's OK for me to help and to stay for supper. But I have to be home before dark. And she said to say thank you."

Walter showed the boys how to work as a relay team to remove the rubble that he dug up. It wasn't long before the boys turned the team idea into a game, so it didn't feel like work. A periodic reminder from the straw boss was all that was needed to harness the horseplay.

Rudi said, "But Hildi isn't helping mom dig the cooking pit anymore."

His father wiped his brow, which made a sooty smear. "Can you smell why?"

Mother and daughter had suspended digging operations thirty minutes ago in order to begin cooking supper. The fragrance was beginning to beckon. "Oh, yeah," said Rudi. "I get it." Half an hour later, all were sitting on chunks of debris around the cooking pit.

"Frau Mauser," said the little hired help, "this is even better than what my mom makes!"

Both parents tried to stifle chuckles. Charlotte quickly said, "Please do not say anything like that to your mother. I happen to know that she is one of the very best cooks around. You can tell her I said that."

"Hansie, I hate to make you go," said Walter. "You've been a great help to me. But it's almost dark and I don't want your folks to worry."

"Can I help again tomorrow?"

"If it's really all right with your folks, we'll see. Hurry on now, young man."

As Hansie sauntered away, the chief engineer said, "OK everybody, we all need to act quickly before the night makes it impossible for us to see."

"See what, Daddy?" asked Hildi.

"We need to quickly get ready to sleep," said Father. "We have no extra clothes or blankets to keep us warm. So, we have to keep each other warm tonight in the hole. I sleep next to Rudi and he sleeps next to Hildi and she sleeps next to mom."

Hildi said, "I don't want to sleep next to him! He kicks!"

"Hush now," said Charlotte. "This is not going to be easy for any of us. Daddy and I have to be on the outside so you kids are the warmest in the middle."

All four reluctantly climbed into the sleeping hole. A full hour of grumbling and shifting around was followed by a half hour of stories in total darkness, followed by prayers followed by a little more jostling. Fortunately, everyone was so exhausted that sleep overtook them all . . . until the deafening crash of a collapsing building, just three houses away.

CHAPTER 47

GREATER THAN OURSELVES

1964
St. Bartholomew's Hospital
London

It had been twenty-four years since Hitler's Luftwaffe had dropped twenty-three thousand tons of bombs on London, totally obliterating thirty thousand people and seventy thousand buildings. Government officials said that almost two million buildings had been damaged to one extent or another. These structures were described in categories such as "doubtful if repairable," "repairable at cost," and "general blast damage without structural damage." The same thing could have been said about many of the surviving eight million Londoners.

Some neighborhoods were already being rebuilt for the second time. The first hastily built replacements were already falling down, just like many of the so-called survivors. Many of the young nurses at St. Bartholomew's Hospital had been born in the rubble. They too knew something of struggle since they had been raised in those cobbled together neighborhoods and families that also now had to be rebuilt.

"So, what was that all about?" said one nurse to another.

"Oh, The Sarge is at it again," said Maggie.

Kate checked in. "What now?

"The shoes," said Esther. "Found a scuff mark on the left heel. Can you believe it?"

"Don't feel bad. Yesterday she got me for a cracked button," said Maggie.

Bea Hopkins said, "That's nothing. Last week she sent Liz home for not wearing her pin."

Supervising Nurse Lyn Ensfield had a reputation at Bart's. Her unit was the best in the entire hospital. That was for a reason. Her standards were high and she brooked no variance.

"I'll say this for her," said Maggie. "She plays no favorites. I even saw her correct Dr. Stansfield yesterday on handwashing protocol."

"And she's still around?" said Esther.

"He thanked her! Management always backs her," said Bea.

"Not surprised," said a passing orderly. "She looks like she's been around as long as Bart's itself."

"How old is she?" asked one of the nurse's aides.

"Who knows? Maybe sixty? Seventy?" said Bea. "Nobody knows anything personal about her. Nobody knows anybody who knows her. She never shows any kind of emotion. Everything is always business."

Maggie said, "And what's with that Rita Hayworth up-do and those government issue glasses? It's like she's stuck back in World War Two."

"Did she serve?" asked the orderly.

"Who knows?" said Esther. "Who knows anything at all about her?"

"Nurse Hopkins. My office, please."

"What now?" said Maggie.

Bea quickly answered the call and stood at the door.

"Have a seat, please," said Ensfield who took her own place behind her desk. In one hand, she rotated a tube of lipstick. With the other hand, she was writing something in someone's personnel file. She did not look up at the young nurse across from her. "Please close the door, Nurse Hopkins."

The one who was still an employee returned to the hot seat. Nurse Sarge continued writing in silence. Then she abruptly closed the file, put down the pen, took a deep breath and locked her gaze on Hopkins for several more moments of silence.

"Nurse Hopkins, standing about in chit-chat does not project a professionalism to our patients or to the rest of the staff."

"Yes, ma'am."

"Do you know why we all work so hard on this unit?"

"To be the best unit, ma'am?"

"It is not about us, Miss Hopkins. It is never about us. Come with me."

The Supervisor launched herself out of the office at a velocity that left a wake through the rest of the staff that had not had the sense to busy themselves elsewhere. Hopkins struggled to keep up, but never got closer than two of Ensfield's strides. No words were spoken, which the young nurse didn't have the breath for anyway. One hallway led to another which led to a flight of stairs, down another corridor to another flight of stairs and then to another hallway. Hopkins was overheating until she was cooled by a sudden drop in blood pressure when she realized where they were. She hadn't been in this wing since she had been hired. Ensfield abruptly stopped at the door to an office labeled "Personnel."

"Wait out here," she said to the wilting Hopkins. This had been the young nurse's first career position. She had never been disciplined for anything. How could she face her parents? How would she ever be able to get another job as a nurse? All for talking in a group on the floor? This did not make any sense. Why her? Why only her? She had never had any trouble before with Sarge.

Ensfield came out of the office and said, "Follow me."

By the time they stopped, Bea had no recollection of how they had found their way to a set of massive oaken double doors. This was only getting worse. Hopkins could only guess that they were about to enter the inner sanctum of whoever ran this hospital.

Before entering, Ensfield turned and faced the confused understudy. "I want you to meet some people." The condemned nurse started to feel a little light headed.

Sarge had to pull back with the weight of her entire body to open just one of the doors. She held open the door for Hopkins. "Some friends of mine."

Nobody else was in the hospital chapel. Low angle, late afternoon sunlight cast a dim illumination through the sanctified space. The antiseptic atmosphere that permeated the rest of the hospital did not enter here. The memory of extinguished beeswax candles mixed with the faint traces of a musty incense. In the deafening silence, Bea thought she could hear her own heart beating. She followed her boss to one of the walls which displayed a massive tripartite stained glass window.

"Miss Hopkins, what do you read on the left pane?"

"Six names, ma'am."

"Read them, please."

"Annie Jobling, Brenda Irene Wells, Daphne Geraldine Strange, Dorothy Muriel Stratford, Jean Frances Watts, Mary Whitehead."

After almost a minute of total silence, the young nurse said, "Your friends, ma'am?"

"Yes, though I only knew two of them. Dottie came from Sussex. She and I went through TANS training together." She had to explain what TANS referred to. "Her ship was torpedoed three months after mine. She was one of the six hundred and fifty-six people who perished. Only one soul survived on the *Ceramic*. Her parents also lost their only other child who was a soldier. In Africa, I think it was. Dottie was just eight years older than you, Miss Hopkins."

"I . . . I'm sorry, Miss Ensfield."

"No need to be."

"You said that you knew two of these people, ma'am."

"Indeed." Ensfield walked right up to the window and very carefully placed her fingers over the second name.

"Bren was one of the Sisters. She was thirty-two, as well. She came from Lincolnshire. Miss Hopkins, have you ever heard of Pom Pom Island?"

"No, ma'am."

"I never had either. Apparently, it is somewhere in Malaysia. East Malaysia, I think they told me."

Bea said nothing, sensing that this was Ensfield's hallowed space.

"Bren enlisted in the 17th Corps of Queen Alexandra's Royal Army Nursing Corps. She was on a ship called the *SS Kuala* which the Japanese sank not far off-shore from Pom Pom. They say that she helped wounded swim to shore. That is when the Jap pilots had their fun, chasing people down the beach and picking them off, one bomb at a time. They called it slaughter bombing. On Valentine's Day, of all days."

Bea was streaming tears and could not understand how Sarge could be dry-eyed. Without a word, the senior nurse handed a tissue to the junior who blew her nose, took a deep breath and said, "Miss Ensfield, did you say that you yourself had been on a ship that was torpedoed?"

Lyn kept touching the name on the window. "What happened to me is not important. It is not about me."

The protégé said, "But . . ."

"Please read what it says in the middle window, Miss Hopkins."

Bea cleared her throat and recited: *Praise God, remembering those nurses from this hospital who gave their lives for their country.*

"Now," said the supervisor, "tell me about the nurse who is standing in the right window."

Bea had always chastised herself for not seeing what was right in front of her face. She took an extra-long, second look at the window and still could not see what Ensfield was talking about. "But I don't believe that she is standing, ma'am. I think she is kneeling."

The younger nurse was not certain if she detected the faintest trace of a smile on her teacher who said, "Precisely. The nurse is kneeling. Now tell me about her hands."

Bea felt a little more confident to call it as she saw it. "They are both palms up, like she is offering something," said Hopkins.

The instructor wanted to be sure that the student understood how the dots were connected. "So, the nurse is kneeling to offer something," said Ensfield.

"Yes, ma'am."

Lyn Ensfield turned away from the window to face the young woman. "Nurse Hopkins, in my opinion you are an exceptionally fine nurse."

"Ma'am?"

"From the way you perform your duties, it is clear to me that you see this as a professional career and not just a job."

"Yes, ma'am."

"The other staff see this in you, as well. They take their example from you. That is one reason why you are the one whom I have taken aside. Understand?"

"I think I do, Miss Ensfield."

"The idle gossiping I saw is not the professional example that I want the others to follow from you."

"Yes, ma'am."

"In my office, I asked you why we work so hard. Do you recall what you said?"

"I think I said that it was so that we could be the best unit?"

"Yes, you did. But what we do and why we do it is not about ourselves. It's about our patients. It is about offering ourselves just as our six sisters here offered themselves. That is what it is all about. Have I made my point?"

"Absolutely, Miss Ensfield."

"Before long, you will occupy a position like mine. I hope your expectations will make the same point."

"Yes, ma'am."

"That will be all." Lyn looked down and quietly added, "For now."

EPILOGUE

Not one U-boat that had rescued the survivors of the *Laconia* was still in this world a year later. Only six of the one hundred and sixty-one sailors would ever live to tell the story. None would be from the *U-156*, the one hundred and eighty-sixth U-boat to die. The men and their boat joined the infamous club of the eighty-five percent of all U-boat sailors who perished in action.

Years later, the captain of the final ship sunk by *U-156* would recall the last words ever spoken by Werner Hartenstein to a vanquished enemy: "A good journey and a safe landing. We hope to meet you again in a better and more peaceful world."

REFERENCES

UBoat.net was an invaluable database of all things U-boat.

Casey, Susan. *The Wave: In Pursuit of the Rogues*. Doubleday: New York, 2010.

Doenitz, Karl. *The Memoirs of Karl Doenitz*. Yorkshire: Frontline Books, 2012.

Hawkins, Doris. *Atlantic Torpedo: The record of 27 Days in an Open Boat, Following a U-boat Sinking, by the Only Woman Survivor*. UK: Victor Gollanz Ltd., 1943.

Mulligan, Timothy. *Neither Sharks Nor Wolves*. Annapolis, MD: Naval Institute Press, 1999.

Niemöller, Martin. *From U-boat to Pulpit*. Chicago: Willett, Clark and Co., 1937.

Stein, Leo. *Hitler Came for Niemoeller*. Gretna: Pelican Publishing Co., 2003.

Stoever, Renate. *Escape From Plauen, A True Story*. New York, NY: iBooks, 2013.

HISTORICAL NOTES: FACT VERSUS FICTION

The sinkings of the *Laconia* and then the *U 156* happened precisely as described, in both world wars. Werner Hartenstein and his senior staff were real. So was Pastor Martin Niemöller and all the events in his life which were described. Hartenstein's personal struggles are imagined, though Niemöller documented his own personal struggles in his memoirs, as did Karl Dönitz who really did serve under Niemöller in the Great War. The connections between Hartenstein and Niemöller are fictitious as were the characters of Lyn Ensfield and Tony Corbetta.

All aspects of *The Laconia* and Master Roger Sharpe, except for the rogue wave encounter, are accurate. The pilot of the B-24, and the top commanders at Ascension Island were real, though the actual plane, the conversations, thoughts and motivations of all American personel are fictitious. To my knowledge, there is no information available to explain why the Americans took the actions they did with the information that was available to some. I made the decision to portray the tragedy as the result of a cascade of errors, a perfect storm, where players did what seemed reasonable at the time, with the information that they had.

Events, campaigns, ships, military units, the command staff of all ships and boats, key figures, statistics, and locations on specific dates and times are historically documented and accurate. The head of commands like Dönitz are real, but the others figures under such a person are usually fictitious.

The Author

Photo credit: Karl Oberjohn

Dave Garwick was a speech and language pathologist and is a retired Lutheran pastor. His military experience was as a cannoneer and then a First Lieutenant in the U.S. Army Field Artillery during the years of the Vietnam War. He and his wife live in Edina, Minnesota. This is his first novel.

Made in the USA
Lexington, KY
15 November 2017